MW01697924

Sydney Biddle Barrows

The Mayflower Madam

with Dan Kennedy

PRESORTED FIRST CLASS

$600+ OF PURE MONEY-MAKING INFORMATION

UNCENSORED SALES STRATEGIES

XXX-RATED SECRETS

A Radical New Approach to Selling Your Customers What They Really Want—No Matter What Business You're In

For Mature Sales Professionals and Entrepreneurs

EP
Entrepreneur Press

Editorial Director: Jere L. Calmes
Cover Design: Desktop Miracles
Production and Composition: Eliot House Productions

Library of Congress Cataloging-in-Publication Data Available

ISBN 10: 1-59918-193-2
ISBN 13: 978-1-59918-193-6

Printed in Canada

13 12 11 10 09 10 9 8 7 6 5 4 3 2 1

DEDICATION

For his courageous belief in me and his stalwart support beyond anything I could have ever hoped for, I dedicate this book to Dan Kennedy.

CONTENTS

PART THREE

OUTSIDE INFLUENCES: GUEST CHAPTERS

ACKNOWLEDGMENTS

James Roche for giving me the inspiration and direction that made the actual writing of this book possible; Nancy Gerber for being the best fairy god-friend anyone could ever have; Marlene Green for her generosity with her time and advice, and her unwavering support and belief in me; Alexandria Brown for her wise counsel; Karen Glazer for all of her indefatigable assistance and support; Bill Glazer for humoring Dan; Vicky Tolleson for all of her assistance and meticulous follow-up; everyone at GKIC for their help, cooperation and hard work; Darnay Hoffman for his vital and indispensable assistance in making it possible for me to keep my head above water; and Patty Heffley, my hard-working and invaluable assistant without whom I wouldn't be able to survive.

I am also very grateful to everyone who made a contribution to this book, both spiritually as well as in writing, including: the members of my Sales Design programs; the members of Alexandria Brown's Platinum Mastermind group, particularly Bonnie Hutchinson and Ileana Kane; and the members of my New York/New Jersey Glazer-Kennedy Mastermind group. I thank Chris Mullins for her counsel and support, Cheryl Kimball for her brilliant editing skills, and Jere Calmes, my long-suffering editor at Entrepreneur Press. I am very appreciative of Harmony Tenney and Sheila Spangler for giving me someone to "run things by." For anyone I have not mentioned who should have been, this omission is completely inadvertent; please accept my sincerest apologies and know that even though your name may be missing here, my gratitude is not.

FOREWORD

I have to admit the first time I heard Sydney Biddle Barrows speak—at an event hosted by my mentor Dan Kennedy—I was so distracted by her former profession as "The Mayflower Madam" that I failed to hear her message.

"How COULD she?" I wondered. "How DID she? WHAT did she . . .?" I completely missed out on all the savvy sales strategies I had traveled in anticipation of learning.

Then I thankfully was able to have the chance to hear her speak again; by now I'd gotten past the shock of her former business.

Now, I was really listening. Not only to her exciting stories and her sales strategies, but her thoughts about the big picture. For me, Sydney's most profound message was one particular piece of information she shared.

"In my high-end escort business, we weren't selling sex," she explained. "We were selling a FANTASY." (You'll hear more about that from Sydney in Chapter 2.)

The common definition of fantasy is: "imagination, especially when extravagant and unrestrained."

Fantasy is the ideal, end-all result. The dream. Whether it's outlandish, or practical. And fantasies CAN come true, whether you believe that or not.

You see, as adults, we've basically been programmed over time to be "DISbelievers." Your job, when you are selling your product, program, or service, is to turn your prospects back into believers again. To get them to see the fantasy. Taste it. Feel it. Believe it can be theirs.

When we are young, we naturally have vivid fantasies all the time. As children we dream of flying to the moon, riding on a unicorn, being a king or queen or cowboy, slaying a dragon and rescuing the princess or being rescued from the burning tower.

Then, as we enter our school years, we're discouraged from using fantasy. We're taught to stick to facts, use reason, and be practical. Our working years are much of the same. We hear: "Don't go dreaming, just focus on the real world." Blech! No wonder most of us have pretty much discarded fantasy all together.

But I welcome you now, as you hold this book, to rediscover fantasy. If not only for your own sake, for the sake of your SALES.

Conscious or not, fantasies are the underlying fuel of life (even for the "disbelievers"). Fantasies get us excited, inspired, motivated . . . and they also make us whip out our wallets faster than anything else.

We ALL buy fantasies every day.

The man buying the Maserati has the fantasy of the world knowing he's powerful and successful. The woman in the dentist's chair receiving cosmetic work has the fantasy of wanting to look like a movie star. The parents buying the swimming pool have the fantasy of having the ideal backyard for happy family memories. The client hiring the best attorney in town has a fantasy of, well . . . kicking his ex's ass.

I find often, as I'm coaching my students—almost all of whom are women entrepreneurs—that they get caught up in the details of the day-to-day offerings of their business, their different products and services, these "commodities" that they sell.

But what we are ALL REALLY selling is a fantasy.

Myself included.

If one were to dissect my business from an outside eye, my commodity is basically marketing and success information. There are thousands of places and people from whom one could buy this type of commodity. But I know, because I've been told over and over, that there's a fantasy behind what I offer: The dream of living a truly extraordinary life as a female entrepreneur. (To me that means a life filled with wealth and prosperity, happiness and joy, love and rich experiences that touch you . . . and the world.)

And sales is, well, a bit of a seduction. Why not enjoy the process?

You hold in your hands one of the most titillating (and useful) guides on sales I've seen in print. Prepare to be entertained, advised, informed, enlightened. The basis underlying all of sales is psychology, which Sydney and Dan know much about. Then you'll be walked through all the steps in sales themselves, from prospecting to keeping those clients and customers coming back for more. And you'll also get all the nitty-gritty tips and tricks that Sydney, Dan, and the other experts in the book have to share.

Arousing, isn't it?

Why not let yourself get excited about selling again?

Let yourself go there.

Enjoy the ride.

I think you'll like it.

—Alexandria Brown

INTRODUCTION

Never Work with Children, Never Follow an Animal Act

Dan S. Kennedy

There are two chief points I'd like to make to help you get maximum benefit from this "uncensored" book that I'm privileged to have contributed several chapters to.

First, Sydney Biddle Barrows brilliantly addresses hidden, overlooked, and neglected aspects of selling as well as sophisticated psychological and emotional aspects of selling that virtually no other book ever written on selling tackles as candidly. That's a big claim. But I've personally been writing about, speaking about, teaching and working with sales strategies—as well as advertising, marketing, and direct marketing strategies—for 30 years. My personal library contains over 300 well-read, well-used books related to sales, and I've discarded at least twice that many. Many of America's leading sales experts and trainers including Tom Hopkins, Brian Tracy, and Zig Ziglar are my friends and colleagues. I can say authoritatively that much, maybe most written and taught about selling is about *mechanics*. Like dancing lessons with feet decals on the floor—do this, then do this, then do this. Inevitably many cover the very same steps in the same manner. Not to say that these mechanics aren't important. But then there is a more advanced, sophisticated, dare I say elegant, *stylish* use of these mechanics that truly top professionals arrive at. Intuitively, observationally, and experientially, Sydney takes you past the important foundational mechanics to this higher plane. Hers is an authentically fresh perspective.

When I first started in professional speaking, I was given advice that is a cliché from the entertainment industry, reportedly given to vaudeville performers way back when: Never work with children. Never follow an animal act. A third piece of advice that some quickly tried giving me when Sydney and I first began working together was: Never associate yourself with a former madam.

It turns out the animal act advice was pretty sound. I have twice been on programs with or following animal acts, and neither one worked out very well. In one case, the stage was covered with the product of the animal's stage-fright-induced diarrhea and in it I stepped, skidded like a vaudeville comedian with foot on a banana, and went airborne. And I said a word that should not be said into my lapel microphone for everyone to hear.

I have often had young kids in my audiences and occasionally engaged them in discussion and risked giving them a microphone with, so far, no embarrassing moments. But I've never actually worked with any children, unless you want to count several Hollywood celebrities I've been on programs with or produced TV infomercials with, who are brats, and who shall remain nameless here.

Winding up working with one of the most famous or infamous, if you prefer, madams who once graced the front pages of the New York tabloids and later made the rounds of most of the talk shows including Larry King is not something I would ever have foreseen, and certainly not anything I would have sought.

People often ask me—given her controversial background regarding her first business—why I have chosen to associate myself with her. There is no shortage of people seeking association with me. And my publishers are quite content to publish more books authored by me alone. My answer is simple. At this stage of my life I have little interest in walking over the same steps walked before, in gluing a new label over the old on the same bottle. I can certainly profit by doing so, but I am not motivated by it. Sydney has unique experience, unique insight, and a unique viewpoint that intrigues me, and that is proving very valuable to some of my smartest and most successful clients and coaching members. We are all in constant need and search for opportunities to improve our businesses in general and our sales practices in specific; but the more experienced we are, the harder these are to come by, and the less likely we are to discover them by reading or hearing about or being exposed to the same kinds of experience, from clone-like traditional sources. Sydney *is* a distinctively different, provocative source. And you are to be congratulated for your own openness to this.

Second, the "broken bridges" in most businesses have long troubled me. My primary role has been creating, reinventing, or strengthening business' advertising and marketing that brings ideal customers, clients, or patients to their doors, eager and willing to pay premium prices or fees for a particular, promised experience—only to have the sales practices used deeply disappoint or frustrate those customers, rendering all my good work impotent, and even having it erroneously blamed for the ultimate poor results. We call this problem "broken bridges."

When you fix the loose boards, gaps, wear and tear on your bridge, your sales and profits automatically increase. Even one loose board can ruin the walk across a ten-mile bridge. And little tweaks have big leverage. Sydney often goes on-site to businesses, combining personal mystery shopping, observation, interviewing staff and customers, to identify these powerful points of leverage. Many are *inside* the business' sales practices. In this book, she equips you to fine tune your sales process and practices for yourself. This, too, is a very different approach to selling. It's not about the same old mechanics. It's about finding creative opportunities.

Finally, about the "XXX-rated" background and origin of many of these concepts: One of the richest entrepreneurs I've ever worked with gave me what I call a "writer-downer" about 20 years ago. He said: "You learn little from the familiar."

His wisdom prompted many habits I've maintained my whole working life that have served me well, that have to do with deliberate exposure to the unfamiliar. As an example, I pick up and read magazines of zero personal interest to me, trade magazines from industries I have nothing to do with, magazines published for women, teens, model railroad builders, and martial arts practitioners, etc. And from time to time, I have found unexpected opportunity or information or contacts of enormous value that never would have come my way if I read the same periodicals of direct relevance to me month in, month out. If you are a dentist and pay close attention only to what other dentists do and what dental marketing experts have to say . . . if you sell insurance and pay close attention only to what sales trainers in the insurance field have to say . . . you learn little; you merely reinforce what you already know. While great opportunities are usually found right underfoot, the means and motivation for liberating them usually comes from far afield.

In this book, through her own experiences, Sydney takes you where no other sales expert has ever taken you. From there you can return to your own day-to-day sales practices with fresh eyes. The fact that many of these experiences come from what is commonly thought of as "the sex business" (but as Sydney will tell you, has less to do with sex than you think) is a bonus. Selling even the most mundane of products or services, even in industrial or professional environments distant from the boudoir is, believe it or not, about sex appeal. Some of our best terminology about selling reveals this secret truth—consider terms like "unique selling proposition" and "irresistible offer." Selling anything—investments, car parts, cosmetic surgery—is best done as *seduction*.

Another flaw in much of what is taught, believed, and practiced about selling is the single-minded emphasis on *making* or *closing* the sale—the signature on the dotted line as the victorious outcome. This is short-sighted and simplistic. Even brutish. The most prosperous sales professionals and business owners learn to transcend transactional thought and behavior in favor of creating and delivering exceptionally satisfying experiences that sustain relationships. In this book, Sydney puts the act of selling in the context of experiences and relationships.

I'll be visiting with you several times during this book, in specific chapters, in my own voice. I've influenced a fair amount of the content throughout the book in other ways as well, such as material from my seminars and newsletters. And I'm happy to be here, to have discovered Sydney, brought her to my most progressive clients, and now to you. If you are open to a new psycho-emotional, experience-oriented approach to selling that richly satisfies customers, you will be happy with your discovery as well.

X X X X X

DAN S. KENNEDY is the author of 11 books, including the popular "No. B.S." series with Entrepreneur Press as well as the editor of four monthly newsletters including *The No B.S. Marketing Letter*. He can be contacted ONLY by FAX at 602-269-3113 or by mail at Kennedy Inner Circle, Inc, 5818 N. 7th Street, #103, Phoenix, AZ 85014. Information about Dan's books at NoBSBooks.com.

PART ONE

PREPARING YOURSELF TO BE A SEDUCTIVE SALES PRO

Chapter 1

WHY LISTEN TO A FORMER MADAM?

Why Not?

Most successful people will tell you that one of the best ways to make it to the top is to model yourself after other successful people. Model yourself after a Madam, you ask yourself? No way!

Why not? It's not called "the world's oldest profession" for nothing! The "Ladies of the Evening" business has had centuries to test every conceivable marketing and selling strategy, adapt to all kinds of challenges and changes, and devise innumerable, creative ways to cater to more niche and sub-niche markets than any other business I can think of.

How Did A Nice Girl Like You . . . ?

So how did a nice girl like me end up in *that* business? I started off my career on the Executive Training Program at Abraham & Straus, at the time the jewel in the crown of Federated Department Stores. As an Assistant Buyer in the Bath Shop, it was my job to not only take care of myriad daily behind-the-scene details, I also was responsible for buying all of the accessories, like soap dishes, tissue box holders, toothbrush stands—you get the picture. Eventually I was promoted to a branch store where I was the Department Manager of Fine Jewelry, Watches, and Sunglasses.

Burned out from working weekends and holidays when every one else I knew had time off, I found a position as an assistant to the buyer of Ladies Fashion Accessories at the New York corporate buying office of the May Company Stores. And when the opportunity to become the head buyer of Fashion Accessories at an independent residential buying office presented itself, I quickly took it.

Business Basics 101

The retail business couldn't have been a more terrific learning experience. Retailing gave me a very solid business foundation in so many areas. I learned about the importance of image and how to create it, maintain it, and change it. I learned very valuable lessons about selling: the mechanics of how to make a sale, the importance of product presentation, and how to price a product in various ways, depending on your purpose at the time. I learned how critical it was to see your business through your customer's eyes, to find out and give them what *they* want, not what you think they should have (or whatever is sitting on your shelves).

I learned that repeat business and loyal customers make up the foundation of every successful business and how vital it is to find ways to maintain and expand that relationship. And I learned how to treat employees in such a way as to instill unwavering loyalty, to create in them a desire to uphold the image of the business, and to make them feel they are an integral part of the business' success.

I also received an unintentional education on how to ruin a flourishing business by personally observing a management team literally destroy decades of success by completely ignoring all of the above. Learning what doesn't work is just as critical, if not more so, than learning what does. I received a firsthand education in both.

In a Nutshell

I lost my job at the independent resident buying office because I refused to participate in a kickback scheme—I may be a little crazy but I'm not dishonest. Living on an unemployment check is all but impossible in New York City; a friend who knew I was struggling told me about a part-time, off-the-books position answering the telephones in the office of an escort service. I didn't even know what an escort service was! Once it was fully explained to me, at first I didn't want to have anything to do with it. But at the time, $50 a night off the books was very good money so eventually I said yes.

It was obvious from the very first night that while this may have been the World's Oldest Profession, this particular proprietor wasn't running it very *professionally*. He ignored every good business practice in existence and came up with even more bad ones on his own! All the lessons I had learned were being *so* flagrantly flouted, it was a mystery to me how this guy had managed to stay in business for even a month, let alone the nearly 20 years he had been operating.

The girlfriend who had told me about the job was making a little extra money herself by working in this office, so we usually called each other the next day and did a lot of Monday morning quarterbacking regarding every unprofessional and irrational, not to mention sleazy, thing that, upon direct orders, we had had to do. It didn't take either of us long to realize there were a lot of really terrific guys out there who were looking for an upscale and elegant experience and there was absolutely no one who was providing it. The challenge was just too irresistible.

Recognizing the Niche

I didn't know the term at the time, but of course now I realize these gentlemen constituted a niche market, actually a sub-niche market, which had gone totally unrecognized and underserved in New York City (and just about everywhere else in the United States as well). Nobody was giving these very wealthy clients what they *really* wanted. No one was even paying attention to what they wanted, *and* had the means to pay for!

And what *did* they really want? They wanted the most beautiful, the most elegantly dressed, the most charming, the most expensive New York City call girl to walk through *their* door. They wanted her to listen to their stories, laugh at their jokes, admire their financial success, and be enjoyable company. They wanted to relax, escape their everyday life, and feel like they were "still in the game" with a beautiful girl whose only agenda was to make them happy. At the end of that wish list was "a sure thing," but the full experience just described was the main attraction.

The business we were in was not the sex business; the business we were really in was the *fantasy* business. Yes, there was sex involved, but if that was their main objective, they could have gotten it for a lot less. What they were really paying for was a unique Experience.

Once we realized that we had a goldmine *and* that we knew exactly how to mine it, it was a no-brainer.

SYDNEY'S XXX-RATED SALES SECRET #1

Stop! Do not do another thing, do not spend another penny until you have figured out what business you are really in and what your customer really wants.

All Businesses Are Alike

When Bill Novak (who also co-authored books with Lee Iacocca, Nancy Reagan, Tip O'Neill, Oliver North, Magic Johnson, and others) and I set out to write my first book, *Mayflower Madam: The Secret Life of Sydney Biddle Barrows*,

Sydney says

The challenge of running a successful escort service is the same kind of challenge your business and every business faces: creating a unique Experience for the customer, one which your target market really wants and, ideally, is willing to pay a premium price for. The fewer people there are who provide a similar Experience, the more you will be able to charge.

we thought we were writing a book about "nice girl starts escort service and ends up becoming the Mayflower Madam." It turns out that the book we really ended up writing was, for the most part, a business book.

Fortune magazine picked up on it immediately; I give them a lot of credit for having the creative vision, and even more importantly, the courage to name it one of the Top Ten Best Business Books of the Year when it was published in 1986. In spite of the unusual nature of the business, they understood that because all businesses are alike, there were lessons in my experiences that any kind of business could profit from.

Unbeknownst to me at the time, there were other people who also knew a good business case study when they saw it. I don't know how it came to their attention, but it turns out that numerous business schools put *Mayflower Madam* on their reading lists for courses on Small Businesses and Entrepreneurship. I have the feeling this was one book everyone found the time to read!

One night I was having drinks with a group of friends at the Harvard Club when someone who turned out to be a recent graduate approached me and asked if I was Sydney Biddle Barrows. Then he told me that he had read my book because it was on the reading list for an entrepreneur course he had taken while at Harvard. One of the guys in our group promptly ordered a bottle of champagne to toast this momentous news, and although it happened years ago, I still feel a thrill whenever I think about it. And I give Harvard and all those other business schools a lot of credit for understanding that all businesses really are alike and that a well-run business is a well-run business, even if it is the call girl business!

One day I received a phone call out of the blue from the head of the Education Committee at the Long Island, New York, chapter of the Young President's Organization (YPO) who asked if I would be interested in speaking at one of their monthly chapter meetings on marketing a high-cost service. I had never heard of YPO; he had to explain to me that it was a by-invitation-only group of company presidents and CEOs, all of whom had attained these positions before the age of 40, and whose companies had to do a certain number of millions of dollars a year in business, have a certain number of employees, and so on. I thought this was such a ludicrous request that I was sure someone was putting me on. It took him quite a bit of convincing before I was satisfied he was legit! Apparently his wife had read *Mayflower Madam* and said something to the effect of, "You are always looking for successful business people to invite to speak at a meeting, here is someone who is a successful business woman—why don't you invite her?"

I have to give her and her husband a hand for extending this invitation and for having the same courage and creative vision as *Fortune* magazine and Harvard because they, too, understood that all businesses are alike. And a relationship that lasted a good eight years was born; I have presented at local chapter meetings, regional meetings, and twice overseas to an international audience for YPO. A similar group called The CEO Club, whose members are made up of only presidents and CEOs, have also invited me to present at numerous chapter meetings of theirs all across the United States.

THE MADAM SPEAKS

While I have never been invited to speak at Harvard, I have been a guest lecturer at many many colleges all across the country, including some in the Ivy League, such as Brown and Columbia. And over the years, numerous business groups have had the creative vision, and in some instances the courage as well, to understand that all businesses are alike, and have invited me to speak to their members about sales and marketing.

I always got a kick out of some president or CEO of a multi-million dollar company coming up to me after my talk and telling me they had either learned something or had a "eureka!" moment during my presentation. The one who sticks in my mind most vividly was this gruff, burley, good-old-boy president of a cement company who couldn't thank me enough for giving him the insight to solve this big problem he said had been plaguing him for quite some time. The only thing cement and call girls have in common is they both begin with a "c" so I don't know what the big insight he got was. But he was smart enough not to fall into the "but my business is different" trap, and walked away with a solution to his problem. There is more than one way to make a man happy!

Fresh Eyes See What You Cannot

When I speak to business groups, some of their members approach me afterwards to ask if I might be available to do some one-on-one consulting. It took a few of these consulting engagements before I understood that I have a gift for seeing things with Fresh Eyes—for picking out the incongruencies between the image a business is trying to project and the reality a customer actually encounters, for understanding what "mental movie" a prospective customer is seeing in his or her head when imagining what it would be like to do business with you, based on the image your advertising and marketing are conveying. For figuring out what business a client is *really* in, as well as

CONSISTENCY IS KEY

One of my cosmetic surgeon clients moved into a beautiful new office. The decorator had obviously been told to create a very upscale atmosphere. The chairs and couches were upholstered in heavy cotton damask, the Queen Anne style tables and side chairs were made of mahogany, and the prints on the wall were of horses and hunting

continued

CONSISTENCY IS KEY, CONTINUED

scenes. But the various brochures describing different products or procedures were displayed in tacky plastic holders scattered around the waiting room and the clipboards holding the usual forms were that standard brown kind with a cheap plastic pen attached. The forms themselves had been photocopied so many times that they were gray and grainy.

The plastic display boxes, brown clipboards, cheap pens, and poor-quality forms were totally incongruent with the design concept of the waiting room and detracted from the upscale image the practice was trying to project.

I suggested either mahogany wood or perhaps antique-looking metal display holders for the brochures and clipboards in a burgundy color to match the upholstery fabric. Operating on the premise that the nicer the pens were, the more quickly they would be "appropriated," I recommended he buy them in burgundy too, and have his name and phone number printed on them—as long as people were going to steal them, at least get some free advertising in return! As for the forms, not only did they need to be redone so they were sharp and clean, but I advised printing them on a cream-colored paper to go with the overall color scheme and on paper with the name and logo of the practice at the top.

Now these may seem like small and perhaps even petty details, but it is subtle details like this that affect the perception of the image a business is trying to project. In this example, the patient very likely did not even realize exactly what it was that made her experience feel so "complete." It was because of careful attention to all the little details that made the reality she experienced while in that office feel totally consistent with the plot or story the doctor wanted to tell.

what business it is their customers want them to be in—and how to reverse engineer it so the customer actually receives that experience. It's a lot of fun to get paid "the big bucks" for something that comes so naturally and that I enjoy doing so much.

Your Business Is Not Different

The legendary Dan Kennedy, the highly esteemed and totally brilliant co-author of this book, has for years been admonishing members of the Glazer-Kennedy Insider's Circle™ to stop thinking "but my business is different." Glazer-Kennedy Insider's Circle™ consists of hundreds of entrepreneurs with six-figure to eight-figure businesses, all of whom owe their phenomenal success to adopting Kennedy-style marketing and various other Kennedy-style business practices. Members attend bi-annual conferences and have the opportunity to take advantage of the dozens and dozens of educational information products GKIC produces. They are also exposed to countless successful entrepreneurs who present at these conferences and share what they did and exactly how they did it to become so successful themselves. And it frustrates the hell out of Dan when he hears someone say after such a presentation, "But that would never work for me, my business is different."

So to prove the point that all businesses are alike, he invited me to speak at their annual SuperConference in 2006. I had never heard of Dan or this group before and had absolutely no idea what kind of business principles he advocated. I just got up there and told my story and shared how I ran my business. It turns out it was almost an exact blueprint of every bit of business advice he always writes and speaks about, and the audience was just blown away. Here was someone who had run an escort service of all things, whose "product" if you will, was call girls, and she was successful because she employed, unwittingly of course, everything they had been hearing Dan say

SYDNEY'S XXX-RATED SALES SECRET #2

So many businessowners let themselves be blindfolded when they fall into the "my business is different" trap. That is not just sensory deprivation, that's opportunity deprivation.

and had been reading about in his books and monthly newsletters for years! How could you not get the message that all businesses are alike and that your business is *not* different after that?

Be America's Next Top Model-er

Nearly every successful business owner will tell you that one of the ways they have achieved that success is by modeling themselves after other successful businesses. The theory is that if another person was able to achieve great success by doing XY&Z, then in all likelihood *you* can achieve great success by doing XY&Z too. Look around you and make note of things that other successful businesses are doing that you could introduce into your business, particularly businesses outside your industry.

For example, cosmetics companies more than any other business use the gift-with-purchase approach to encourage sales, to boost a higher transaction amount, and to introduce new products or acquaint purchasers with products they might not already be familiar with. I have used Estee Lauder's perfume, Knowing, for years after receiving a little vial of it in a gift-with-purchase bag. And because I use the perfume, I also regularly buy the bath powder, the lotion, and pretty much everything else with that scent, and have done so for years. They created a customer for life with a little vial that probably cost them pennies.

How might you model the cosmetics companies in order to boost your transaction size, introduce new products or services, and/or reward people for being good customers? Let me tell you how I did it.

We wanted to thank/reward our best clients for not only spending a lot of money with us, but also for being so terrific to the young ladies who saw them. Each year, right before the holidays, Sherry-Lehmann, a very ritzy liquor store on Madison Avenue on the Upper East Side of Manhattan, has a sale on champagne by the case. (Note how they upped their transaction size by having the sale on the champagne by the case, not by the bottle.) Because we wanted to support the image of ours being a very upscale, premium-priced business, only the very best champagne would do. So every year during the big sale we placed an order for two cases of Dom Perignon.

At first, we just had the young lady stop by the office on her way to the call and gave her the bottle to give to the client. It didn't take but one or two times to figure out that if we chilled it, most likely he would decide to drink it on the spot. Well, since nobody gulps down a bottle of fine champagne, a call that might otherwise have been one hour turned into two, and a two-hour call turned into three. Now this is precisely what they coined the term "win-win situation" for: The client was impressed and flattered he was being acknowledged as a valued client, and we increased the dollar amount of the transaction with the increased hours. And there were ancillary "wins" as well:

SYDNEY'S XXX-RATED SALES SECRET #3

ALL BUSINESSES ARE ALIKE!!

If the call girl business can pick up viable strategies from the cosmetics business, then your business can implement strategies from an escort service. Just keep it clean and legal!

We provided the client with a special Experience, subtly reinforcing in his mind that we were a prestige business by gifting him with the very finest champagne, and we put more money in the pockets of the young ladies, also reinforcing our top-drawer image with them and providing them with a special Experience too.

Businesses are all alike in more ways that you could ever imagine. Look around you and make careful note of what exceptionally successful businesses in other fields are doing. Pay attention to what the businesses *you* patronize are doing. Keep an open mind and creatively modify the successful practices of others, and you will see your sales and profits soar.

Just because you have a service business, resist making the assumption that there is nothing to be learned from one that sells products, and vice versa. Mine was a service business, yet I got the idea for champagne-with-purchase from cosmetics companies, which sell products.

Don't make the mistake of thinking your business is different and you couldn't possibly learn anything from a former Madam. I can tell you from personal experience that all business *are* alike, and that if you keep an open mind and exercise a little creativity, I can show you how to be just as successful as I have been.

XXX POWER IDEAS

- **X** There are lessons to be learned from every job you have ever had, and they can be used in every job or business you will ever have.
- **X** Niche markets are lucrative, but sub-niche markets are even more lucrative and it's very easy to command premium prices.
- **X** Your business will really take off once you understand what business you are really in and give your customers what they really want.
- **X** Look around at what other successful businesses and businesspeople are doing and model your business and yourself after them.
- **X** Ideas come from unexpected sources and not necessarily from businesses similar to yours: Keep your eyes alert and your mind open.
- **X** "Gift-with-purchase" is a strategy that can be used in nearly every business—you might have to get unusually creative, but the opportunity is there.
- **X** Gifts must always reinforce your image and position in the market and enhance the "mental movie" you are trying to create in the mind of your future and current customers.
- **X** Gifts should be fun and create an experience—into every life a little champagne should pour!

Chapter 2

AIM TO PLEASE

What Business Are You Really In?

You want to be in the business your customers want you to be in. So before you spend another dime on advertising, marketing, a new website, an expansion, or anything else, sit down and make sure you know what business you are *really* in. As I mentioned earlier, contrary to what you may believe, I was not really in the sex business, I was in the fantasy business—and the trust business. Our clients were looking for a Fantasy Call Girl Experience. They were looking for a business they could trust to give them that Experience on a consistent, discreet basis. And they were willing to pay top dollar for it.

SYDNEY'S XXX-RATED SALES SECRET #4

The needs and desires of your customer determine what business you are ***really*** in. What is it they dream about, aspire to, fantasize doing or having? Satisfy these basic, often secret, desires and watch your business take off!

Look around you and think about the places you patronize—what business are *they* really in? Why do you really buy the products you do? What below-the-surface needs are you satisfying when you make these purchases? Once you get the hang of it, then focus your attention to what hopes, needs, fears, desires, dreams, fantasies, self-affirmation longings and aspirations your customers are hoping or expecting to have satisfied when they dial *your* number, walk through *your* door, or log onto *your* website.

Bad Execution Foils the Best Efforts

The sales process begins with this understanding of what business you are really in and what your customers are really looking for. The primary objective of advertising and marketing is to make prospective customers aware of your business and to communicate that you have the ability to provide them with what they are really seeking. Effective advertising and marketing creates prospective customers who, based on the information they have been able to obtain, are lured to your business because they believe you are selling what they really want. You have the solution to their problem, a product that will satisfy a particular need or desire they secretly harbor, or you are going to give them an experience they have always wanted to have. If your advertising and marketing have done a *really* good job, they have already been "sold" and come to you already prepared to make a purchase, once they confirm the product or service is what they are expecting.

But what often happens is customers are thwarted in their attempt to give you their money. Some ways the sales process screws this up are:

- The right hand does not knowing what the left hand is doing—everyone involved in the sale needs to be on the same page delivering the same message and working towards the same outcome.
- The old Boy Scout motto, "Be Prepared," is ignored. Anyone interacting with a customer needs to be ready with all the information a customer might ask for and/or realistically hope to receive.
- Pure and simple carelessness and laziness.
- Being oblivious to what a customer actually experiences when doing business with you.

SCREWING UP THE SALES PROCESS

Loehman's, an off-price store that primarily sells clothing, spent a considerable amount of money mailing out a gorgeous brochure advertising a big event featuring a large selection of Italian designer women's clothing. It was beautifully photographed and printed on heavy, glossy stock. So far so good: Their advertisement made the prospective customer aware of who they were and what they were selling.

Upon walking in the front door, the customer is greeted by an employee. The customer shows the brochure to the greeter. This employee informs the customer he has no idea where in the store this event is, has no idea there even is such an event in the first place, and makes absolutely no effort to track down any further information. When asked how he cannot have even heard of a sale the store went to such great lengths to promote, the answer was: "I'm just security." A lot of money and effort spent to get a customer into their store foiled by the first point of contact in the sales process!

continued

SCREWING UP THE SALES PROCESS, CONTINUED

A subsequent visit to this particular Loehman's is no better. A very large sign standing just inside the front door announces they have just received a new shipment of designer shoes. The sign is clearly intended to inspire nearly every woman who walks in the door to make a beeline for the sale. But where, exactly, is it? Again, no employee in the vicinity knew anything about it, although one helpfully noted that the shoe department was "downstairs somewhere."

An effective advertising campaign and a perfectly good in-store promotional effort sabotaged by a totally ineffective sales process.

The Broken Bridge

Think of the sales process as a bridge your customers have to cross to get from the side that represents their initial interest in buying from you, to the other side—the consummation of the sale. What are the potential gaps or slats they might fall through as they make that journey?

The first broken slat in the bridge is not knowing what business you are really in. Unless and until you fully understand what that is, you will:

- be unable to communicate via your advertising and marketing that you have "it."
- be unable to design your sales process so you can effectively sell "it."
- have such an incomplete idea of what "it" is that you may be offering the wrong thing, an inaccurate version of the right thing, or an incomplete version of the right thing.
- be charging less than you could easily get if you positioned "it" properly.

The Biggest Hole in Most Bridges

The next gap in the bridge your customers need to maneuver around is your sales process, the most common and biggest broken slat customers encounter as they try to cross the bridge. Can you answer these questions about your sales process?

- Does the first person the customer comes into contact with have the knowledge and ability to answer questions and move the customer on to the next step (e.g., an appointment, a follow-up call, a mailing, etc.)?
- Is the first action a customer has to take simple and easily understood (e.g., contacting you through your website, leaving a specific message with specific information on a voice mail, etc.)?
- Is it easy to contact you in the first place or are there irritating or confusing hoops they must jump through first (e.g., voice mail hell, lots of personal information to fill out, etc.)?
- Is it easy to find you, either online or in person? Is your website easy to navigate? Is there adequate parking, etc.?
- Is the person actually making the sale both very knowledgeable about the product or service and a good salesperson? If you sell online or by direct mail, does your copy fully explain the product or service? Are there clear and detailed photographs, where applicable?
- Do you make it easy for customers to give you their money? Is the actual financial transaction simple and straightforward?
- Do you deliver the product or service in an appealing and timely manner? If the customer is not actually walking out with it in her hot little hand, is the transaction finished up with a full understanding of when she will receive the product or service? Do you have options for those customers who are willing to pay more to get it sooner?

SYDNEY'S XXX-RATED SALES SECRET #5

Mother may have warned you that being easy was a bad thing, but I am telling you that being easy is not only a good thing, it will make you good money too.

THE LEOPARD'S SPOTS: A LITTLE STORY

On my way home from a three-day trip with a consulting client, I found myself cooling my heels in Air Canada's private club in the Montreal airport due to a flight delay. I decided to kill some time by going online and searching for a much more interesting computer bag than the boring black one I was currently carrying. While it may not have had any style, it was extremely well-designed, and I wanted a new one that had as many of the same features as possible. In leopard.

A Google search turned up many potential sites. The selection was not as extensive as one might have hoped—apparently leopard computer bags are not in high demand. They don't exactly bestow a "corporate" image, but I wanted something fun and since I'm not exactly the corporate type, this was not a concern. Besides, it would match my leopard luggage. And I was willing to pay just about anything for it the very second I found one I liked.

It was immediately obvious that whoever decides how these bags are displayed on these websites has no idea how women buy a bag. There is no woman on earth who would even consider buying a bag until she has opened it up and looked inside. Not one of these leopard bags had a close-up photo so you could see the specifics, nor did they show, or in most cases even describe in any kind of detail, how the inside was designed. I thought to myself, "How dumb is that? Do these people really think I'm going to dig out my credit card for a complete and total crap shoot? I don't think so." As of this writing, I still do not have a new leopard computer bag.

Know who your customer is *and what that customer needs to know* before she will place an order. If you sell products online or in a catalog, make sure your prospective customer, particularly if a female customer, has as much detail as possible about its appearance and its "attributes" so she feels she has sufficient information to make the decision to make the purchase. If she is not sure the item meets her criteria, you will never get the sale; the hassle to return it is just not worth it.

Experiencing the Potholes

The Experience a customer has while going through your sales process is very important; most businesses don't even bother to fill this pothole. Of course, being able to make the purchase as easily and quickly as possible is the only Experience a customer wants under certain circumstances, but this is not always the case. High-ticket purchases in particular require careful attention to the environment, personal service and amenities, knowledgeable and patient salespeople, and a little extra pizzazz whenever possible and appropriate. Better restaurants are masters at creating an Experience for their patrons, especially those in very competitive locales.

TWO WORDS, TWO MINUTES, AND ONE SALE

Ileana Kane
milliondollarmuse.com

The new home building industry was in a downturn cycle. I was marketing and selling stacked Santa Fe-style condominiums in a suburban neighborhood—that is, if potential buyers could find this community. Not a good mix for vigorous sales.

I looked up from my desk to see a potential prospect was about to walk in the door. I immediately recognized him—it was Clive. Clive had been in five times in the last six weeks and even though he was bright, warm, and outgoing, his answers to my questions were always elusive. Today I made the decision he was not going to walk out without choosing his home, authorizing his purchase agreement, and giving me a big fat deposit check.

Clive came in and I flashed a warm welcoming smile. We made small talk as I escorted him through the home models again. We went to look again at the condominium he had been interested in. We climbed the stairs to the master bedroom and a whole new world opened up with a forever view of the valley with the privacy of an estate. He liked the home, he wanted the home, and then the brakes went on. He saw the hillside and asked about the weeds.

"Where do you see weeds? Oh, you mean the natural chaparral?" And then I shut up (the first one who speaks loses) and smiled. Clive said nothing. Our eyes were locked in and I made no change in expression. That very moment seemed to be suspended for hours. Then I noticed his eyes crinkle at the side and a smile followed. I heard the words "yes, natural chaparral." He had seen the private hillside through a different lens. Clive purchased his first new home that day.

All it takes is a new intention, deeper listening, and a new simple perspective to give two words two minutes to make one sale.

How Much Money Do You Want to Make?

Another very common hole in the sales bridge is focusing on selling the features of your product or service; this approach makes the least amount of money. You start to raise income when you sell solutions and benefits instead of things. But your income will skyrocket when you sell aspirations, hopes, dreams, even fantasies—Experiences people want. And depending on how much this Experience means to a customer, they will pay more for it.

The Most Misunderstood Gap in the Bridge

One gap in the bridge that most business owners fail to fully understand and appreciate is the incongruency between the movie playing in the customer's mind and the reality they actually encounter. When your advertising and marketing efforts lead a prospective customer to believe they are going to have a certain Experience when buying your product or using your service, and the reality is different, that incongruence dismays and confuses them. When the environment they find themselves in, the people they interact with, the manner in which they are treated, or the actual product or service itself does not match up to what they are expecting, it is unsettling and disappointing. They either do not buy, do not spend as much as they might have otherwise, or they simply never come back.

The Performance Hole in the Bridge

Another very common hole in the bridge many businesses fail to recognize or fill in is the actual performance of the sale itself. If you are simply selling commodities, the only performance a customer cares about is how quickly you can accomplish the transaction so they can get out the door. When you are selling solutions and benefits, the customer usually wants some sort of "proof." This may be visual (graphs, charts, photographs), written (a report or testimonial), or verbal (a detailed explanation). A physical demonstration of the product can be very effective. How and when you introduce these elements

MINDING THE STORE

Recently, I walked past the liquor store on my corner and noticed that both the front and side windows, comprising a good 50 feet of display space, were filled with bottles of Piper Heidsieck rose champagne, my very most absolutely favorite kind of bubbly. Clearly Piper was launching the debut of their first rose champagne with a big marketing push, and was paying this store for the exclusive use of their window space for an entire month. They certainly got my attention; I headed right inside to find out how much a bottle was going to cost me. I was already sold, the only thing left to do was give them my money.

The store was not very busy and there were three employees standing around the front desk, as well as another one in the back. I gave everyone a big smile and announced how excited I was that Piper Heidsieck had come out with a rose champagne, I wanted to buy one, and how much was a bottle? Blank looks from all three. Not a single one of them knew Piper Heidsieck was a brand of champagne nor were they aware they had a 50-foot window display of it. One asked me to accompany him outside to show him what I was talking about!

When we returned inside, he walked me back to the champagne section and asked the man stationed there where the rose Piper was located. Another blank stare. After carefully searching every shelf, he finally located it, and seemed surprised to see it. Then it took a while to look up the price. Had I not been so absolutely determined to have a bottle, I would have walked out in disgust long before. This store didn't just have a missing slat in their bridge, their bridge had totally collapsed.

is important. Selling a product or service with a strong emotional component (aspirations, hopes, dreams, fantasies) requires a carefully scripted presentation that sweeps the customer into feeling they are already experiencing it, which triggers the decision to experience it for real.

SYDNEY'S XXX-RATED SALES SECRET #6

If you do not make sure your employees are fully briefed about your advertising and marketing campaigns, you are just pouring jeroboams (four ordinary bottles of champagne!) of money down the drain.

Sales choreography can be physical or psychological, and is a subtle, often subliminal influence that sways (one might even say manipulates) customers to perceive you or your business in a particular way or encourages them to respond or behave, or not, in a certain manner. Lack of effective choreography is a pothole that exists in most sales bridges; filling it in can make a considerable difference in your bottom line.

SYDNEY'S XXX-RATED SALES SECRET #7

You need more than good foreplay to consummate the deal.

What You Say Affects What You Get

Another gap in the bridge, and one of the simplest to repair, is sales language. The words you use to sell, be they written or spoken, can make or break a sale. Customers need to hear or read words that resonate with them—words that make them feel you understand who they are, that you know what they need or want, and that lead them to believe you have or can do that which they are seeking. Using the wrong words can break a sale and, in a worst-case scenario, cause a customer to never want to do business with you, ever.

MAKE IT WORK FOR THEM

Ileana Kane

milliondollarmuse.com

I had been handed a coupon for a "free, no-strings-attached" manicure. This was good timing for me because I was looking to find a manicurist closer to home.

One problem—I was away on a trip during the dates on the coupon. So I called to see if the owner would consider extending the offer for two days for me. The young lady who answered told me no. When I returned home, I had another coupon from the same shop that was mailed out to our neighborhood with a different free offering (which would have worked for me). However, since there are many nail salons where I live, my experience made me decide to pass on the new mailing.

The loss to the company? The lifetime value of this client would have been approximately $9,000, plus purchasing products, plus referrals. When you have someone interested in your product or service and they are ready to try what you have to offer and you have them on the phone right there ready, willing, and able, what do you do? You make it work for them! No excuses!

Bringing Your Bridge Up to Code

In the following chapters, you will find the information you need to identify where the holes in your bridge are and how to fix them.

XXX POWER IDEAS

- **X** Always remember that you want to be in the business your customers want you to be in—as long as it's legal!
- **X** Make it easy for people to do business with you.
- **X** Customers are not just buying a product or service, they are also buying the Experience of buying it, owning it, and using it.
- **X** The movie in your customer's mind must correspond with the reality he experiences.
- **X** The manner in which you perform the sale must be congruent with what you are selling.
- **X** Sales choreography can be psychological or physical, and when properly designed and executed will have a measurable impact on your bottom line.
- **X** It's not just what you say, it's the words you use to say it.

Chapter

3

ATTRACTION

Making Your Business Irresistible

Before you can make your business irresistible, you have to be sure you know what business you are really in and what kind of customers you most want to have. So many businesses feel their ideal customer is anyone who wants to, or can afford to, give them their money. I would argue that this is faulty thinking.

I regularly turned down potential clients who could have and would have paid our fees. I also declined to do further business with a client who proved to be someone who did not fit my definition of an ideal client. And I had a very specific list of criteria as to who an ideal client was.

As I mentioned back in Chapter 2, we were not in the sex business. Yes, there was sex involved, but, as I also mentioned, if that was all a client really wanted, he could have gotten it for a lot less. There are plenty of agencies in New York City in the crude, cheap, sex-as-a-commodity business. We were in the *fantasy* business—a very specific fantasy for a very specific kind of client. Not to be disrespectful, but I described our ideal clients as "straight, conservative, successful businessmen." They had to be very successful because our prices were very high and they were paying us with after-tax dollars. (I'm sure a few of them found creative ways to expense it, but for the most part this was a personal outlay.)

What You See Is What You Get

How did we attract this particular type of client? How did we communicate to them the message "This is exactly what I'm looking for, this is for me!"? At the time we started the business, our only advertising option was a "newspaper" called *Screw*—and if you find the name distasteful, I assure you it was the classiest thing about it. The majority of the pages in this august publication were devoted to classified ads, most of which offered the company of various types of women for various types of sexual encounters. Just to give you an example of the tenor of these ads, my favorite one had a photo of a nude girl seated with her legs in a wide V and the headline screamed, "Cum into my valley." Real classy, right? The others were slight variations on this one, and they basically all looked the same too.

Our ad, by comparison, was very simple—no photo and a lot of white space. There was a heavy black border around the perimeter, a narrower one inside that, and the name of the company, Cachet, was prominently placed in the middle in a bold, deco-style font that I have never seen anywhere since. Below our name was our tag line, "New York's Most Trusted Service." In the lower left corner was the price, $150 per hour (that was the price at the time we advertised in there) and underneath were our hours, 5:00PM to 1:00AM. In the lower right corner were the two phone numbers, and that was it. This ad literally jumped right off the page; you couldn't miss it, it was so different and so unique in its understated style compared to all of the others.

This Is for Me!

Men who are seeking to patronize this type of service business fall into several categories; most of the advertisements in *Screw* appealed to the majority of their readers. But there was a sub-niche of men who were looking for a more refined, upscale experience, if you will, and were totally turned off by those ads. As soon as they saw ours, their immediate reaction was, "Wow! This is for me!" and dialed our number. If a prospective client couldn't tell we were expensive and markedly different than the other businesses just from the style of our ad, one look at the price, which was usually at least twice as much as everyone else, certainly got that point across. Finally, most of the other services were open 24 hours a day and we were only open in the evening for eight hours—just one more thing that differentiated us from all the rest.

So we attracted those clients who were looking for an upscale service, who were willing and able to spend top dollar, and who were pretty much only available in the evenings because they were doing business during the day. It was my experience from working for Eddie that most people who called to make an appointment after 1 A.M. were "up to no good" and drugs were involved. Definitely not the sort of client I wanted my girls exposed to.

The style and content of our ad eliminated those who were not in a high-income bracket, who wanted to party late into the night, have a quick roll in the hay during the day, or were looking for a "hot chick" or a sleazy experience (don't kid yourselves, the sleaze factor is extremely appealing to a lot of people).

Ideal, Yet Not Ideal

One aspect of customer acquisition that most business owners rarely think about is: What kind of customers do you want your *employees* to have to deal with? Just because someone can afford your product or service and is willing to accept other terms involved with the transaction does not automatically make them an ideal customer. I was very particular with respect to the caliber of client I wanted my young ladies to see and the standard of behavior that was acceptable while she was with him. I declined to do business with numerous clients for all kinds of reasons: one was a doctor who liked to see someone after working a 48-hour shift, during which time he did not shave and did not want to shave before she arrived (the stubble tore up the girls' skin); another had several cats and was, shall we say, less than fastidious about cleaning out the kitty litter boxes on a regular basis; another had an apartment that was so minimally furnished, the only place to sit was a mattress on the floor (and this was someone on Wall Street who did *very* well); and so on and so on. These were all perfectly nice guys and fit all of our "ideal client" criteria in every way except for the fact that it was an unpleasant experience for the girls to see them.

SYDNEY'S XXX-RATED SALES SECRET #8

Just because a prospect fits into your ideal parameters, they are still not an ideal client if they are difficult or unpleasant to do business with.

Are You the One for Me?

An effective advertising or marketing campaign should make it clear what kind of person your product or service is for. And remember that the more specialized the sub-niche, the easier it is to attract ideal customers. If your product or service is appropriate for more than one distinct sub-niche, run totally separate marketing and ad campaigns and definitely use a different, specifically appropriate name for each one. Just like when prospective clients saw our ad and felt, "This is for me," your ads should evoke the same response in your prospective customers.

Many businesspeople erroneously think that the more mass appeal they have, the more business they'll do. This might be true if you are in a basic commodity business (think orange juice), but it has been proven over and over again that almost all products and services do better when they target a specific clientele. By trying to be everything to everyone, you end up attracting a lot of incompatible prospects who are going to waste your time, energy, and resources because in the end, you are not a fit for each other.

We Are Not for You

Some businesses go out of their way to make it clear who is *not* a welcome customer. Harry Winston, the world-famous jeweler whose flagship store is on Fifth Avenue in New York City, has the most effective tactic for doing this I have ever experienced. When I was in high school, I used to take the train into the city by myself and spend the day window shopping at all the big department stores that were then on Fifth Avenue. The rule set by parents was, I was allowed to walk two blocks east on 34th Street (where the Penn Station is located) to Fifth Avenue, and then up Fifth Avenue to 57th Street as far as Bergdorf Goodman. Nowhere else. On one trip I decided to go into all the jewelry stores—Cartier, Van Cleef & Arpels, Harry Winston, Tiffany, and others. When I got to Harry Winston and went to go in the door, a uniformed guard greeted me and asked if I had an appointment. Well, of course I didn't, at which point he told me I needed one if I wanted to come inside. Most people don't know that this is illegal in New York but it sure is an extremely effective way of repelling the Looky Lous, their less-than-ideal customer.

HERE COMES THE BRIDE

Ciara Daykin

rockstarweddingplanner.com; fireflyoccasions.com

The bride is an interesting consumer. She's only in my target market for a year to two years maximum, then she's off and married and has no longer has a need for my services. But while she's there she is voracious for information, and more specifically, FREE information.

(Every bride is on a budget regardless of how large or small that budget is.)

I use a targeted client attraction process specialized for brides, involving a lot more than simply placing an ad in *Bride's* magazine. To draw them into my market reach, I offer a free report called "The Top 10 Tips to Take Your Wedding from Cookie Cutter to Couture." This report addresses most brides' biggest concern: "I don't want my wedding to look like everyone else's." I tap into that concern right away with my free report, and then I continue playing on the same theme throughout all my marketing materials. One of the most highly read e-zine articles I ever wrote was, "Will Your Wedding Look Like All the Rest?" I think every bride who read it must have e-mailed us for more information!

My fees are uncommonly high for the wedding planner industry. In order to attract brides with a wedding budget that can accommodate my fees, my marketing copy and pictures convey a glamorous, haute couture look and feel. Every bride is the star of her own wedding, and wants to be showcased as the star. We took advantage of this natural desire to have a wedding befitting the celebrity that she is. And we help her fulfill that desire.

I have found that the more I charge, the more exclusive my services are perceived to be—one of the primary reasons affluent brides choose to work with me. I have found a way not to exclude those brides who don't have as big a budget but still want my help by providing them with my wedding information products, which help them design a celebrity wedding day experience on their own.

If It Looks Like a Duck . . .

One of the easiest ways to communicate what kind of business you are and what kind of person would be comfortable being your customer, or would be an appropriate customer, is your décor or your packaging. If you walk into an office and see oriental rugs, period furniture, and beautifully upholstered sofas and chairs, you can be pretty certain the prices are going to be high. You probably won't get a conservative haircut at a hair salon with wild, wacky décor and stylists who have purple hair. Even if you were from another country and not familiar with the names, you could walk into a Gap or Old Navy and know a T-shirt there is going to cost a lot less than one from the Chanel or Versace boutiques on Madison Avenue. Face cream in a heavy, frosted Lalique style jar is going to set you back a lot more than face cream in a plain glass jar. And lip gloss in a hot-pink-with-red-polka-dots tube that sells for $9.99 is unlikely to appeal to anyone's grandmother.

You need to devise a way to let people know whether or not they will be a good fit for what it is you do or sell. It saves both buyer and seller a lot of time and energy. Neither you nor your staff need to spend time on customers who, in the end, are not going to do business with you because what you offer does not fit their bottom-line criteria, whether that be functional, financial, emotional, practical, etc. And they don't need to waste their time with you either.

SYDNEY'S XXX-RATED SALES SECRET #9

Time is money, whether you are in the business of charging by the hour or not.

The Customer Is Always Right

At one point I noticed that we were being asked, "If I paid more money, could you send me someone prettier?" Or, "If I pay you more money, could you send me a 'ten'?" And, "Do you have any girls who are more expensive?" Ninety percent of the time, it turned out that what they meant by "prettier," a "ten," and "more expensive" was, tall, blond, beautiful, busty, and under 25. (I always used to joke that thank goodness they didn't also want one more B—brainy—because it was my experience that this last B rarely came along with the other three.) Having never been someone who voluntarily offered to pay more when I could get it for less, I was fascinated by these requests. We were already charging top dollar for the most fabulous girls in New York City, yet here were these guys who were all but begging to pay more. So I did what any responsible businesswoman would do: I charged them more.

I already had a few girls who fit the standard please-let-me-pay-you-more-money description—any client could have seen them for the regular price. But we stepped up to the plate, responded to the obvious market demand, and tacked on an additional 25 percent, which made the clients happy, the girls happy, and my bottom line happy. In many businesses there are customers who will almost always choose the highest-priced option, regardless of whether or not there is a corresponding increase in value in the product or service. The real value to them lies in having the ability to spend the money or the knowledge that they own the most expensive option, and how that makes the customer feel about *themselves*.

Give Them What They Really Want

You are leaving money on the table, or more precisely, in your customers' wallets, if you do not offer a premium-priced version of your product or service. You needn't necessarily create a whole new or different product or service, just come up with something you could add to what you are already offering: more personalized follow-up or customer service, ancillary products that complement the regular product, a special phone number with a dedicated person who will respond immediately to their call, an opportunity to take advantage of "special offers" only available to them—let your imagination soar.

You should have one or two options whose prices fall in-between your regular price and your premium price for those who want the emotional validation from spending more, but who can't afford or simply cannot rationalize taking the highest-priced option. Always keep in mind that the features or services you add on to the regular product or service must have an intrinsic or emotional value to the customer in the niche you are targeting; in other words, they must be appropriate for that market as well as appropriate to the business you are in. Just as an example, a bottle of Dom Perignon was an appropriate gift for my former clients because it was an expensive, premium champagne and we were an expensive, premium service. Champagne is also associated with extravagance and festive occasions, definitely an association we wanted to emphasize.

Remember, just because your customers aren't actively clamoring to pay you more doesn't mean they wouldn't appreciate and take advantage of the opportunity to do so if you gave them the option.

RICHES IN NICHES

Karen Campbell
campbellscotties.com

Who knew that when we purchased Robbie, our first Scottish Terrier puppy, that he would lead us to a collectibles business many years later? We began our own collection, purchasing the older Scottie collectibles from the 1930s and 40s, learning what we could of their history. We even attended the Scottie Collector's Convention in Ohio.

Twelve years ago, I was at a wholesale gift show shopping for another business and saw some charming new Scottie collectibles. On the spur of the moment, I ordered the products and advertised them in the *Scottie Collector's* magazine. The response was immediate; this new business took off so fast, our heads were spinning. We published a catalog, used direct mail, and went searching for someone who could fashion a website with a shopping cart before the days when turnkey website solutions became readily available.

We quickly learned that Scottie collectors wanted to purchase from someone who has a "history" with collecting, knows what is collectible, knows quality, and knows what is likely to increase in value. Most of all they want to build a relationship that centered on excellent customer service and the love of the breed.

Because of the old "Black and White" Scotch advertising, many people own both a Scottie and a West Highland Terrier, or "Westie." Those customers started asking for us to carry Westie collectibles and we have gradually added some to our line. Our segmented list of Westie collectors has grown, mainly by word of mouth and Westie chat lists.

We have published an e-mail newsletter for over ten years, but in the last year have changed it to an e-zine format with incredible response.

Most people say "Oh, you sell figurines" when they hear about our business. Actually, figurines don't sell very well! Amazingly, our biggest sellers are greeting cards, especially boxed Scottie Christmas cards. Last year we shipped out over 2,000 boxes—who could have known? Yes, "there are riches in niches" but also undreamed of satisfaction, pleasure, and fun.

There Are Riches in Niches

If you had a Shih Tzu dog, wouldn't you pay more for doggie biscuits that claimed they were created just for the special dietary needs of Shih Tzus? If you were an attorney, wouldn't you pay more for a word processing program that was designed specifically for lawyers? If you were a woman over 50, wouldn't you pay more for a face cream that claimed it had ingredients that would diminish the appearance of fine lines and wrinkles? Sure you would—and every day people spend more for products and services that they believe have been created or designed specifically for their particular needs or situations.

CATERING TO YOUR CLIENTELE

I have a friend who is in the catering business. He has set up three separate entities with three different names for three different types of clientele. One is for his corporate clients, and there are certain menu choices available, certain choices in linens and tableware, and certain price packages. He also has a thriving business in catering private parties in client's homes. The menu choices are different from the menus for corporate clients, as is the quality of the linens and table and glassware, and clients pay by the hour. Lastly, he has a wedding business with all the food, etc., tailored to that kind of event; he charges more than he does for the other two because wedding clients are much more difficult to work with. The staff is made up of the same people, he uses the same linen and party rental service, and the same chef makes all the food. In fact, the food items are sometimes identical, but are given names that are more appealing to the clientele and/or are presented in a different manner.

Could you create a version of the product or service you sell for a niche within your market? The product or service can be identical to, or a slightly tweaked version of, one you offer to all your other customers. But if the niche customer believes there is something special and different about it, if it sends the message "this is for me," that is the one they will buy. And they'll happily pay more for it because if it costs more, then it must be better! All you might need do is use different packaging, for example. The cosmetics industry has that trick down cold. Did you know that all lip liner pencils are made in the same two factories? The only thing different is the appearance of the pencil itself and the packaging. But the one you buy from Dior in Neiman Marcus is going to cost you five times more than the one from Maybelline you get in a drugstore because of the name and the packaging.

THE STORY THAT LAUNCHED MY BUSINESS

James Roche

InfoProductGuy.com

I was spotlighted at a networking event for five minutes. Instead of focusing on what I do, which is developing information products, like the other presenters did, I talked about the benefits my business provides to my clients. At the end of my five minutes, I told everyone to get out one of their business cards and write, "I want passive revenue" on the back. Then I offered a Special Report to everyone in the room who gave me their card and the next day sent it out.

But that's not the end of it! In the e-mail accompanying the report I told them to stay tuned because in a couple of days I was going to send another e-mail with an even MORE valuable offer. Two days later I sent out that second e-mail offering the first 10 people to respond a free 45-minute consultation, which at the time was valued at $97.00. Ten people responded immediately. After giving the free consultations, I ended up making four sales worth over $7,000. Not bad for my first five days in business!

The best part is that three of the four referred other potential clients, and that was what really got the ball rolling for my business.

Yes Virginia, There Is a Sub Niche (In Your Business)

Take a good look at whom your present customers are. Do they fall into two or more distinct groups? Do you have certain customers who have predictable needs or desires that you could create a "separate" business for? It's not unusual to be unable to see opportunities like this in your own business; I'm sure you are familiar with the saying, "you can't see the forest for the trees." This is where the usefulness of fresh eyes comes in. Fresh eyes are able to see what you cannot. Fresh eyes are able to see your business from an entirely different point of view and come up with fresh ideas you would never have thought of on your own.

A few people are able look at their own business with a totally dispassionate and objective eye, but this is a very rare gift. Most others find they need to bring in someone from the outside to help them identify the sub-niches in their client base in order to create individual entities for each one. Then, of course, you need to have individual marketing plans, sales processes, packaging, and the like, that reflect that entity's unique character and appeals to their customer. I spend a lot of time doing this for clients and believe me, it pays off.

XXX POWER IDEAS

- Be sure you know exactly who your ideal customer is and design your advertising and marketing campaigns to attract them, while at the same time have them be unappealing to the customers you do not want.
- Be clear with yourself about who you do not want as a customer and devise ways to send the message "we are not for you."
- Offer a premium option for everything you do or sell.
- Break your customers down into sub-niches and create separate business entities appealing specifically to each one.

Chapter 4

SEDUCTION

Satisfying Your Customer's Secret Desires

When I talk about my former escort service, I always point out that the business we were *really* in was the fantasy business. Why? Because that's the business our customers wanted us to be in.

Eddie, the sleazeball who owned the agency where I moonlighted as a phone girl all those years ago, believed his customers wanted him to be in the sex-as-a-commodity business, and certainly many of them did. But I figured out pretty quickly that many of the men who were calling were looking for a lot more. How did I know this? *I listened to them*. Instead of focusing solely on asking the customer to describe the physical features he wanted in an escort, which is the way Eddie told us to do it, I encouraged him to talk about the kind of person he was hoping to see. By engaging him in a dialog by asking questions and really listening to the answers, I learned about what he was like as a person as well as the type of young lady he was seeking.

Eddie ran the most expensive escort service then appearing in *Screw*, the only publication at that time in New York that took ads of this nature. Operating on the theory that if it was the most expensive it must be the best, many of the men who called Eddie's service were looking for an upscale experience. The problem was that Eddie had no idea what that was. In his mind, men were attracted to "hot chicks"; the more stereotypically "hot" they were, the better. He made the typical mistake that so many businesspeople make: He assumed that his customers had the exact same taste as he did. So he only "sold" what he would have wanted to "buy" because it never occurred to him that some people might actually prefer something else.

SYDNEY'S XXX-RATED SALES SECRET #10

It's not about you. Your customers couldn't care less what you like or what you think they should buy. Customers only care about what *they* want. So if you are interested in getting their money into your pocket, you'd better find out exactly what that is.

Who Is *Your* Customer?

Eddie's approach was in a way understandable, because Eddie didn't know what these men might want—he didn't know any successful, affluent, upper- or upper-middle-class men. But I did. These men were just like my girlfriends' fathers, my parents' friends, all my male relatives, all the men at the beach club, the country club, the yacht club—pretty much the only kind of men I'd ever known. Most of them would be absolutely horrified if they called an escort service and an hour later have some hootchie mama prance in their door wearing a short, tight dress, "bed head" hair, and sky-high platform shoes. Add a heavy New York accent and some chewing gum, and some of these guys might have gone into cardiac arrest! You may be laughing, but considering just about every escort service at that time was run by men like Eddie, this was not an unlikely scenario.

Things have been improving since then. Most of the better services are now being operated by women who were former working girls themselves; and they have a much better idea of what upscale clients are looking for. All the ones I know or know of were once independent girls—girls who have their own private clientele and are usually part of a network of other independent girls. For the most part, the clients of independent girls are wealthy, or at least very well off, and usually extremely nice and well-behaved, if for no other reason than these girls wouldn't see them were they not.

What Do Your Customers Really Want?

My clients formed a very specific sub-niche of men who

a) frequented escort services
b) were more comfortable with and preferred to see "young ladies" as opposed to hot babes
c) could afford to pay top dollar
d) were willing to pay top dollar.

As it turned out, the majority of the men in this sub-niche were also seeking a particular EXPERIENCE. They were not solely interested in the appearance of the young lady, nor were they focused on the sexual act. It was an entire Experience they were seeking, the Experience of *the* most beautiful, *the* most elegant, *the* most charming, *the* most attentive New York call girl walking in *their* door.

This perfect girl had no agenda of her own; she was there to listen to him, to have fun with him, to hold an interesting conversation with him, and to be pleasant and relaxing company for him. Whenever he decided to move on to what we euphemistically called "the nitty gritty," this meant that he was ready for the evening to wind down. The young lady (who, of course, had a great figure) would disrobe down to her matching bra, panties, garter belt, and stockings and make him "happy" in whatever manner he desired (and we allowed). Then she would dress, they would take care of the "business end" of the evening, and she would leave looking as elegant as she did when she first arrived. This was the Fantasy Experience our clients wanted and this was the Fantasy Experience we provided.

You Are Not Your Customer

One of the easiest traps to fall into is to think like Eddie—that your customers want what you want and like what you like. This is particularly easy when you do not understand who your customer is and what they value. You must always be asking questions or testing different items or versions of items to refine your selection or offering, as well as keep up with your clientele's changing tastes.

What magazines and newspapers do your ideal customers read? You should be reading them too. If you are a local business, which stores and restaurants do your ideal customers frequent? Go there yourself and try to identify what the customers you see there have in common. What search keywords do visitors to your website use and what other websites come up when you do a search with the same words? Figure out what those customers are looking for. Do surveys to help you find out this information; everyone likes to be asked their opinion.

YOU ARE NOT YOUR CUSTOMER: A CASE STUDY

George Sierchio
consultantscoach.com
info@consultantscoach.com

I recently had a client who was trying to start up a new technology company while still working full time at a "real job." He became exasperated because he couldn't understand why his prospective customers didn't "get" the help his new venture was offering.

My question to him was "What makes you think they *want* the help you wish to give them?" His answer was as expected: They needed his help.

But did they *want* it?

I explained to him that his point of view was not necessarily, nor usually, the same way his prospects viewed their situation. My advice to him was to avoid a business model based on convincing people that they need what he is selling and position his company as one that understands the needs of his target market and offers the assistance and expertise to fulfill those needs.

The first thing I told him to do was to make an avatar of his ideal client and then put himself in that client's shoes. Evaluate the services his business is offering this client and then tell me whether he still thinks he has a winner of a business plan. I gave him a week to do this. I knew he was not going to come back with the answer he was hoping for.

He did the exercise as assigned and came back to me with a sad and glad conclusion. He was sad to realize that he was fighting an uphill battle to convince his prospects that he had what they needed and that they were going to have to pull money out of their pockets in order to get it. But he was also extremely glad because he had only pursued this fruitless quest part-time for a few months instead of full-time for several years.

He headed back to the drawing board with a better understanding of the necessity to get into his target market's head to find out what they wanted, not put his energies into trying to convince them that they should buy what he thought they needed.

Up Close and Personal

If you do not have a good handle on whom your customer is, how are you going to determine what it is he or she really wants? Don't delegate all of the interaction with prospects and customers to your staff; by doing this, you are missing out on a huge opportunity to hear what they want directly from them. There is absolutely no substitute for working personally with customers. You cannot imagine how much you will pick up—little nuances, hesitation, and uncertainty. These nuances give you the opportunity to interpret what they are saying they want vs. what they really want but are unable to articulate. You can test what approach and which words are most successful and then create effective scripts that everyone can use.

If you have a customer service department, commit an hour or two a week to answering those e-mails and phone calls yourself. Don't isolate yourself in your office. Review service and complaint logs, meet with staff every week to go over everything that went on that week, have your website tracked to see what people are clicking on and how long they are staying there, evaluate which products are selling better than others and if people habitually purchase the same two or three products together. Do A–B tests on your website, alternately directing visitors to different sales pages to see which is more effective. Send out different direct mail pieces and track which one pulls better. Continuously evaluate, evaluate, evaluate.

Good Evening, May I Help You?

The sales process for my escort service was specifically designed to both complement and enhance the Fantasy. After viewing our tasteful ad (described in Chapter Three), the prospective client would dial our number and a warm, friendly woman with a beautiful speaking voice would answer the phone. She would give him a very carefully scripted overview of the business, and then ask him what kind of young lady he was hoping to see. She did not inquire just about physical attributes. She encouraged him to describe his dream girl as completely as possible, usually by gently asking leading questions, making it clear she was taking note of every word (which she was) and genuinely cared about determining exactly what would make him happy (which she did).

He was then given the description of anywhere between one and three young ladies who most closely matched his wish list, highlighting the similarities and also noting, but subtly downplaying, the differences. Once he made his choice, the assistant (that's what we called our phone girls) would then work out the logistics and call him back to confirm the booking.

The assistant was always very professional, which established and maintained the caller's trust. She was also very warm and friendly, not cold and "business-like," which supported the fantasy that this was not really just a commercial transaction.

Everything but the Kitchen Sink

The customer is not just buying your product or service, your customer is buying everything that goes along with that product or service too. In the next chapter we will discuss the significance of the "mental movie" your prospects and customers have about you and your business. In Chapter 9 we will cover the "customer experience" and how to reverse engineer it so the experience is congruent with the movie in the customer's mind. The sales process is part of both the mental movie and the customer experience; if your process matches the expectations that appear in the movie it enhances the experience—which leads to a very satisfied customer.

The point I am trying to make is that the *process* by which you engage and sell the customer is just as much a part of the sale as ringing it up, and the manner in which you perform that process will influence whether you even get a sale. And it will certainly influence whether or not that customer returns to make a second purchase. Do your customers feel heard? Do they get the distinct impression their satisfaction is extremely important to you? Do they feel they are getting what they asked for and are they fully aware of any discrepancies? Do you or the people who handle your sales know how to highlight those elements the customer requested, while at the same time subtly

Sydney says

The "customer experience" is the next wave in the evolution of our economy. Get ahead of the curve and design customized experiences that enable you to command premium prices and ensure increased customer loyalty and retention. You may need to bring in a consultant who specializes in working with businesses to create a unique customer Experience to get you started in the right direction.

downplay the inconsistencies? This is where the value of scripts comes in. This particular part of the sales conversation could benefit from role play too, until everyone feels confident and comfortable with doing it.

It Depends on Your Definition of the Word "Guarantee"

Most people would say there's no way you can make a guarantee in the call girl business. Now while we couldn't guarantee the, ahem, "happy" part of the experience, we could in fact guarantee something that was actually more meaningful. Let me explain.

We'd only been open for a couple of months when I was on the phone one night with a prospective client describing a couple of young ladies who might suit him. When I asked which one he might prefer, he said, "How do I know that's what she really looks like? What if she gets here and I don't like her?"

Considering it was standard practice in the industry to lie through your teeth and say anything to get the booking, this was a very legitimate question. I was so confident he would see that she was exactly as I told him she was, I answered, "I'll tell you what. If she gets there and she doesn't look exactly as I have just described, or if you don't want to keep her for any other reason, just give her $20 for her taxi fare and send her home, no hard feelings, and I'll send you somebody else." There was nobody who had ever made a guarantee like that before, and how could you refuse? All you'd ever be out is a measly $20. I made that a standard policy immediately!

Note that we were not guaranteeing the experience, we were merely guaranteeing that the physical appearance of the young lady would correspond with the description we had given him. This is what could be called a "creative guarantee."

It's Worth the Risk

Do you offer any kind of guarantee? If you are thinking, "What I am selling cannot be guaranteed!" then do what I did—get creative. There is something in every business that can be guaranteed if you give free rein to your imagination.

Guarantees reassure, they reduce the perception of risk thereby making a prospective buyer feel safe, and if they feel safe, they will likely take a chance and make the purchase. It is very common for business owners to fear customers will take unfair advantage of a guarantee. But the truth of the matter is, while there is always going to be a very very small number of people who may take unfair advantage, the money you give back is way offset by all the additional sales you make because you offered the guarantee in the first place. If you are truly delivering what you claim to be delivering, returns should be pretty low. If you are getting returns because your product or service does not live up to a customer's expectations, expectations you yourself have created, then you have a bigger problem than having to make good on a

SYDNEY'S XXX-RATED SALES SECRET #11

There is no business in which a creative and persuasive guarantee cannot be made. You may just need to dig a little to find it.

GETTING TAKEN BY THE CLEANERS

A local carpet cleaning company here in New York City gives a very creative guarantee. They do not guarantee the work they do, which is what you would expect. They guarantee that you will not have to pay extra for moving the furniture, apparently a common extra charge that other carpet cleaners don't tell you about until after the fact. The prospective customer hears the word guarantee, hears that other carpet cleaning businesses don't disclose they charge extra for moving the furniture, and the prospect instinctively feel like this business is a better, safer deal—that the final bill won't be a big and unwelcome surprise. Knowing that other carpet cleaners may end up taking you to the cleaners, who would you pick up the phone and call?

guarantee. When you get a return from a difficult or unrealistic customer, this may be a customer you are better off without anyway.

Tell Me Lies, Tell Me Sweet Little Lies

It is not at all unusual for people to need to prove, convince, or reassure themselves that they have made the right decision when it comes to a purchase, especially an expensive purchase. This is one of the reason celebrity endorsements are so popular. People rationalize that if Ms. Celebrity owns or is using something, there must be something special or particularly worthy about it. Since Ms. Celebrity ostensibly has her choice of anything and everything out there, not to mention the money to afford it, if she owns or uses XYZ product or service, then it must be "the best." What the consumer either doesn't know or chooses to ignore is that the celebrity has usually received the product or service for free, or is being paid for their endorsement.

As long as people are so influenced by celebrities or other persons of influence or high standing, think about how you might align yourself with one. It must be a person who resonates with your target market, someone your ideal customer admires or respects. Your ideal customer must also be impressed that this person has chosen to do business with you. Depending on your particular business, this person need not be someone of national stature. Often someone with stature in your community is actually more credible.

For example, occasionally by mid-evening, we were completely booked and had no young ladies available to even describe to a client. This was usually because we were very short-staffed that night, but we certainly didn't want them to know that. I remember this happening shortly after we had opened. Out of nowhere I had this inspired stroke of creative genius and told him, "I'm afraid all of our young ladies are spoken for tonight. The Italian embassy phoned and booked every single one for the entire evening, I'm so sorry." "The Italian embassy?" the caller is thinking. "So *this* is the place where the diplomats and the movers and shakers get all those beautiful women." Well, if we were the service of choice for ambassadors and the like, obviously we must be the best! OK, it was a little white lie, but if the Italian Embassy *did* find itself in need of a dozen stunning women on short notice, we could have obliged.

SYDNEY'S XXX-RATED SALES SECRET #12

Determine what perception you want prospects or customers to have about your business, and also *the perception your customers want to have about you*. Then work out a plausible story or strategy that will create or enhance those perceptions. If the story includes some "creative" elements (in moderation, of course), don't think of it as being deceitful, think of it as giving your customers the opportunity to experience feeling good about themselves and their choices. They will appreciate you for being the source or catalyst of those positive feelings of pleasure, and validation.

This little white lie was all about creating a perception, a perception that our clients and prospective clients *wanted* to believe. It made them feel pleased with themselves that they, too, also had access to the most elegant, sophisticated and beautiful women New York had to offer. It validated their belief that they had the same taste level and financial means as these (presumably sophisticated and glamorous) European diplomats. It made them feel good about themselves and good about seeing our girls. And what's the harm in that?

MOTIVATING WITH SOCIAL PROOF

Harmony Tenney
Charlottesville Radio Group
harmony@businessempowerment.com

Years ago, I became aware that testimonials were supposedly a "huge help" in acquiring new customers. I started asking for testimonials, writing them up for my clients so they could sign them, and keeping them in a folder. When I received Bill Glazer's testimonial booklet "Retailer's Speak," I immediately modeled it. First, in a small binder, then in a comb bound booklet with a cover. I added some stories from my clients (small features like in a business journal) and a bio. No one else where I work has one, and I'm sure hardly any other radio reps do either.

The importance of the testimonial book is twofold: one, prospects realize they're not some "experiment" and that I'm NOT gambling with their hard-earned resources. Many times, they grab it to see if any of their business peers are in the book—the ultimate assurance. And two, I share with them that they can, one day soon, have their own "page of success."

Testimonials are another way to reassure a buyer that they are making the right decision. When the testimonial is perceived as legitimate—the claims seem plausible and the words sincere—the customer feel safe, justified, or both, making the purchase. Remember, what others say about you is much more impressive than any claim you could ever make about yourself.

The Time Is Right (Now)

When a customer has shown sufficient interest in what you have to offer that they have come to your premises, called you on the phone, responded to your direct mail piece, or clicked on the "more information" link on your website, it is in your best interest to have them buy right then and there. Once they have slipped out of your grasp, you may not get another chance to make that sale again. A customer who is wavering on making a commitment can often be influenced to do so if you give them a reason to act immediately. The most common ways of doing this are

- offering a limited number of the item
- offering a bonus the customer would find appealing, but only for a limited time
- offering a bonus for the first X people who make a purchase
- making it clear you will be raising the price on a specific date
- informing them you are discontinuing the item once they are all gone

All of these maneuvers create the impetus to make the commitment now.

We told our clients and prospects that our young ladies were only permitted to see one gentleman per evening, and that if he waited to book the call, the girl he preferred might no longer be available. Or if a client called and asked to see a particular type of girl and we did have someone like that on staff but she wasn't working that evening, we encouraged him to call ahead the next time and "pre-book" her. This way, she would make a point of being available that night "just for him." He was so thrilled that he would be able to see the girl of his dreams the next time that he often booked someone "less ideal" for that night anyway because he was on a high anticipating Miss Perfect and didn't want to have no company at all until then.

"I Make Special Just for You!"

Business owners should never underestimate the value of making a customer feel they are going out of their way to find or create a product or service just for them. Just because you do not have whatever it is they want available right then and there doesn't have to mean the sale is lost. Make them feel that by waiting, the whatever-it-is will be better because it will be just the right one for them. It will be newer, fresher, have the latest updates, be the preferred color, the person delivering the service will be the most senior person on staff, the service person specializes in their specific situation—use your imagination and add perceived value to whatever-it-is so they feel waiting for it is actually in their best interest!

XXX POWER IDEAS

- **X** Your customer wants to buy what *they* want to buy, not what you *think* they should want or should buy.
- **X** It is critical to understand just who your customer is, what they do professionally, what they do in their leisure time, what kinds of clubs or organizations they belong to, what people they spend the majority of their time around, and who they respect and admire.
- **X** Your sales process must complement the business you are in and be appealing to your ideal customer.
- **X** Remove any reluctance a prospect might have to make a purchase by offering a guarantee.
- **X** People like to be reassured that other people like them have done business with you and were satisfied.
- **X** Give a customer a reason to make the decision to purchase now.

Chapter 5

SATISFACTION

Make Them So Happy They're Eager to Come Back for More

A truly happy customer is not someone who is satisfied merely with the features and/or performance of the product or service they bought. The truly happy customer also feels an *emotional* connection with you personally; your business, which usually includes and is because of your staff; the actual product they purchase; the service they ultimately receive; or a combination thereof. The product or service may not even be of the highest quality available, but if the consumer feels good about buying it, using it, and/or the experience of doing business with you, the trade-off is worth it to them.

At first, this may seem counter-intuitive. Doesn't everybody want the "best" product, the most comprehensive service available? Yes, ideally they do, but if "the best" doesn't create a positive emotional connection, second best will be their first choice. And consumers *will* pay more for a product or service that satisfies their emotional needs. What are these emotional triggers that make customers feel happy and satisfied?

Sydney says

The way your customer feels about the product or service, as well as the people they deal with and the business itself, controls everything.

Feelings

In my former business, it didn't take long to realize that our clients really liked doing business with *us*. They liked talking to me, they liked talking to the assistants (the phone girls). It was not at all unusual for a client to phone us from another city just to chat. I'll always remember the night a client told me, "I would never demean myself by calling another service after having done business with you."

They also really liked the girls who worked for us. I would never hire anyone who had nothing going on in her life and just rolled out of bed at 4:00 in the afternoon and "hooked for a living." Most of the young ladies were students, but because New York is a magnet for those seeking a career in the fashion and entertainment industries, there were also quite a few aspiring models, actresses, dancers, singers, writers, artists, you name it. We also had girls in the fashion magazine, book publishing, and PR businesses—all notorious for paying little more than a pittance to new hires. But no matter what they did with themselves during the day, they were fun, they were interesting, they were sweet, and they were a pleasure to be with. It would have been impossible for even the most curmudgeonly client not to like them.

Your customers and clients must feel about your staff the way my clients felt about mine. People naturally gravitate toward those who make them feel welcome and special. Nearly all of us have competition, and customers have a choice with whom they do business. If your staff makes them feel special by greeting them with a big smile, remembering their name or recognizing their voice on the phone, recalling something from a conversation they had the last time they spoke, asking how they've been since they were last in the office (particularly important for doctors, dentists, spas, and other personal-services businesses), those customers are going to have an anticipatory smile in their hearts when they think about doing business with you again. One of my best friends has told me numerous times that she loves going to her cosmetic surgeon, "because they are always so happy to see me." How many referrals do you think *this* guy has gotten?

One of the best examples of someone who understands how important staff is to the success of a business is New York restaurateur, Danny Meyer. He wrote a book called *Setting the Table* about his life and business adventures. In it he outlines exactly what he looks for in a prospective employee and what he expects of his employees. His restaurants, the Gramercy Tavern, Union Square Café, Tabla, and many others are consistently listed in the "Top 50 Most Favorite Restaurants" in the Zagat restaurant guide; it is not just because of the food, which happens to be spectacular, but also because of the way his staff makes his customers feel. I urge you to get a copy of his book; it is not only a great read, it is very instructive as well.

MAKE THEM SO HAPPY THEY'RE EAGER TO COME BACK FOR MORE

Chris Hurn

TheSmartChoiceLoan.com

We finance commercial real estate purchases for owners of small and mid-size businesses. In our industry—and specifically in our niche—it's not very common to have repeat customers. The deals we work with are usually the biggest decisions/purchases in our clients' lives, and they are rarely able (or would need) to go through the process more than once.

However, we've had numerous clients come back as repeat customers. Two in particular stand out for the sheer number of times they've come back for more. The first is a cell phone retailer and repairer. He's now closed three loans with us on a total of four buildings. Another, a childcare/daycare business owner, has completed four separate transactions on four different buildings. Both of these clients returned to us for several reasons.

First, we provide the absolute best experience for their individual projects. Many of our competitors strive to deliver good customer service, so their customers are "satisfied." But we know that our clients aren't looking merely for good service or just to be satisfied—good service and adequate satisfaction can be found in lots of places. But a complete and delightful experience (which is what we provide) will cause them to rant and rave to others about what we've done for them.

Second, we help them understand how owning their businesses' commercial property can create wealth for them and pave the road toward a worry-free retirement. We always emphasize that they made a great decision to work with us the first time around, and that any ensuing properties/loans would only enhance their wealth creation. Once our clients own their properties, they can have a steady stream of income from rental payments (made to themselves or from future tenants) even after they sell or shutter their businesses. This "mindset-shift" is not the way a typical banker talks with his prospective business owner clients, so we stand out because of the entrepreneurial way we educate our clients about increasing their net worth.

Third, we do our best to recognize and reward our clients. We host an annual client Appreciation Event—a Mardi-Gras-themed bash in conjunction with our company's anniversary—and we give "Boatie" awards (named for our ship-like logo) to our best and favorite clients. The cell phone and daycare businesses each won one of these awards in years past. The recognition we gave them and appreciation we showed them played a large part in them returning multiple times—very rarely in today's business climate do businesses demonstrate publicly how much they appreciate and think of their clients.

More recently, we closed a commercial loan for a martial arts academy owner. Before we met with this client, he had gotten the run-around from six other lenders. The majority of them wouldn't even take the time to fully listen to his story. When he came to us, we did listen, and afterward, we told him his project was doable with us. He was thrilled that we simply sat down and took the time and showed genuine interest in hearing his story—his hopes, his struggles, his dreams, and why he finally wanted to own instead of lease. The exceptional experience we provided was all icing on the cake for him. Now, he plans to expand his academy in a few years, and I'll let you guess who he'll talk to about financing that next project with . . . especially after he wins the "Boatie" award for "Client of the Year" at our next anniversary bash.

Illusions

Illusions are the attributes or meaning customers attach to a product or service, as well as to the person or business they are buying it from. This is directly related to "what business are you *really* in?" Illusion is particularly relevant for those selling high-end, luxury products and services. Just as an example, nobody buys an $8,000 Hermes Birkin bag simply because they need something to tote their stuff around in. In fact, the entire luxury handbag business is based entirely on the emotional rewards those bags give to the women who shell out thousands, sometimes tens of thousands, of dollars for the latest one.

Designers like Oscar de la Renta, Carolina Herrera, and the recently retired Valentino Garavani, all three of whom travel in the same crowd as their wealthy and often very social clients, inspire a fiercely loyal following. Many women who are not actually part of this inner circle still feel a personal connection when buying and wearing these designers' clothes. And, of course, there is the illusion that the purchaser, too, is a part of that elite crowd. In addition, there is the feeling of validation the wearer gets that they also have the taste, the money, and the lifestyle to wear these very expensive and special creations.

Many people vacation in St. Barts or Aspen during the holidays, not because St. Barts has such spectacular beaches or Aspen has the best skiing, but because they want to vacation where all the other wealthy, successful movers and shakers and people-in-the-know vacation. They may never even interact with any of these people; they derive emotional satisfaction by just being there and from being able to tell their friends and colleagues they were there. In part, they choose these particular destinations in order to feed the illusion that they, too, are in-the-know, successful movers and shakers.

"Marquee-name" plastic surgeons aren't better than every other plastic surgeon in town; in fact, some of them don't even perform all aspects of the surgery, nor do they spend much time with the patient one-on-one during office visits. I know of a few who have terrible reputations when it comes to their bedside manner. I distinctly recall one of my friends telling the rest of us girls at lunch that she couldn't believe she had "spent so much money on a guy who was so nasty to me." But having your face done by Dr. Marquee-Name grants that person a degree of prestige and gains her admittance to the elite group of other women who have the money and are "in-the-know" regarding who is (presumably) "the best" plastic surgeon. It is not necessary that they are actually acquainted with these other women; the illusion that they are included in the price tag, and means a great deal to those for whom this is important.

Much of the time the illusion factor is associated with luxury purchases, but it could also be derived from doing business with a person or business that has considerable prestige due to position or expertise. What can you do to position yourself as "the best" or "the most prestigious" in your geographical area or your field? Is there a local magazine or newspaper that you could write a column for, positioning you as the expert on that subject? Local TV and radio stations need new and different content every day; how might you "spin" your product or business to sound different, interesting, exciting, sexy?

One of the reasons so many people are influenced by the fact that a celebrity uses a certain product or service, or patronizes a certain establishment, is the illusion of a connection with that celebrity when the purchaser patronizes the same place or uses the same products or services. Are there any influential men or women you could entice to become your customer and then very discreetly get the word around that they patronize your business? Or even better, might they give you a testimonial? Not every business is in a position to do this, but if you take some time to sit down and think about it, you might very easily come up with a creative way to use the emotion of illusion to attract and keep clients and customers.

CELEBRITY SHOES

Sex and the City has made Manolo Blahnik shoes a household name, but at a starting price of $500 a pair (and usually much more) you aren't going to see large number of women teetering around in them any time soon. Shopping at the Manolo Blahnik boutique in Manhattan is a bit of an "insider" experience. There is no sign on the front of the red brick townhouse located on West 54th Street; either you know where it is or you don't. A doorman clad in a dark suit opens the door and admits the client into a store that is the Holy Grail for those who collect beautiful shoes. Regular clients have their own salesperson who knows their size, their taste, and which shoes they have purchased previously. New customers can look around at their leisure without being accosted, but there is always a salesperson discreetly within eyesight should they wish to try something on. Until recently, there were no prices on the shoes; if you wanted to know how much a pair cost, you had to ask.

The store itself is unremarkable in appearance. The shoes are the stars and there is nothing to distract the customer away from their beauty. In the back there is a pretty little garden with a fountain for you to look out on as you're trying on the shoes.

While a significant number of women can afford to buy several pairs of Manolos, as they are known, at one time, for many others, Manolos are a major purchase for which they have saved for months. The blue satin pump with the rhinestone buckle featured in *Sex and the City* (and which really cost $900, not the $500 cited in the movie) were so sought after that the factory had to go into overdrive to satisfy just a fraction of the demand. This shoe was a huge status symbol for young women who wanted to identify with the movie's main character, Carrie Bradshaw, played by actress Sarah Jessica Parker. For nearly all of the purchasers, this was their first pair of Manolos. Considering the tab, it may well be the last. But the bragging rights, the envy of their friends, the telling and retelling of the buying experience, and the personal connection to the *Sex and the City* phenomenon is well worth the months of belt tightening needed to make that special purchase.

Manolos are such a status symbol and one that is so out of reach for most women, that whenever there is a sale, there is nearly always a story in at least one of the newspapers

continued

CELEBRITY SHOES, CONTINUED

reporting on the hordes of women eagerly waiting to get in and the physical altercations over just who is going to walk out with a particular pair. Survivors of these sales often get more mileage out of telling the details of the experience of the purchase to their friends than they do from actually wearing the shoes themselves. eBay does a brisk business in previously-enjoyed Manolos, where they can be had for $100 or less a pair. Whoever dreamed there would be such a market for used shoes?

When someone attaches a great deal of meaning to something or it is important to them to be identified with something or someone, they will go to great lengths to acquire it.

Surprises

Unexpected gifts and extras have a very positive influence on customers. Everyone, no matter who they are or how much money they have, loves getting a gift, a little something extra, particularly when they don't expect it and have not had to do anything to get it. Cosmetics companies have always had little samples their salespeople drop into the shopping bag, and they have also popularized the free gift-with-purchase concept with great success. Certain hotels and some offices hand out freshly baked cookies to clients and guests, and some customer rewards programs give a free something when a member has accumulated a specific number of points.

We gave a gift of a bottle of Dom Perignon champagne to our best clients during the holidays or on their birthday. The client was thrilled to be acknowledged and appreciated as someone special, and the fact that Dom Perignon is widely considered to be a very prestigious brand underscored that we were a very prestigious service and he was a highly esteemed client. Do you see the emotional rewards and ties this created between us and our clients?

Extra gifts and goodies do quadruple duty when properly executed. They delight your customer; they make your customer feel special and appreciated; they reinforce your customer's belief that you are the perfect resource; and, when chosen carefully, the right gift subliminally supports the image of your business that you are trying to project. Start thinking today about what you might gift your customers with that will produce this home run for you.

Recognition

Enormous power is attached to expressions of thanks and gratitude. There is a reason your mother put such emphasis on saying "thank you." Everyone likes to feel their efforts have been recognized and are appreciated, particularly when those efforts are over and above what the recipient might realistically expect. Just as you and your staff probably go out of your way to accommodate customers and clients who make it a point to express their gratitude to you, customers and clients will go out of their way to continue to patronize those who make it a point to express gratitude to them for their continued loyalty.

When was the last time a business sent *you* a thank-you note or made a follow-up phone call to thank you for your purchase? Most of you will probably answer "never." Imagine how good it would have made you feel, particularly if you had spent a significant amount of money. And imagine how impressed you would have been if the note was handwritten on a nice card or piece of stationery instead of some form letter on generic paper spewed out by a computer.

We always called our clients after the young lady had left to ask them "Was the evening everything you were hoping it would be?" And then we thanked them for calling us and told them we looked forward to hearing from them again. This took new clients by surprise, but the regulars were accustomed to it and usually enjoyed giving us feedback on the young lady's positive attributes as well as suggestions on areas that might use some improvement. The latter was very useful because we had no way of knowing how the girls handled themselves on a call; this gave us the opportunity to advise them on how they might tweak their MO to make themselves more effective.

Flowers are an excellent way to express thanks, particularly to female clients. When I was interviewing people for a book I was writing on cosmetic surgery and dermatology, you cannot believe how excited and appreciative those patients were who received a bouquet of flowers after their procedure. They mentioned it every time we spoke for weeks. And you might be surprised at how many men enjoy receiving flowers or a plant, too.

Do not be lured into taking the easy way out and giving a discount or some kind of deal or freebie from your business as an expression of thanks or gratitude. Such "gifts" are self-serving and are usually recognized as such. Items like key rings, baseball caps, or T-shirts with your logo on them, a calendar, and the like are not a great idea either; rather than engendering feelings of being appreciated, they are more likely to produce the thought, "Why did they even bother . . ." and "What the heck am I going to do with this?" Alcohol is not usually an appropriate gift because many people do not drink or should not be around alcohol. (When we gave our gift of Dom Perignon, we tried to be certain the client was someone who would appreciate it. If we inadvertently sent champagne to someone who did not imbibe, we hoped they would consider it a very nice pass-along gift.) And certainly don't give anything of a personal nature, such as an item of clothing, perfume, etc. Gift cards suggest a lack of thought, as do items that look as if they were purchased in bulk or were given to you by a vendor. Remember, an expression of thanks should make the recipient feel appreciative of *you* for being the kind of person who has obviously gone out of their way to validate the importance of their patronage.

Belonging

Ongoing relationships create a bond and give clients/customers a sense of belonging. You have heard it a million times: People like doing business with someone they know, like, and trust. If someone were to ask you why you patronize coffee shop A when the one right around the corner is newer and has a more extensive menu, it's likely your response would be "Because I've always gone there." And why do you always go there? Because you know, like, and trust the owner and/or the people who work there. The fact that coffee shop B is spiffier and offers a choice of three different kinds of bacon to go with your eggs is irrelevant; you *like* going to coffee shop A because you have a relationship, a bond, with the people who work there, and often with some of the other customers too. You feel you belong there.

Why do people stay with the same doctor or dentist for years, decades even? Because they feel that doctor or dentist knows them and their history, cares about them, and if he or she has ever helped them get through a rough period, can be counted on to do so again if need be. Why do people stay with the same bank, pest control company, pool service company, auto repair shop? Because the owner and/or the people who work there make them feel like a valued customer. Not only that, when you have been doing business with someone for a long time and they know the name of your dog and you know the names of their kids, they start to feel like old friends. One of the primary elements in a friendship is loyalty.

Familiarity creates a bond. While it was true that we had the most beautiful girls in New York, even if a competitor came along and had girls who were just as pretty, we would have lost very little business. Our clients knew us and liked us and they knew we liked and cared about them. Many felt they had a special relationship with my two assistants, Ashley and Jamie—and it's true, they did. They felt like they belonged because they knew we genuinely cared about them and were happy to hear their voice, which we often recognized the second they said hello. They felt they belonged because when the young lady arrived, she'd tell them all the nice things we had told her about them. They felt they belonged because, in fact, they did belong.

Make your customers and clients feel recognized, special, valued, and appreciated. Get to know them, take an interest in them, and while you should always remember it is a professional relationship, let them feel they know a little something about you too. What might you have in common? What might their children have in common with yours? What kind of a pet do they have? If you know they like a certain something, let them have first

SYDNEY'S XXX-RATED SALES SECRET #13

Regular and frequent contact is key. You don't want to be perceived as the occasional one-night stand.

dibs when it comes in. If yours is a seasonal business, get in touch with them before the season starts so you can make sure they are on your appointment schedule before you get booked up. Have special "insider" sales or specials just for regular customers. Give them advance notice before you raise your prices so they can take advantage of the old price before it goes up.

Send monthly newsletters that include more than just information about your business. If you support a local charity or children's sports team - and if you don't, you should - always report on how it is doing, and name names. Everybody loves to see their name or their children's names in print! Include something interesting and if possible, amusing, about yourself and your employees. It doesn't have to be long, one sheet is fine, but it does have to be consistent. You could do an e-zine (an electronic newsletter), but know that e-mail boxes are so full now that many people do not read them.

XXX POWER IDEAS

- **X** All other things being equal (and sometimes even when they aren't), a customer will choose to do business with people they have a relationship with, people they know, like, and trust, and who they feel know and like them.
- **X** Many people will buy a product or patronize a business for no other reason than it is considered "the best" or the most prestigious.
- **X** Everyone loves to receive an unexpected gift.
- **X** A little gratitude goes a long way.
- **X** Give your customers a reason to be loyal to you; make them feel recognized, special, valued, and appreciated.

PART TWO

TOOLS & TACTICS OF SEDUCTIVE SELLING

Chapter 6

Creating and Directing the Movie in Your Customer's Mind

The purpose of advertising and marketing is to pique a prospect's interest in doing business with you. This interest could be minor, such as merely getting your product or service on their "OK, let's consider that one" list. Or it could jump right to " I've got to have it *now*, how quickly can you get it to me?" Marketing also serves to create an overall perception of your company, as well as a specific image of you and your product or service in the minds of your customers and prospects before the buying process even begins. The message your marketing sends begins the process of forming a "movie" in your prospect's mind, an expectation of what doing business with you will be like.

For obvious reasons, there really wasn't much we could do in the way of marketing in my former business, but we did advertise. We were limited there too, since most publications don't accept ads from escort services. I would have killed to have been in the *Wall Street Journal*, and I know certain readers would have liked to have been able to find us there too, but it was just not in the cards.

As previously described, our ad was very clean with lots of white space. It contained the name of the company, our tag line, "New York's Most Trusted Service," our phone number, hours of operation, and, in one publication, the price. It was very elegant and refined looking; anyone seeking an upscale experience would have been drawn to it immediately. Right from the start, someone reading our ad began to develop a sense of the type of service we provided, the caliber of young ladies we had available, and what doing business with us would (hopefully) be like. I think of it as a "mental movie" taking form in their imagination—and I was determined that movie was going to be Academy Award material.

We were in the enviable position of being in an industry with such abysmal standards that just about any alternative was better than what was already out there. Our niche market hoped and dreamed about finding a business on the level of ours, but they had been horribly disappointed over and over again for so long, that most of them were understandably pretty cynical. For example, assuming most readers aren't familiar with Standard Operating Procedure in the escort service business, Rule Number One is: Lie through your teeth and tell the prospect anything necessary to book the call and get their money. Rule Number Two: When in doubt, refer to Rule Number One. So one of the first things we needed to do was dispel our potential customers' natural suspicion that we were just as deceitful as all the others.

Creating Your Mental Movie

In order to create and direct the movie you want playing on your prospect's mental screen, you first need to know the exact nature of the need or desire they are looking to satisfy. Second, you need to understand the experience they are hoping to have during the purchase process. And third, you need to understand the experience they want to have as the service is taking place or once the product in their hot little hands. You need to know the end result they hope, want, or expect so that you are able to convey in as much detail as possible what it will be like for them to have or experience that outcome.

You also need to be aware of what potential customers *fear* their experience might be like, both during the buying process as well as during the course of the service or once they receive and use the product. When you know what those fears are, you can allay them by building in reassurances during the course of the sales process. All these elements will influence how you formulate your plan to create the "mental movie" you want them to have. These elements form the basis for your script, which is based on your story, your plot.

Developing the Script

No director can do his or her job without a script; you, as director of the sales process, must also have a script. Your script must communicate a coherent, understandable, and believable story. We've talked about the importance of your business having a plot or story, and planning how you are going to develop your prospective customer's mental movie is the first thing you are going to do with this story. A script is a written document that not only tells the story, it also describes the set, depicts the characters, and contains the characters' dialog.

The Set

The set is where the action takes place. This could be your office or store if this is where you interact with your customer. If you have an online business, it is your website—or your direct mail piece, advertisement, or brochure if that is how you "interact" with your customers.

What is the image you wish this set to convey? Take into consideration the plot or story you have developed for your business and create a set that supports that storyline. Be sure your set delivers the experience your prospect or customer hopes or expects to encounter.

The Characters

Scripts describe the characters in a movie by appearance, demeanor, actions, and the like. What image do your prospects have in their mind about what they hope or expect interacting with you or your employees will be like? Does this correspond with the image you wish them to have? How should your employees be dressed for their roles? Does their dress reflect the perception you want to convey? Is this consistent with what your customers or prospects expect or hope to see?

The Dialog

What should the characters—your employees—be saying to prospects and customers, and how should they be saying it? If you want specific information covered and you want it said in a certain way, do your characters have a written script with specific dialog to follow? How do you want your cast of characters to answer the phone, greet a customer, say goodbye to a customer? You must create a script for your employees so they know what you expect them to say and how you want them to say it. All this needs to be carefully thought out in the context of your story so it supports and reinforces the image you intend to project.

Background

Do your employees have all the information they need to answer a prospect's questions so the prospect can make the decision to book an appointment or make a purchase? Do employees have sufficient knowledge of the product or service that they can not only describe it accurately, but also answer any questions about it? If communication with your customers is primarily by e-mail, have templates your employees can use, and customize where necessary, in their correspondence.

One extremely effective way to familiarize your employees with what they are selling is to actually give them the product or have them experience the service themselves, whenever feasible. If you have ever been unsure about buying something and the person selling it to you tells you about their personal experience with it, presuming that experience is positive, wouldn't you be more likely to make the purchase?

Reality Check

Once you know what you want your customer's experience to be like, do a compare and contrast with the experience your prospect or customer is actually receiving. Be brutally honest; what is your customer actually encountering right now? How big is the discrepancy between the experience you want your customer to have and the one they are actually getting?

It is usually very difficult to do a realistic assessment of your own business; this is, again, where the benefit of those fresh eyes we discussed earlier comes in. Your business must be mystery-shopped on a regular basis both in person and on the phone. Have your website "tested" by someone who is not very tech-savvy to assess how user-friendly it is. Some people call it The Mom Test or, if your mom does know her way around a computer, the Grandma Test. I have personally beta-tested numerous websites for clients because I am so technologically blonde that if I can figure it out, any one can!

Sydney says

Almost every business category can take advantage of a Fresh Eyes analysis or a "mystery shopper." You can have a consultant mystery shop your phones, your website, your store, or use your service and report back their findings to you. Chris Mullins, a contributor to this book, has such a service; you can find her contact information in the Resource section.

Get Me Rewrite!

Once you have identified the inconsistencies between what you want your customers to experience and what they are really experiencing, you need to do a rewrite. At the very least, this new script must match the mental movie you have learned that your customers are hoping for and/or expecting. Wherever possible, it should be even better than the customer's version. Is everyone who interacts with a prospect or a customer saying what they should be saying in the exact way you want them to say it? Does the language used, whether it be spoken or written in a direct mail piece or on a website, resonate with your target audience? Do your employees look and act the parts they are playing? Does your set (your website serves as your set if you have an online business) support your story? Is your sales process congruent with your plot and the perception you are trying to create?

Obviously there's a lot to this, but it's critically important to get it right because there's so much opportunity when you do. It is very much in your best interest to take care of this ASAP. Once you have your new script, you are ready to re-shoot the movie you are currently showing so that you and your business are in a position to live up to the positive expectations your prospects already have as well as additional ones your new script is going to suggest they can anticipate.

Expectations Management

Diffusing unrealistic expectations was extremely important in my former business. I always had to keep my eyes from rolling 180 degrees back in my head when a prospective client told me he wanted a "10" to show up at his door: Tall, blonde, drop-dead gorgeous, the body of a voluptuous Victoria's Secret model–some even specified blue or green eyes. Every once in a while I did have someone who fit that description, but let's be realistic, girls who look like that do not usually go into the call girl business. As ludicrous as this request was, we still wanted to tell him in a way that worked to our advantage that we weren't going to able to meet it. For one thing, we didn't want it to sound like we just did not have what it takes to attract girls like that. My technique for diffusing unrealistic expectations such as this was to give a little laugh and say sympathetically, "I sure wish I had someone who fit that description–hell, I wish I had ten of them. Then I could start looking for penthouses on Park Avenue! But as you know, girls who look like that are extremely rare to begin with, and while I do occasionally find one, I don't have anyone like that at the moment, so I think we need to move on to Plan B." It worked like a charm; we were able to tell him "not happening" in a way that did not imply we thought he wasn't playing with a full deck, and gave just a little hint that possibly in the future, we might have such a young lady available.

Every business needs to address this "perfect 10" issue. Perhaps you are in the advertising business. Someone calls to place a full-color, full-page ad hoping it will cost a third of what your going rates are. A response you could use, similar to my "perfect 10" response, would be something like "Geez, I wish I could do it for that rate, I would sell out my ad space in a day and be able to take the rest of the month off! But I am sure we can work out an attractive ad that meets your needs and stay within your advertising budget."

They Can't Get No Satisfaction

You may find that some of *your* prospects or customers have unrealistic expectations—and there are some of those who, no matter what you do, are not ever going to be satisfied. The minute you feel you are dealing with someone like this, get out as gracefully and quickly as you can. These people will cause you and your staff far more work and grief than they will ever be worth. You don't want to anger or alienate them, because you don't want them badmouthing you all over town; you just want to discourage them from doing business with you. Tell them you just don't have the staff to handle it (which you don't if they are going to be a time-consuming pain in the butt), you do not have the technology, you are unable to get all of the components—whatever it is, you are unable to do it. And because you agree that they absolutely should have everything they want, you suggest they find another vendor who has whatever it is that you are claiming you don't. Do not leave any room for them to "decide" to compromise and go with you anyway; some people play a game where they ask for the moon, knowing full well you cannot deliver, so

SYDNEY'S XXX-RATED SALES SECRET #14

It's not just about the money,
it's what you have to do to get the money.

they can make you feel like they are doing you a favor by giving you their business in spite of your shortcomings. Or they'll use it to weasel on the price. Get rid of them; life is too short to have anything to do with these troublemakers.

Higher Education

There are prospects and customers who just want to see how much they can get out of you. But there are also people who have unrealistic expectations because they just don't know any better. This is your opportunity to educate them about the product or service in general, and why *your* product or service is superior to the competition in particular. You never ever want to badmouth the competition, you merely note that XYZ Company has or does so-and-so, but you do thus-and-such because [fill in the blank as to why your way is better]. And, of course, why this benefits *them*, why it is better for *them*.

If you are selling via direct mail or through a website, you will have to do all of this in writing with little give-and-take to draw upon. This will take research on your part to discover what it is that uneducated prospects usually have misconceptions about so you can address them in your copy.

Getting the Right Perspective

Spend time talking with your prospects and customers to learn not only what they believe they want or need, but *why* they want or need it. What problem are they trying to solve, what pain are they seeking to alleviate or avoid? What pleasure or gain are they hoping to experience? What do they see as the ideal outcome and how will that make them feel? Once you have all that information, use it to tailor your sales pitch specifically to those problems, needs, and feelings. This should be done with verbal sales scripts as well as with web copy and direct mail pieces. Highlight that which you are able to deliver and describe how it will solve their problem, relieve their pain, or give them the positive experience they are seeking. Downplay that which you cannot deliver; you must *always* be honest and forthcoming about what you cannot do if you ever want to do business with that person again.

A "damaging admission" makes you sound much more credible and trustworthy; most people are suspicious of someone who claims they can do it all. For example, if a client told us he was looking for someone with long blonde hair, I'd talk up her beautiful, long, lustrous hair and then ruefully mention that it isn't blonde, but that it is really gorgeous. And would follow that damaging admission by emphasizing all the other attributes she had that were on his wish list. There were times when we had no one who was even close to physically resembling a client's original request, but we described a couple of the girls we did have in such a flattering and enthusiastic manner that he would often book anyway because at least he knew exactly who was going to be knocking on his door. The whole spiel was a damaging admission; in the end, he was buying the honesty more than the actual product (with apologies for the analogy).

You must have an accurate handle on what your typical customer is looking for and why, what problem she is trying to solve, and what she sees as the ideal outcome. Construct your sales presentation, whether written or verbal, to reflect these points. Always include "damaging admissions" using examples your research has found prospects and customers often have about your product or service.

Doing the Research

Let me give you an example of the way we gathered information about what our clients wanted their personal fantasy experience to be like. After we had established that a prospect was someone we wanted to do business with, we then needed to get an idea of the type of young lady he was hoping to see that evening. We were interested in what age he had in mind, whether he preferred someone short or tall, slender or with a little something more to her, glamorous or girl-next-door looks, that sort of thing.

There were two things we never asked: What hair color do you prefer and how busty would you like her to be? The reason we avoided asking about hair color was because the answer would invariably be "blonde" and there were never enough blondes to go around. If blonde was that important to him, he would have mentioned it himself. Why use up the blondes working that evening on someone who didn't think it was important enough to ask for it? The next caller might be someone who would only consider a blonde and we'd lose the call because we didn't have one.

We applied the same reasoning to bust size; if we asked they'd usually say busty, and busty girls were not all that easy to come by either. So if they didn't care enough to specifically request it, we didn't bring it to their attention.

Hierarchy of Needs and Desires

Once we understood the type of young lady a client was seeking, we tailored our sales presentation as described above, highlighting what we could do and "admitting" but downplaying what we could not. First, we selected one or two girls who were available that evening who most closely fit his specifications. Let's say he was looking for someone tall and busty with long blonde hair but we had no one available that night who fit that precise description. We might have a tall flat-chested girl with long blonde hair, or a tall girl with an average chest with long brown hair, so the next step was to ascertain which of these features were the most meaningful to him. In a conversational, story-like manner we would describe the available young ladies, highlighting those qualities that matched his request and downplaying the disparities. Once we had worked out a combination of attributes that appealed to him, we had a

Sydney says

You can downplay the disparities between what your customer wants and what you have to offer, but you must never ignore them. The trust factor is critical; you can never go wrong being honest about not only what you can, but also cannot do for someone. What you really need to pay close attention to is determining what it is about your product or service that is most significant to them. Once you understand that, you can emphasize those points and hope there are enough checks in the positive column to outweigh those in the negative one.

sale. And we had a client who felt we really cared about him and were genuinely trying to satisfy him.

We never described more than three young ladies; if they couldn't make a decision after the three best choices, giving a fourth wasn't going to make it any easier. If we really did not have anyone on that night we could plausibly claim might suit him, we came right out and said so, even though we might risk losing his business. Repeat clients were easier to book because we knew from our records the type of young lady he preferred; many of them left it up to us once they got to know us well and felt assured that the caliber of our young ladies was so high, anyone we sent was going to be terrific.

While your customer is unlikely to care about hair color or bust size, they do have a list of things they hope, want, or expect of your product or service. In order to make the sale, you need to determine just which features or benefits are the most important to them.

Managing Negative Expectations

As I mentioned earlier, the escort service business has a terrible reputation, and deservedly so. The First Big Lie is the description of what the girl they are sending looks like. After finding out what type of girl the client wants, the phone girl claims to have just that very girl available, and spouts back to him a description that is nearly identical to that which he just gave her. They were operating on the theory that after waiting at least an hour for her to arrive (that's Big Lie Number Two: She'll be there in half an hour), he'll keep her because otherwise he'll have to wait an hour or longer for a replacement. Yes, they pocket his money that night, but he is unlikely to ever call them again.

These places function on the bird-in-the-hand principle—go all out to grab his cash now and don't worry about tomorrow.

I countered a prospect's perfectly natural skepticism by saying, "Sure, I could lie to you and send you just anybody, and take your money tonight. But then you'd never call us back, would you? But if I'm honest with you and send the type of girl who is just as I describe her, you'll know you can trust us and you'll call us again. That's my goal—for you to call us back. And for you to tell your friends about us too. You'd never do that if I ripped you off, would you?"

Remember, these guys were businessmen and they had that same long-range outlook too. They understood the importance of building a relationship, and that repeat business is critical if you plan on being around for the long haul.

While it is unlikely the field you're in has as dismal a reputation as the one I was, you are still going to encounter skepticism from time to time. Honesty is really the best policy; if you talk with your customers the way I talked to mine and make it clear that their satisfaction is extremely important to you because you want to do business with them again, they will usually make the leap. And remember the value of a good guarantee, which takes the fear out of the risk of making a mistake.

Honesty Is the Best Policy

One of the most effective ways to manage negative expectations is to let the customer know right up front about any possible dubious aspects of doing business with you. Southwest Airlines is commonly cited as a classic example of a company that delivers a less-than-ideal experience with negligible customer dissatisfaction. Southwest lets their prospects and customers know right from the get-go that there are no assigned seats, no free food or beverages, and that they are going to stuff as many people into that airplane as they possibly can. Nobody complains because they know that's what they're getting before they even buy the ticket. If American Airlines were to do that, there would be an enormous hue and cry, with people ranting and snarling and carrying on, not to mention letters to the FAA and nasty blog postings.

If adverse events might occur during the course of doing business with you, even if only occasionally, you must mention it, but also make it very clear that you are fully prepared to deal with them. Inform the customer exactly what you intend to do about the situation in general and for them personally in the hopefully unlikely event something untoward were to happen. Reassure them; when people know you are aware of a potential problem, have a plan to deal with it, and are committed to taking care of them should something go wrong, they will trust you far more than someone who acts like everything is going to be perfect and therefore has no contingency plan. In fact, that could

SYDNEY'S XXX-RATED SALES SECRET #15

Always have a Plan B.

be your guarantee: if such-and-such happens, you will do so-and-so to fix it. This is another example of a damaging admission that can be used to work in your favor.

It's a Wrap

It is vital that the image you project, the "movie in their mind" that you have created, be consistent with the product or service and experience you deliver.

CREATING A POSITIVE MENTAL MOVIE

Does your advertising demonstrate the benefits the prospect will receive if they give you their business? A terrific example is an ad with a before picture of someone with crooked, broken teeth, and an after picture of the same person with a beautiful smile and perfect teeth. That dentist has made it abundantly clear he has the solution to your problem, if your problem is crooked, broken teeth.

But most people have a negative Mental Movie when it comes to going to the dentist. So our dentist creates an environment designed to make the patient feel at ease. His waiting room is decorated to resemble a comfortable library. His staff wears uniforms—but not clinical, white uniforms; theirs are a soothing shade of blue, crisply ironed, and the same style as typical uniforms. They look professional but not intimidating. The prospective patient is offered a beverage in a real cup or glass, just if they were in someone's home. The patient feels comfortable and reassured, which makes it much easier to get her to sign up for a new $20,000 smile.

When a business delivers the product or service the customer has been led to believe they are going to get *and* the experience that goes along with it, customers respond in a very positive way. Under promise and over deliver—exceeding their expectations—makes a strong first impression. When customers see that the movie in their mind is congruent with their actual experience, when they know they can trust you to deliver on your promise, you are on your way to cultivating a customer for life.

XXX POWER IDEAS

- X You cannot begin to work on creating a movie in your customer's mind until you have an accurate sense of what movie the customer hopes, wants, or expects to see.
- X It is just as important to know what customers do not want, what they fear, and what negative expectations they might have.
- X In order to write an effective script, you must be aware of what your customer hopes or expects to get out of the transaction as well as what you are able to deliver.
- X Your script consists of the storyline (the plot or story about you and/or your business), a thorough description of the set (where the "action" takes place), the characters who have parts in the script, and the dialog spoken by the characters.
- X You absolutely must have a reality check done by an impartial observer (aka "fresh eyes") so you have a clear picture of the current situation.
- X Compare and contrast your script with the fresh eyes analysis and make careful note of the discrepancies.
- X In order to properly manage their expectations, you must understand not only what your customers want or need, but also why they want or need it.
- X Damaging admissions make you sound more credible and cultivate trust.

XXX POWER IDEAS, CONTINUED

- **X** When you are unable to satisfy all their initial requirements, establish which criteria are the most important to them and highlight those, while downplaying the differences.
- **X** Diffuse negative expectations by being very honest about what you will not be delivering.
- **X** If there is even a modest possibility an "adverse event" might occur, make it very clear you have a Plan B and what it is the customer can expect you to do about the situation.

Chapter

7

WHAT MOVIE ARE YOU CURRENTLY PLAYING?

As business people, we all have so much on our plates every day it is understandable that we aren't particularly anxious to add anything more. As long as it looks like everything is running relatively smoothly, we don't go out of our way to look for trouble. This is why most people stick their heads in the sand when it comes to doing a reality check on what is really going on at the sales level.

Sure, we look at the numbers, but as long as those numbers are within an acceptable range, we figure our sales process is humming along smoothly. We assume our website is operating properly, all the links work, and the shopping cart is doing what it is supposed to. We assume our staff is doing their job "properly" because we gave them some direction when they came on board. Or we assigned someone else to do it and we give them credit for doing the right thing in the right way because as far as we're concerned, the right thing and the right way is so inherently obvious that anyone with an IQ above room temperature would naturally make the correct choice and perform the correct action.

I hate to break the news to you, but you're dreaming. And that pipe dream could very well be creating a horror movie in your customer or prospect's mind.

We go back to that old saying "You can't see the forest for the trees." You, and your employees if applicable, have become so accustomed to the status quo that familiarity blinds you to anything that might be amiss. And remember that it is usually not in an employee's best interest to point out any problems they might end up being assigned to fix or for which they might be blamed. Unless a problem directly affects the size of their paycheck or makes it difficult to perform their duties, most will figure it's your business and therefore your problem. And in reality, ultimately it *is* your problem.

Well, you can't fix a problem you don't know you have. Since the likelihood of you or your staff being able to see your business through the eyes of your prospects and customers is dubious at best; you have to call in an impartial observer. If you think you might have a leak, you call a plumber; if your website is acting up, you call your webmaster; if you think you may have a pest problem, you call an exterminator. If you want to get an accurate reading on what a customer experiences when they try to do business with you, you hire

SYDNEY'S XXX-RATED SALES SECRET #16

You can only fix it if you know it's broke.

someone who has fresh eyes to do a professional analysis. Realistically, it is your only option.

They're Saying What??!!??

The first place you must start in your analysis is your telephone—or in the case of a web-based business, your customer support department or live chat feature. We all assume everyone knows how to answer a telephone, and to a certain extent, that's true. However, they might not actually be answering it the way *you* want it answered. Or in a way that is most effective for your business.

Your staff might not have a clear idea of how *you* want them to interact with a customer. And in the absence of clear direction, they will do or say what they think is best, based on their own values, which might not be the same as yours. They likely know the end result they are supposed to achieve, such as capturing a prospective patient's information before booking an appointment. But exactly *how* are they asking for that information? You might be appalled when you find out. If you have not made it a priority to thoroughly train everyone who might ever come into contact with a customer, you are doing the equivalent of letting the inmates run the asylum—who knows what crazy things they are subjecting your prospects and customers to?

Listening In

The first order of the day is to have a professional "mystery shop" your phones. Chris Mullins, one of the contributors to this book, has a business that does just that. She has an army of people who make numerous calls to a client's business, answering service, or call center over a period of days and records them. Her people are trained to ask all sorts of questions and conduct themselves in various manners, all in order to capture a response to many different situations. She then analyzes the tapes and makes the appropriate recommendations.

Chris says clients are shocked when they hear what their employees are actually saying! For online businesses, her mystery shoppers e-mail the customer service department and use the Live Chat feature to see how those people interact with customers over a period of a week or two.

The very first thing I do when working on a consulting engagement is call the client's business several times on the phone to see how the staff handles themselves in various situations. On one call, I make an appointment and upon my arrival, anonymously go through the experience of being a first-time client, patient, or customer. In addition to observing how I am shepherded through whatever it is I am ostensibly there for, I also make careful mental notes of the physical premises, the actual sales presentation, and the actions and behavior of all the staff members I interact with as well as those I see in the background. You would be amazed at what I find is *really* going on. Nearly every time, it is far different than what the client believes is going on. One actually fired the office manager on the spot after I submitted my report, he was so horrified.

Employees behave very differently when The Boss is around; didn't you do the same when you had a boss? Many business owners are so busy running the business in a global sense that they either "let the business run itself" or hire a manager to do it for them. Putting the inmates in charge of the asylum is a dubious business model. Unless the manager is your spouse, you absolutely must have weekly meetings not only to stay on top of what is going on, but to let the manager know you are paying attention plus you need to make sure they are taking care of whatever it was you discussed at the last meeting. Trust but verify, as Ronald Reagan was wont to say during the negotiations of the nuclear disarmament treaty with the former Soviet Union.

Sweat the Small Stuff

It is not just the way your staff answers the phone and interacts with customers in person. Yes, this is extremely important, especially during that first contact a prospect has with your business. It's not just what they say, nor just how they say it; it is also their ability to give the prospect sufficient information in a coherent and understandable way that the prospect is able to make the decision to take the next step and make an appointment or a purchase.

One thing many business owners overlook is the impact the physical environment has on a customer's perception of your business and, often, on their decision to buy. What is it like to be in your space? How does it feel and what kind of associations does a customer make when looking at his or her surroundings? What messages, both overt and subliminal, does the appearance of your space signal to the customer?

You and your employees are so accustomed to being in your space that it is all but impossible for any of you to see it through a customer's eyes. Once again, this is why it is so imperative to have fresh eyes come in and do a completely impartial analysis. Fresh eyes can see the inconsistencies between your customer's "mental movie" and the reality they actually experience. Fresh eyes can also help you rewrite the script for your business so that the movie you are showing is the same one your customer is expecting as well as the one you want them to see.

Fresh eyes do not only look for problems, they also identify additional opportunities to create, reinforce, and maintain the image you want your customers to have of you and your company. Fresh eyes also contribute fresh ideas to revitalize your business, and are often able to recognize sales and marketing opportunities you may never have considered.

They're Doing What??!!??

Let me give you a few examples from some of my on-site consulting engagements. I do a Fresh Eyes analysis and consulting for a number of day spas and medi-spas; in fact, spas are probably my favorite clients. Nearly all of them want to project a luxurious and upscale image, which makes sense considering their clients are relatively affluent. One of the ways one of my client's employees decided to cut down on the size of the daily laundry was to put paper towels in the bathrooms instead of using the usual terrycloth towels. That would not be incongruous with their upscale image if the paper towels were of good quality—but not only were they not good quality, they were probably the cheapest grade on the market. Another spa had pieces of paper taped to the wall of the very elegant dressing room describing new services the spa offered. In another, the minute a client walked in the front door she found herself in a very beautiful, luxurious, and serene space, but when she was shown to the consultation room where the sales presentation and decision to make the purchase takes place, suddenly she found herself in a dismal and chaotic environment. Do you see the incongruency between the image or story these business owners thought they were projecting and the reality? Can you understand that a client would feel confused, dismayed, and disappointed when confronted with a very different experience than the one she was led to believe she was going to have? And you know what they say: "A confused mind always says no."

Sydney says

Your business must project a consistent image at all times. If elegance is the image you want to project, elegance must be evident in every detail. If simplicity is the image you are after, there must not be a speck of clutter in sight. A pair of fresh eyes will catch things that you cannot see, because you are involved in your business on a day-to-day basis and just don't notice.

THE DEVIL IS IN THE DETAILS

Harmony Tenney
harmony@businessempowerment.com

Business owners "let things slide" all the time. What the business owner fails to see is how their mixed messages confuse their prospects and customers, distort the mental movie they want them to see, and clash with the mental movie they already have playing in their minds. The confusion these mixed messages causes cuts through a business owner's profits "like a hot knife through butter." Here are other examples:

1) A tiny, used-car business had a huge sign by his front door in an adjoining window. It was at eye level, and had huge letters that warned "NO TRESPASSING."

2) Dried-up plants in waiting rooms clearly show that the business owner does not care about details, and is NOT capable of cultivating/sustaining customers for life.

3) E-mails without a signature line, or with an incomplete one, impede the flow of communication. How is anyone supposed to get back in touch with you unless

you enable/facilitate communication? Make it easy for someone to send you a handwritten note, or to take the next step by phone.

4) Cell phone discourtesy is truly distasteful. A business phone should never be answered with "yeah?" or "hi"—script a greeting and think of every caller as the next million-dollar customer. Never answer a cell phone in a meeting—that immediately signals to the person whom you are with that they are not your top priority. Each time this happens, you're chipping away at your reputation—and your income.

Petty Annoyances Add Up

There are issues related to practicality and user-friendliness that business owners and their employees often don't catch. For example, if your business is in an area of the country where everyone wears coats seven months out of the year, doesn't it make sense to have a place where customers can hang them? One of my clients did not. If your customers need to disrobe and store their belongings while having a treatment, shouldn't the lockers be deep enough to fit a hanger and long enough to accommodate a dress as well as leave room for shoes or boots and a handbag? The person who designed the dressing room for one of my clients didn't think so. If a customer needs to use the restroom in your store or office, shouldn't there be a place to set her handbag and somewhere to put her coat, other than the bathroom floor? I myself have been in more bathrooms than I care to count where the floor was the only option. Such things might sound petty in the grander scheme of things but they are irritating and annoying to your clientele. Several little things can easily add up to one big disappointment—which may lead to her choosing to take her business elsewhere.

Looking Beyond the Big Picture

The area in which a business is most vulnerable is the Sales Process. The only indication that something might be amiss is if the conversion rate is lower

A VERY BAD HAIR DAY

The Rita Hazan hair salon is spending a great deal of money on PR agents to get the salon mentioned in all the women's fashion and beauty magazines in order to establish themselves as the latest, greatest, most fabulous place to get your hair done in New York City. After seeing the salon written up in several "Best of" columns, I decided to give them a try. I phoned for an appointment to get my hair highlighted, told the person I had never been to the salon before, and we spoke at length about what I wanted so she could recommend an appropriate colorist. Upon arriving on time for my 7 P.M. appointment, I was greeted in a perfunctory manner, eventually shown to the colorist's station, and the two hour process was pretty uneventful. We were finished by 9 P.M. Well, not entirely finished, it still needed to be blown dry. I assumed the colorist would tend to that, just like every other colorist I have ever been to in every fancy salon I have ever patronized. You can imagine my surprise when he informed me he did not do blow drys but there was a dryer and brushes "behind that mirror."

I wasn't about to spend the hour plus it takes to do that myself—after all, isn't the point of going to a hair salon to walk out looking professionally coiffed and fabulous? I inquired if there was an assistant who could do it. That would be an additional $75, he informed me. Considering it was already costing north of $300 plus the tip, that seemed pretty outrageous, but the only other option was to go out into the winter night with sopping wet hair and do it myself at home. Not at all happy about it, I agreed to shell out the $75. Then it turns out that there is no assistant available because I had not booked one. Wouldn't you expect that the girl I spoke with when making the appointment would think to mention that? It's practically a guaranteed upsell, for heaven's sake!

I pointed out that this was the first salon I had ever been to that did not include drying the hair after a color treatment, and that this little factoid should have been brought to my attention when booking the appointment. All I got was a shrug and was basically told there was nothing they could do about it because it was my fault I had not booked a blow dry.

This is a perfect example of a sales process operating with no scripts, no training, and no common sense.

than might be reasonably expected, higher ticket items are not being purchased as frequently as might reasonably be expected, and/or overall sales are realistically disappointing. Do you really know what your employees are saying during their presentation? Do you have scripts, or at least an outline of the salient points they need to cover? Do they thoroughly understand the products or services they are selling and can they give a coherent explanation of all of them? Do the people who most often make the sales really know how to sell? Not everybody has the talent to be a good salesperson!

I spent the afternoon sitting with the receptionists at one of the spas where I was consulting. The receptionists were inarticulate and uninformed (well, if they were informed they couldn't articulate that information to the customer!). After half an hour I was so on edge I started looking around for where they stashed the Xanax! Prospective clients would call to inquire if the

YOU NEED TO CLEARLY SET YOUR OWN STANDARDS

Here is an example of what can happen when an employee does the job by her standards, not yours. One of my medi-spa clients does a brisk business in products, aka "Lotions and Potions." A patient who had been there a few times before brought back a bottle of some sort of lotion she had just purchased. After she got home and took it out of the box, she saw that it had separated and she felt the color looked funny. So she came in to ask for an exchange, but the receptionist had to run it by the manager first.

The manager became very indignant at this request, saying that all it needed was to be shaken and that the color was fine. She would not authorize the receptionist to make the exchange. Knowing the prices this spa charges, this woman had easily spent $1,000 on treatments plus products, and was very likely to come back for more. She couldn't believe they would not make the exchange and, not surprisingly, got pretty steamed about it. She was not going to take no for an answer.

continued

YOU NEED TO CLEARLY SET YOUR OWN STANDARDS, CONTINUED

This woman got on the phone and called the office of the doctor to whom the spa belonged and with whom she had a prior relationship as a patient. Of course he authorized the exchange and had to spend a considerable amount of time placating the woman as well. I was on site at the time but did not witness the exchange. I heard about it from the doctor, my client, later at lunch. He was pretty steamed himself.

This was a classic example of an employee who does not understand the level of service her employer expects her to deliver. Instead of giving the level of service the doctor assumed she was giving, and that the patient was rightfully expecting, she set and followed her own standards instead.

spa had a treatment to address a particular problem; frequently there were two or three treatments offered by the spa that might be appropriate for the problem, all a little different. Of course the prospect wanted to know what those differences were but the receptionists were unable to give them anything but vague answers, either because they didn't know themselves or they were simply unable to articulate it. It won't surprise you to hear they weren't converting many calls into appointments. This spa had a huge problem they were totally unaware of. Because the people answering the telephones—the first point of contact in the sales process—were unable to give a prospect the kind of information she needed in order to book an appointment, the spa was not doing nearly the volume it could have, should have, and needed to do.

Do not take it for granted that the people who answer your phones are knowledgeable about what it is that you do. They probably have a good idea, but that is not good enough. If you don't like the idea of scripts, at least have spec sheets on every item you sell or type of service you provide so the phone person is able to have a credible conversation with a client or prospect.

Your customer service/customer support department is part of the sales process too. In many cases these departments don't get involved until after

THE TRIUMPH OF HOPE OVER EXPERIENCE

I had been looking for someone who would give me a hair cut that was less boring than the ones I'd been getting, so I asked the colorist at Rita Hazan if he knew of anyone. I wanted something that was young and fun, yet still age-appropriate. He recommended a colleague we'll call John, who was good at doing "something classic but a little edgy," which was exactly what I was looking for. Understandably hesitant to go back there after the blow dry incident, vanity got the better of me and two weeks later I warily made an appointment for the following Thursday (confirming, of course, that styling was included with the cut). That Tuesday I realized I wouldn't be able to make it and gave them a call.

"Hi, this is Sydney Barrows and I need to reschedule an appointment I have this Thursday at 4:30 with John." Silence while she brings me up on her computer screen. "Barrows? Sydney?" "Yes." "OK, it's cancelled." CLICK!! I couldn't believe it. Did I not say I wanted to reschedule that appointment? And even if I hadn't, shouldn't she have been trained to immediately ask, "When would you like to reschedule?"

Once again, a classic example of no scripts, no training, and employees with no common sense. A less charitable person would add "brain dead" to that.

the sale. But they are as much a part of the sales process as the person who makes the sale, because if an unhappy customer is not handled properly, he will return the product or cancel the service and may very well never do business with you again.

It is also not unusual for a customer to return a product or cancel a service because he is unable to figure out how to use it. Easy-to-understand written directions are crucial as is a support person or team who can walk the customer through how to set up and use their purchase. In fact, if you are selling a product or service that is not easily usable or understandable, part of the sales presentation should include assurances that you have a support person or team who will be available to answer any questions or help the customer with any confusion that might occur.

XXX POWER IDEAS

- **X** You can't fix a problem you don't know you have.
- **X** Your phones and website must be mystery-shopped on a regular basis.
- **X** A professional analysis of your store or office uncovers problems as well as contributes fresh ideas to improve your business.
- **X** Prospects and customers feel uncomfortable and confused when they encounter incongruencies between what they were led to expect and what they actually experience.
- **X** Do not take for granted that your employees understand what you do and what you sell thoroughly enough that they can coherently or effectively explain it.
- **X** Never assume your employees have the same values as you do; make it very clear the level of service you want and expect them to deliver.
- **X** Your customer service and customer support people are just as important a part of your Sales Process as the salespeople.

Chapter 8

THE IRRESISTIBLE EXPERIENCE

In less sophisticated economies, people buy a product because they need whatever features it has or whatever function it serves. They purchase a service because they need something done, usually because they are unable to do it themselves.

In more advanced economies, the Experience Economy is replacing the basic act of buying and selling; merely providing products and services is no longer enough. Consumers are now seeking to have an experience while buying and/or using an item or service; the more memorable or meaningful an experience you present, the more you will differentiate yourself from your competitors, the more you can charge, and the more successful you will be.

THE TIFFANY EXPERIENCE

Millions of women grow up fantasizing about shopping for their engagement ring at Tiffany with Mr. Right, and walking out with a diamond on their finger and the signature blue box in a Tiffany blue bag. In fact, giving someone *anything* in a Tiffany box is perceived as a special experience.

You can walk exactly ten blocks down Fifth Avenue in New York City from the Tiffany flagship store and purchase a diamond in the jewelry wholesale market for far less. But who dreams of going shopping for an engagement ring in the kind of atmosphere the stalls on 47th Street provide? One of the businesses Tiffany is *really* in is the fulfill-my-dream-of-shopping-for-an-engagement-ring business. They are providing an Experience their customers have fantasized about for years. And their customers are happy to pay a premium price for that Experience.

The Escort Experience

My former business is a perfect example of providing a service versus providing an experience. Sex, or more accurately the sex act, can be considered a commodity, even though it pains many people to think of it that way. If you want X, it will cost you Y; money exchanges hands, the service is provided, and the transaction is over. That is as much of an "experience" as the sex-as-commodity purchaser wants to have.

We catered to a very elite sub-niche market for whom the "service" was incidental; it was the *experience* surrounding the service that had far greater appeal. And our particular niche was not looking for just any experience. Our clients were seeking a refined, sophisticated, fantasy call girl experience.

Sydney says

Adding value to what you sell or do by providing your customer with an Experience is the key to differentiating yourself from your competition. Businesses that create a meaningful or memorable Experience for their customers can command premium prices and inspire a very high degree of customer loyalty.

The fantasy we provided extended beyond spending a few hours with a beautiful, charming, elegant young lady; the fantasy began the minute he dialed the phone and continued to the moment he closed the door after her departure.

This experience added value to the basic commodity. Our clients were more than willing to pay a premium price to obtain it—and we had to spend a considerable amount of planning in order to deliver it. Everything we did, no matter how minor or seemingly inconsequential, had to be consistent with our story or plot. The appearance of our ads and the conduct of the person who answered the phone had to be congruent with the fantasy. The sales process had to be designed to support the fantasy. The young ladies themselves had to look the part, act the part, and communicate in a way that maintained the fantasy.

We created this experience using a process called reverse engineering. I like to joke that I did reverse engineering without a degree from MIT! I began with researching just what it was our clients were seeking, what they were ideally hoping to find. Then I built on that foundation, adding one element to the next and the next. What needed to happen after they dialed the phone? Exactly how should that interaction be designed to be congruent with the plot? What should the person on the phone sound like, what should her demeanor or attitude be? Exactly how should she describe who we were, what we offered, the price, and the payment options? How should she inquire as to the kind of young lady he hoped to see? How should she present his options? If he booked, what would the various steps in that procedure be? What exact wording should she use while extracting the logistical information necessary in a manner that was congruent with the fantasy?

Then, of course, there was the "product." The product had to be packaged (dressed) in a style consistent with our overall story, but also consistent with the type of young lady we were describing. Glamorous fashion model, girl-next-door, budding actress, stylish artist—we had a pretty varied selection. Each girl had to have a name that reflected her look; obviously the girl-next-door wouldn't be called Natasha and the stylish artist would never be named Jane. Every girl needed a background story that basically had to be true, but might be embellished a bit if necessary; certain facts were omitted if they did not add to the story. So if a girl knew how to sail, was a skier, or spent her junior year abroad in Italy, we would weave that into her description, particularly if we knew the client had similar compatibilities or interests. In order to get this kind of information, we debriefed the girls after the call and kept notes on individual client cards.

We also kept careful notes as to the type of girl a client preferred, which we determined the first time he called. This way when he called the next time, we could quickly look him up and, instead of having to ask him his preferences all over again, after a minute or so of pleasantries we could tell him about one or two girls we thought he'd like, accentuating the attributes we knew appealed to him and downplaying the ones that didn't. This contributed to the impression that we remembered exactly who he was, knew exactly what he liked, and that we were picking young ladies who were just right for him. (Of course, if someone was a regular client, we did remember the type of young lady he preferred.)

In order to avoid telling him about someone who would not be suitable, we also kept notes about what did *not* appeal to him. If he told us he didn't like tall girls, it was probably because he was not so tall himself, so launching into a description of a 5′11″ model was not a very good idea. Remember, the goal is for them to think, "They know who I am," and "These people really listen to me and care about me." And they did not come away thinking that because we were good actors, they came away believing that because it was true.

Making our clients feel special was also part of the experience, and fortunately they were such nice guys it was a pleasure for us to do it. I think that was actually an extra bonus that we threw in there because it made *us* feel good, but it certainly didn't detract from their fantasy.

That's how you reverse engineer your plot or story to create such a wonderful experience for your clients and customers that they want to do business with you and only you. That's how you make their experience so meaningful or irresistible that they'll pay you more money because it's worth it to them. If it sounds complicated, it can be. But the ROI is well, well worth it.

EXPERIENCE IN ARCHITECTURE

Larry R. Lane
LaneArchitecture.blogspot.com

It does not matter whether you want to renovate a home, office building, retail store, or even revitalize a has-been downtown, the one design ingredient that is imperative to use in order to make a lasting impression and cause the user to sense the significance of the "place" is *Experience*. Everyone has had their own experiences in life. Emotional triggers differ from one person to another. While one may perceive a space as being cozy and safe, another might view it as cramped and lonely. But, there are some social norms and proven architectural design tools that can be used to make a positive impact.

I was the project architect for Niketown, New York. The store is located on East 57th Street in Manhattan. It is next door to Tiffany's and Trump's famous Tower.

The first step that Nike Image Design made was deciding what they wanted their customers to experience while visiting this major flagship store. Some of the descriptive words and phrases that they came up with were: movement, nostalgia, uplifting aspirations, teamwork, connection with the community, progressive, technologically advanced thinking, and being decisive ("Just Do It").

Nike also choreographed the experience that they wanted their customers to have. The customer was to experience the anticipation that one would have while entering an old monumental school gymnasium that was built in the 1930s. An old gym was found in middle-America that had a large arch with windows and large vertical pilasters on either side of the arch. This became the architectural model to follow. As the customer approached the bronze revolving front doors, they would pass large antique lanterns and display boxes that looked a lot like ticket sales booths. After entering into the "Nike Museum" at the front of the store, they would pass through turnstiles in order to be in the ever-expanding five-story atrium. The old scuffed up gym floor could be seen below a more modern elevated floor. Walls and ceilings were made to move on cue in order to have a "show" every 15 minutes. During the "show," projected images of balls would appear to bounce off of walls, floors, ceilings, and was synchronized with sounds of impact coming from speakers hidden in columns and resonating low tones under the floor. Customers would watch a brilliantly produced video during the "show" that continued to give the customer the experiences that Nike Image deliberately planned long before building this memorable place.

This building was to be like no other building in the world. Yet, it borrowed a lot of classical architectural elements to help tell its story. Curves were used in the public areas, including the shape of the elevator cabs, because they give one the feeling of accelerated movement. The façade had vertical flutes that led one's eyes upward to the soaring flags that were on top of the building. Next time you visit the store, notice that the name of the building is PS 6453. If one was to dial that, they would spell NIKE on their phone.

Having a building that is so deeply based on creating an experience affected even those who were building it. Although the steel arching beams at the top of the atrium were welded, the steel fabricators dusted off their obsolete rivets manual and placed black painted plastic caps exactly where they would be if the same steel beam was connected only with rivets—in order to maintain the 1930s era experience.

When I talked with Donald Trump, the Duchess of York, and Spike Lee during the grand opening, it was evident that they were positively affected by the designed experience.

Experience is contagious. It affects all of us. Focus on how you want your customers and clients to feel and react while doing business with you and your company. Otherwise, you are just another forgettable commodity.

Be in the Business Your Customers Want You to Be In

One of the big secrets to being in the experience business is, "do not try to be everything to everyone." First of all, it isn't possible; second, it is so much easier and more lucrative to be everything to a very special few people ("few" being a relative number). You want to provide an experience that appeals to customers who have very qualifiable wants, needs, and expectations, *and* who have the wherewithal to satisfy them. When you provide an experience that is markedly different from your competition, you are differentiating your product or service and providing a distinctly different *value*, which is why you can charge a premium price for it.

SYDNEY'S XXX-RATED SALES SECRET #17

You can satisfy some of the people some of the time and you can satisfy some of the people all of the time, but you can't satisfy all of the people all of the time (with apologies to Abraham Lincoln).

Categories of Experiences

Remember, delivering an experience is adding *value* to whatever it is you do or sell. Depending on the kind of experience that would most resonate with your customer and would support the story or plot of your business, consider the following:

- What would delight them?
- What would be fun for them?
- How could you surprise them?
- What would make them feel unique and special?
- What would make them feel good about themselves?
- What would reaffirm the way they see themselves and reinforce that identity?

- How could you customize your product or service so they will identify it as being "Just for me!"?
- How might you give them the temporary experience of letting them "be" someone else?
- How might you make it possible for them to do something out of the ordinary?
- How could you create the perception that doing business with you raises or confirms their status?
- How could you create feelings of validity and satisfaction about themselves?
- What could you do to make them feel safe and secure, give them peace of mind?
- How might you help them become the person they have always wanted to be?
- How might you give them the ability to do something they have always wanted to do?

CREATING THEATER

Legendary retailer Stanley Marcus was known for saying that retailing should be entertainment and that a store is a theater. He always maintained that "When customers have fun, they spend more money." How might you create a theatrical environment in keeping with your plot or story? How might your employees be dressed to support that theme? If you have an internet business, how might you design your website to be in keeping with your story? Your direct mail pieces? Consider color, graphics, fonts, photos, or drawings to create a compelling visual message that will engage and delight your customers.

THE KISSING WENCH

Kim Castle
BrandU.com

The summer after I graduated from college I needed to raise money quickly to attend a graduate program in New York City. So, I took a job doing something I had always wanted to have experience with–kissing. I became a kissing wench at the local Renaissance Festival for the summer. After all, I wasn't kissing as myself, I was kissing as a bawdy character born somewhere in late 1600s England.

I spent 30 solid days preparing for my debut at the festival, from my character's back story, to my wardrobe, to the tools that would support me in kissing anyone who would pay me. I was excited!

I set my asking price per kiss at $1. Up until this point, I had never charged anyone to kiss them so I thought this was asking a lot. So . . . people paid me what I asked, one dollar per kiss.

I busted my hump to convince 65 customers to pay me $1 a kiss. Yet, I had asked hundreds. Sixty-five sweaty people. At the end of the first weekend I was exhausted . . . and I had made $65.

Then it dawned on me, I'd have to kiss thousands of people at this rate if I ever was to get to New York. I had to figure out a way to get more money from fewer people.

I wondered if I could let them decide what the kiss was worth–and allow them to do this after I already kissed them. A donation of sorts. I would let them search their soul after I had already planted my lips. Risky? Yes, but bigger payoffs always come with bigger risks. They could easily stiff me but it couldn't be much worse than getting a dollar.

To ensure that I received more money per kiss I had to go beyond what I had done the previous weekend–beyond the character, beyond the story, beyond the tools. I had to create an entire experience for the customer from start to finish.

I needed to make sure that the entire transaction was well worth whatever money they had–it had to be priceless. This played out for each customer in four very specific choreographed acts.

The first act was getting the customer to realize that they needed a kiss from me. Not just wanted a kiss, but that they needed a kiss. No one walking into the festival that day woke up knowing that they would pay for a kiss that day. By the time they crossed my path . . . they did.

Once they said yes, the second act consisted of preparing them for the kiss—the build up. I made them feel great about their decision. I put them on stage by gathering an audience around us to multiply the customer's good feelings about their decision—or at least they couldn't get away without looking like a wimp.

The second act also included offering choices that the customer could make. I got them to take an active part in creating the experience; after all, the sell involved two people—me and the customer. These choices included what flavor and color of lipstick they wanted me to wear and their choice of where they wanted the kiss. They only had three choices of kiss location—the cheek, the hand, and the upper arm, which I turned into a dancing kiss (See the fourth act).

The third act was the actual kiss. And what a kiss it was. Every single time. For every single customer. I didn't rush right into it. I moved as if in slow motion, allowing the customer to savor and anticipate every passing second as I leaned in. So much so that when I did finally placed my lips on them, you could literally feel joy pour out of them. The crowd would burst into applause and laughter. The customer felt that they were not only the recipient of a kiss but that they were receiving the applause as well. They were overjoyed and fulfilled simply by saying yes to a kiss.

In the fourth act I highlighted the service I just gave the customer, allowing them to relive it for a few more moments and reinforce their good feeling about their decision. If I kissed their biceps and the customer had some muscle, I would open and close the arm and make the kiss move—a dancing kiss. After allowing the kiss to linger for about 30-45 seconds, I would turn to them and say in my weekend cockney accent, "Now what was that worth to you?"

My second weekend as a kissing wench I averaged $20 a kiss—20 times more than I got the week before for doing the same service. I came home with nearly $900, as overjoyed as my customers had been, and with energy to spare.

Throughout the summer I continued to perfect the selling process, but sticking to my four acts like clockwork. My donation per kiss continued to rise as did my closing ratio, which went up to an astounding 90 percent. I peaked at $67 for a single kiss on a cheek that a group a friends bought for someone.

I learned that by giving a customer an experience that they could re-live in their mind and heart, beyond what they expected they would get, they would pay more than I could ever figure out to ask. And they'll gladly do it again and again.

It's no wonder that 20 years later that experience plays a big part of my work today—showing entrepreneurs how to craft the whole of their business as a brand, from the reason it exists, to why customers should buy it from them, to how to make it stick in their mind, to how to position it in the marketplace. And their customers are overjoyed because of the experience. It all started with a simple kiss.

A Note to Attorneys, Financial Services, and Mortgage Brokers

Above all else, people in the legal, financial, and mortgage business want to emanate an air of security, reliability, trustworthiness, and *success*. The first place to start is to decorate your office in subdued colors. That doesn't mean the colors have to be drab! And you can add interest with texture. Classic mahogany or cherry wood chairs, bookshelves, and tables, and of course Oriental carpets. Interesting sculptures and *objets*; framed pictures of

PROFESSIONAL PRACTICES

Generic waiting rooms and treatment rooms do not create anything but a basic, run-of-the-mill experience. Add some color, amusing accent pieces, murals on the walls—at the very least paint some clouds on the ceilings! Turn the bathrooms into little jewel boxes. Give away a fun little gift to children and be particularly considerate of your elderly patients.

you with well-known people; framed clippings from magazine pieces that mention or feature you; perhaps photographs of businesses you have helped finance, along with certificates and testimonial letters in wood frames. If you like, the bathrooms can be fun and whimsical, as long as they look expensively fun and whimsical.

Engage Their Senses

The point is, no matter what business you are in, you want your client, customer, or patient to experience a lot of visual stimulation that is not only interesting and pleasurable, but also influences how they perceive you and your business. Give them a lot of different and diverse things to look at, include contrasting textures and colors, display unusual and uncommon accessories, knickknacks, plants, and art work. Delight their eyes at every turn. Play soothing background music (or whatever type of music suits the atmosphere you are trying to create). Some offices even bake cookies, both for the smell and to give their customers/clients/patients a surprise treat. Make coming to your establishment a distinctive and unique experience.

There is a growing uniformity today, everything is becoming more homogeneous not only in our own country, but in others as well. The mom 'n pop stores, family-owned restaurants, quirky little shops, owner-operated pharmacies, and myriad other small businesses are all being squeezed out of existence by rising rents and large chain stores. Consumers are hungering

Sydney says

Enhancing the connection between you and your customers by providing them with a distinctive Experience every time they do business with you. The Experience Economy is the wave of the future, and those of you who get on board before your competition realizes what is going on will have a huge competitive advantage.

for something different, something that feels special and unique, products and services that are customized, encounters that engage them, and experiences that feel more personal and intimate. Businesses that can add value to their offerings by giving their customers such an experience can command higher prices because they are providing more than a basic transaction. And people will gladly pay more money to be engaged, entertained, and to feel special.

MEMORABLE EXPERIENCES AND THE SIXTH SENSE

Kurt Minson
kurtminson@MGroupConsultants.com

To deliver the highest satisfaction in any business, owners must be in a position to create and control a nice slice of reality for their clients. But apart from good old-fashioned SLA brain washing, how can this be done effectively? To build a world, especially one that is favorable to your product or service and promotes the Prime Idea (PI) that must fuel it, you first need to understand the reality of that PI. In other words, what is the compelling value in what you are *really* selling?

Great brands are great precisely because they are built on a Prime Idea that resonates in the market and can be delivered at a high level by the company. For example, Smucker's, that homey, Orrville, Ohio, bastion of jams and jellies . . . what do they *really* sell? With a name like Smucker's, not only does it have to be good . . . it feels so totally nostalgic in the process. Sepia memories of grandmother's kitchen, warm breads, and melting butter are all over this experience . . . the products, as yummy as we all know they are, are just a means to this tasty end. The fact that the company experienced a down tick in sales when a consultant was successful in getting Smucker's to test drive a modernized version of their packaging, shows just how sensitive this perceptual linkage can be.

While Smucker's can make its case to a great experience via a nostalgic appeal to our tastebuds, other brand experiences can be just as rich. What does Tiffany's really sell? If you said jewelry, you are missing the point. A ton of places sell diamonds, gold, watches, and platinum, but there is something special, exciting, and even more to the point, anticipatory about that eggshell blue box. I personally don't know a woman alive (unless she's living in a South American rain forest), who couldn't spot "The Box" in her man's coat pocket, two zip codes away, at 3 A.M., in the middle of a dense San Francisco fog. We all know that the goodies inside are nice, but the absolute glee that comes with just seeing the box speaks volumes.

What about Ferrari? The company's founder, Enzo Ferrari, made it clear when he built his business, that racing was his primary concern. The construction of road cars was a necessary evil to finance track dominance, a sentiment that continues without interruption in the Ferrari brand to this day. While the coach work on these beautifully crafted Italian exotics will always turn heads, the sounds of those eager revved engines tell you in no uncertain terms that you are only a few degrees removed from the track and the sweaty palms that go with it.

Rance, the venerable French parfumier to Napoleon Bonaparte, makes it their business to *really* sell history. The fragrance the French Emperor commissioned for his beloved Josephine and the complimentary scent, Le Vainqueur (The Victor) formulated for him in 1805, were kept under lock and key for more than 100 years before being reintroduced. Hockley, the UK's most famous furrier isn't in the game for the thrill of fighting PETA activists on the runway, nor is the company in the business of selling hot, heavy, need-to-be groomed outerwear for its own sake. Even with all the controversy surrounding its goods and those who buy them, Hockley is really in the business of selling indulgence and pampering via one of the most sensual articles money can buy.

Marketing 101 suggests that perception must be reality, but to orchestrate perception, the six, yes, that's six senses, must be fully engaged, influenced, and well directed. Those senses—sight, smell, sound, taste, touch, and mind—are the tools by which we KNOW our world and situate ourselves within it. If it looks, smells, and draws hemoglobin like a rose . . . then in our reality it must be a rose. It's direct for us, because our brains are essentially high quality pattern recognition devices, similar to, but far more powerful than the self-serve bar-code reader down at Target.

For clarification, brain does not mean mind, which Webster's defines as "that part of an individual that feels, perceives, thinks, wills, and especially reasons." For our purposes, the mind senses the other senses and recognizes the responses that those other five senses elicit in us. Put into practice, this means as a species, we capture information and link it to the current pictures and patterns, complete with assigned smells, textures, sounds, and flavors that we already have mentally on file. This enables us to make buying decisions based very much on the nature of the responses that are elicited from the experience patterns that our brains recognize. *Blink*, by Malcolm Gladwell, asserts that our mind then makes the powerful leap between data driven perception and higher valuation in that sixth sense, mostly and pretty formidably on its own.

Ask yourself, how does anyone ever get anyone else to actually eat caviar? By tapping into the sense of mind that exists beyond the lower senses, we leverage comparisons, status, and personal position in our own spaces. The conventional senses are mostly outward facing, but the mind looks outward, inward, and sideways simultaneously. It is the ability of great brands to address and successfully herd more of these six cats that makes the experiences that they generate more memorable and subsequently more inviting than those brands that simply cannot.

XXX POWER IDEAS

- **X** The more memorable or meaningful an experience you provide, the more you will stand out from the crowd.
- **X** The nature of the experience you provide differentiates you from the competition.
- **X** Experiences add value to a product or service.
- **X** Customers will pay more for a product or service if it comes with an experience that is meaningful to them.
- **X** Create an interesting, unusual, or exciting environment that supports your plot or story.
- **X** A run-of-the-mill experience positions you as just another commodity.
- **X** Engage as many senses during the experience as possible.
- **X** Consumers are looking for something different; they are bored with uniformity.

Chapter 9

INSPIRED OR DISAPPOINTED?

The Result of Customer Interaction

Dan S. Kennedy

It seems to me that there are only three possible outcomes every time a potential customer or an established customer has any interaction with a business, store, office, staff person, or salesperson: one, they can be (merely) satisfied; two, they can be disappointed; or three, they can be inspired. Most hit the first mark most of the time, to little good.

For example, my current dry cleaner holds a record: I've been a customer for four consecutive years without ever getting annoyed enough to switch. My clothes are taken there by my errand-runner, picked up by my errand-runner, and they appear to be satisfactorily cleaned and pressed. That's what is supposed to happen.

But it is in the "nothing less but nothing more" category. In those four years, I have never once referred anybody to him. I suppose if somebody directly asked me to recommend a local dry cleaner, I might name him. But in four long years, in thousands of conversations with potential customers of his, I never once spontaneously told anybody about my dry cleaner. Why? Because I was merely satisfied but never inspired.

Worse, had any other dry cleaner, especially one closer and more convenient—like the one located right in the supermarket where I shop—bothered to solicit me effectively, I would have succumbed to the seduction and switched my dry cleaner. I have no passionate love affair with my dry cleaner nor do I feel the loyalty that comes from a long, intimate relationship. I could be seduced away quite easily, perhaps by convenience, perhaps by price, even by simple soliciting. His retention of me as a customer has nothing whatsoever to do with anything he's done; I am retained only by the utter absence of ambition on the part of the other cleaners around me.

I have just described the reason why business owners grumble about the lack of customer loyalty, lose customers they feel they've served well, and fail miserably at growing their businesses through referrals and word of mouth.

Many even miss this minimalist mark and disappoint potential customers. When they disappoint potential customers, they flush hundreds if not thousands in advertising, marketing, and promotion dollars—money they thought they were smartly investing—right down the toilet.

How do you disappoint a potential customer? By being incongruent with your promise or by selling poorly. This incongruency problem is covered throughout this book, so I'll focus on the disappointing sales process or person. Yes, poor salesmanship is a disappointment.

If You Use Brute Force, Don't Expect to Get a Lot of Valentine's Day Cards

Once a potential customer enters the sales process and ultimately arrives in a sales environment, there are three basic ways to sell:

1. One, by brute force, the experience of being violated.
2. Two, as a skillful, often subtle process resulting in entirely voluntary and probably enthusiastic compliance—the approximate equivalent of consensual sex.
3. Three, by creating a pleasurable and gratifying experience—the approximate equivalent of romance.

Approach One

The first approach guarantees disappointment. The second risks it. Only the third approach guarantees zero disappointment.

But the first is the most common selling approach. It is taught to and widely favored foremost by business owners, sales executives, and salespeople who believe—mostly, falsely—that they are in situations where there are no "be-backs." You either close 'em now or lose 'em forever. Or they believe—mostly, falsely—that there is little or no after-sale, continuing, or reoccurring customer value, so if they wind up feeling violated after the sale is done, so what?

This approach is also favored by lazy salespeople who are disinterested in being more skillful and professional, and by stupid salespeople too dumb to realize they are living life as primitive beasts. This entire group includes but is sadly not limited to large numbers (but not ALL!) of auto salespeople; in-home salespeople in the water filter, security system, vacuum cleaner, etc. fields; life insurance and pre-need (i.e., burial) insurance; time-share and vacation/travel clubs; and numerous other categories.

These brutes give the entire sales profession and even business in general a bad reputation. It is why public opinion polls repeatedly show 70 to 90 percent of people hating the thought of ever being employed in sales and stating that they "don't like" salespeople. It disappoints the customer who began in a buying mood, before a sale ever occurs or a product ever used. Therefore, it is brain-dead stupid to do it or permit it to occur in your business, even if you or a salesperson you employ "gets good numbers" by this means. The bigger picture is long-term damage to your business that will far outweigh the short-term gains. Entire industries and professions have been brought to heel by government regulators or abandoned by consumers en-masse when sanctioning or relying on these sorts of practices.

THREE POSSIBLE SALES APPROACHES

1. Brute force
2. Consensual
3. Romance

Which do most people find more intriguing?

Two Anecdotes

Recently, I worked with a good-sized business with multiple offices in which by-appointment, face-to-face selling occurs. I replaced their brute-force salesmanship style with an entirely different approach—at great temporary pain for the client, but with enormous ultimate gain.

In the short-term, I took their average closing ratio from 20 percent (1 in 5) to only 16 percent (1 in 7)—but the number of non-buyers who responded to follow-up marketing and came back and bought within 30 days went up from only 4 to 14 percent. In the longer term, measured over four months, the referrals from these customers were double those obtained from previous customers.

The other situation I want to mention is from our own Glazer-Kennedy Insider's Circle™ business, where one of the many things we do for our Members is organize two major multi-day conferences each year with outstanding speakers, often "celebrity" entrepreneurs. Each speaker has a sales target at these events–it's called "platform selling."

A couple years ago, we had a highly recommended speaker at our main annual event for the first time. To my shock, he employed the most brutish of brute force sales tactics on stage. He was an over-bearing bully who picked on and embarrassed several in the audience in order to intimidate everyone else; he "hard closed" at unreasonable length, and he virtually beat people into submission. His numbers were quite spectacular–he sold a large amount of his resources to an impressive number of people, and created a better-than-anticipated amount of revenue, shared by formula between he and "the house." And I am very proud to say that despite this excellent financial outcome, my partner Bill Glazer and I immediately agreed that we would never, never, never, never permit him to get within ten miles of our events, platforms, or customers again. Our business is all about relationship, and we cannot let a proverbial rapist hang around. To be clear, this guy was masterful at selling this way, and you certainly can sell this way. But you will leave behind you a long-lingering sense of disappointment in every customer.

Approach Two

The second selling approach is more skillful, leading to compliance rather than submission, and leading to a customer at least satisfied with the way in which he was sold to.

There are many ways this type of selling is described, including diagnostic selling, consultative selling, empathetic selling, conversational selling. I go into these steps further in my *No B.S. Guide to Sales Success*, in which I describe the use of expert positioning instead of prospecting, attraction rather than pursuit, and "takeaway selling," a technique that has the potential customer eagerly asking to be allowed to buy and for the privilege of becoming a client.

Approach Three

The skills used in approach two are foundational skills for the third type of selling. They were used well by Sydney in her old, original business of "ill repute," as she describes in this book and in much greater depth in the audio program I recorded with her, *XXX-Rated Selling Strategies*.

Many salespeople stop at the skill level of the second approach—and that's perfectly satisfactory in many situations. The salesperson can make a good living and his customers will be satisfied with their buying experience. But it is the third approach to selling where the grand opportunities lie. You will be more welcomed, appreciated, and enjoy a better experience in selling by having customers so inspired by their experience in buying from you that their post-sale value is ensured. They are also very likely to proactively tell their friends or associates about you; not about the product or service—but about *you*.

THREE POSSIBLE SALES OUTCOMES

1. Satisfied
2. Disappointed
3. Inspired

Be sure you aim for #3.

The Secrets to Highest-Level Professional Selling

I have yet another "list of 3" for you—the three secrets of *highest*-level professional selling.

1. Make the customer the focus.
2. Use the right language in your sales presentations.
3. Your salespeople need to be Pleasant, Practiced, Personable, and Professional.

The Customer Is the Focus

The first "secret" is making it all about the customer, not about the product, service, price, you, or your company. In face-to-face, person-to-person selling, it's easy to determine whether a salesperson is doing this or not: measure the number of minutes the salesperson devotes to asking open-ended questions and listening intently for buying motives, interests, needs, desires and emotions vs. the number of minutes spent telling and talking. This is completely compatible with using scripted, memorized, and rehearsed sales presentations. Sydney and I are strong advocates of selling as performance which requires carefully crafted scripts. This has you customizing your presentation on the fly, choosing and using different scripted stories, examples, explanations of benefits, and facts responsive to what each different customer is telling you.

Here's an example of non-listening, clumsy, low-level selling fom a transcript of a recording of an actual salesperson talking to an actual, potential customer (a 78-year-old man) in a hearing-aid store. This dialogue is toward the end of the presentation, when price was raised.

Customer:	What will these hearing aids cost?
Salesman:	$5,800.00
Customer:	Hmmm. Gee, I don't feel right about spending that much money on myself. I do have five grandkids, you know.
Salesman:	Well, I can understand that the price may seem high to you. Let me tell you more about why these particular hearing aids require such an investment.

The salesman then went into a long-winded justification of the price, which then led to the customer raising more price objections. Ironically, given that he was selling hearing aids, the salesman failed to hear what his prospect was really saying. The man did NOT say he thought the price high, too high, or even higher than he'd expected. The man did NOT offer any price objection at all. If listening carefully, you would realize the man meant what he said: he didn't *feel right* about spending that money *on himself* when he had five grandchildren's futures to think about.

At this point, buying made him feel selfish, and was in conflict with his personal values: family and legacy. Here's how I would have handled it using a more careful, sophisticated style of selling described throughout this book:

Customer: What will these hearing aids cost?

Salesman: $5,800.00

Customer: Hmmm. Gee, I don't feel right about spending that much money on myself. I do have five grandkids, you know.

Salesman: Tell me about those grandkids. Do you have any pictures with you? (I pull out pictures of my three grandsons.)

Customer: Here they are. Bobby is the oldest, 13, and he wants to be a professional baseball player.

Salesman: Who's his favorite player?

Customer: Derek Jeter.

Salesman: What, a Yankee fan in Cleveland! Sir, you need to work on that boy!

Customer: <laughs> Yes, I guess I do. Charley and Tommy are twins, eight years old, always in trouble. This photo's from Halloween—you can see they're dressed up as a fireman and a policeman. Their dad's a volunteer fireman in Richfield. Susan is six, and Carol is four. So you can see, there's quite a brood.

Salesman: What does your son do for a living—in addition to being a volunteer fireman?

Customer: He and his wife have a very successful insurance agency.

Salesman: That's great. These are my grandsons: John, Lucas, and Mark. Two years between each one. I'm doing my part, putting some money into their college savings funds on their birthdays, but I'm glad my son-in-law has a successful business just like your son does. I'm sure you are too. Now tell me, how much time do you get to spend with those grandkids? What do you enjoy doing with them?

Customer: [Describes various activities]

Salesman: I hope you won't mind me pointing out the obvious: almost everything you described involves being able to hear well to really enjoy yourself, and even for those kids to be safe when they're out with you. As I said, I certainly understand the feeling that you want to put money aside for those kids—and I can see that you are one of the least selfish people on earth and certainly wouldn't want to be thought of as selfish. But I'll put it to you straight: given that the payment can be as little as $87.00 a month for these hearing aids that you really need, do you think your family would want you to go without them, to enjoy your times with them less, to save that money?

Customer: No . . . I guess not.

Salesman: I'll bet you're like me, and your son is like my daughter—we have big photo albums and treasure our moments with these kids. You and I are old enough to know it's that day at the ballpark or at his Little League game that really matters—and it's all those memories that will matter more to him in the years to come, even the years after we're gone, than will whether whatever money is left him has the small investment these hearing aids require in it or absent from it . . . you'd agree with that, wouldn't you?

Customer: Yes, I suppose I would.

Salesman: Look, the last thing I want you to do is feel like you made anything but the very best decision here today—not just for yourself but for your whole family. Let me share three things. First, let me remind you why these hearing aids are such a terrific investment—<use same price justifications as other salesman used, emphasize guarantee>.

The second thing I want to share is a story from one of our customers—let me pull out her letter. As you can see from the photo, Helen's a grandmother of four, great-grandmother of two. I think you'll appreciate what she says here. <Read letter.>

The third thing, well, I'd like to do something special for you if you'll let me. I want to extend the 10-day return privilege to 30-days so you have no time pressure, and have plenty of time to try out your hearing aids and see for yourself how pleased your family is at how much better you're hearing, how much more—how do they say it?—"with it" you seem to them. We'll fit you with these today, you'll be used to them by next weekend when you said you were going with the whole family to the county fair . . . a real noisy place where you'll still hear every word of every conversation and every grandkid, clear as a bell. And if it turns out you aren't feeling good about all this, you can bring them back for a full refund. Is that fair?

Customer: Yes it is.

Now, you tell me: how is this older gentleman going to feel about how he was sold? Pretty good, wouldn't you say? Yes, I did "close." And I did, at one point, pull out and use my best-scripted price justifications. But I mostly talked with him about him, his family, his activities, and ultimately, his feelings and values.

That's the core of this first secret: feelings and values. If you can get to an honest, sincere, and empathetic conversation with someone about their true feelings and important values, they will buy from you and feel good about doing so—no matter what you are selling. When a buying decision is not in harmony with values and aspirations, it does not feel, as this man said, "right." When it is brought into harmony, it feels right. The truly skillful sales professional understands this and works at creating that harmony, whether selling an $18.00 jar of skin cream at a department store cosmetics counter, a $5,800.00 set of hearing aids, a $58,000.00 premium insurance policy, a $580,000 home, or a $5.8-million dollar piece of technology to the owner of a company.

Secret Two, the Old Cliché: It's Not What You Say, But How You Say It

The first secret is creating the right feelings. The second secret is using the right language.

In NLP, Neuro-Linguistic Programming, should you study it, you'll find much made of "mirroring." To be abbreviated and simplistic, a person feels best buying from—trusting someone—who reflects himself and the sense he has of himself. He's unconsciously looking for real understanding and connection. In the example above, I sought this by changing the relationship from salesperson-customer to concerned grandparent-concerned grandparent. The final bit of selling or, if you prefer, closing would have been heavy-handed, unwelcome, and felt inappropriate without that grandparent-to-grandparent relationship; but with it, it was perfectly acceptable.

The NLP practitioners "mirror" in many ways, but one of the easiest to understand, most effective, and, Sydney and I believe, most important is with language itself. In the next chapter, Sydney delves into Sales Language in detail. Just let me say this: As a professional copywriter of advertisements and sales letters, I agonize over word choices, I'm sensitive to how the copy sounds when read aloud, and I strive to match terminology and linguistics to the targeted reader. When I'm being paid upwards of a hundred thousand dollars to write such materials and the client will invest hundreds of thousands or even millions of dollars using it—or at least such sums are at stake in potential sales—there is nothing *casual* about this! Since your income, your stature in your company or organization, your future, your security, your kids' college educations . . . since so much is at stake every time you speak with a potential customer, you shouldn't be casual about this either.

THREE SECRETS OF HIGHEST-LEVEL SELLING

1. Creating harmony with values and aspirations
2. Mirroring with carefully chosen Sales Language
3. Presenting yourself as Pleasant, Personable, Practiced, and Professional

It's Not *Just the Experience of Using the Product or Service That Matters*

The tone of eventual satisfaction or better-than-satisfied enthusiasm for whatever product or service is being sold is set, nearly in stone, long before that product or service is actually experienced—by the experience of buying.

Consider for a minute Sydney's old business. A man calls and arranges for a visit to his hotel suite by a young lady. If he is taken care of by a pleasant, personable, well-spoken woman who answers his questions with well-crafted answers, describes the companion being sent in appealing terms not limited to body part measurements, and thanks him for his business, he will have in his mind a certain expectation. Because of that expectation, he is likely to find and focus on things about the young lady who arrives and the hour or hours they spend together that validate his best, most positive expectation, while also overlooking things that may not perfectly match that expectation. But if his call is handled by a brusque, hurried woman impatient with his questions who uses coarse language and describes only the physicality of the lady being sent, he will have a different expectation. And therefore, he is likely to find and focus on faults that validate his worst, most negative expectation. In short, the experience of buying will greatly influence, possibly even govern the experience of using.

If you want to be inspiring, then you have to give a great deal of thought to this, not just about fulfillment, but about the selling itself that precedes fulfillment. What really is an inspiring buying experience?

I have sat through a number of time-share and real estate sales pitches, as you probably have too, and they're anything but inspiring. But Disney's time-share sales presentation, the way it's delivered, and the people delivering it are inspiring. So much so that not only did my wife and I buy and feel good about it, we told many people about it before even once using the membership. What's the difference? All the things I've talked about in this chapter and that have been talked about in this book overall.

We were pleasantly greeted on arrival at the sales center and ushered into a nicely appointed community waiting area, with beverages, fresh-baked cookies, and comfortable chairs. Next, being greeted by the salesperson, perfectly attired, who comes out and, rather than immediately grabbing his prospects and hustling them into the sales office, sits down and "chats" in a very relaxed way. In the sales office, he presents a gift bag including a book and DVD about the properties. When told we were going directly from the center to a park, the salesperson immediately offers to have the gift bag delivered to our hotel instead of making us drag it around with us.

That plus a scripted, practiced, polished sales presentation supported by state-of-the-art visuals on a large flat screen monitor that he was thoroughly familiar with and adept at manipulating, via handheld clicker, as our conversation and questions warranted meant no pressure was given and none was needed.

Secret Three: Pleasant, Personable, Practiced, and Professional

The third secret, then, I would describe as Pleasant, Personable, Practiced, and Professional. Face-to-face selling situations are usually tense and uncomfortable and, oddly, done in poorly designed environments. But the goal should be for everyone to feel relaxed and comfortable. Being "practiced" for the salesperson is extremely important; customers need to see and sense that you know what you're doing and know what you're talking about. Fumbling about trying to find something, meandering around verbally without clear direction and easy-to-follow organization is not reassuring at all. Being in the hands of a consummate professional is always inspiring—it inspires confidence in that salesperson and in the buying decision.

X X X X X

DAN S. KENNEDY is the author of 11 books, including the popular "No. B.S." series with Entrepreneur Press as well as the editor of four monthly newsletters including *The No B.S. Marketing Letter*. He can be contacted ONLY by FAX at 602-269-3113 or by mail at Kennedy Inner Circle, Inc, 5818 N. 7th Street, #103, Phoenix, AZ 85014. Information about Dan's books at NoBSBooks.com.

Chapter

10

LET ME WHISPER IN YOUR EAR

Sales Language Secrets

Words matter. Language matters. There's just no getting around it; certain words are more effective than others and certain words create an effect better than others. I've always loved words - I'm one of those people you're talking about when you joke about people who read the dictionary!

POWER WORDS

Here are 15 power words according to John Tanner in an article he wrote titled "Magical Power Words That Make People Do What You Want":

1. 100% Money Back
2. Practical
3. Plus
4. Now
5. New
6. Miracle
7. Compare
8. Discount
9. Discovery
10. Easy
11. Exclusive
12. 100% Money Back
13. Important
14. Hurry

And remember, probably the *most* powerful word you can use in your advertising, website, and direct mail copy, as well as in face-to-face selling, is the word "you"!

Knowing these words is only the first step, now you must memorize them and then the most difficult part—use them. You need to know exactly when and where to use these words in your sales presentations. This is why scripts are so effective. These Power Words are just as compelling in ad copy, web copy and in direct mail pieces.

Years ago, I very deliberately picked words to create an effect or influence our clients' perceptions of my business. As I've mentioned before, the escort business is not exactly known for truthfulness. While I couldn't do anything about how the other agencies operated, I was determined that we were going to set the highest standards for honesty and integrity. Above all, I wanted our clients to know they could trust us. That's the reason I chose the tag line, "New York's Most Trusted Service."

Be Consistent

First, we indirectly prescreened our clients by accepting only clients who were staying in the top hotels or who lived in what were considered the "better parts of town." (This was by 1980s standards—New York City has become so gentrified that neighborhoods that were then considered junkie hellholes now have some of the hippest shops and restaurants in town.) When we received a phone call from someone with whom we would not be able to do business because of where they were located, we were always very polite. We wanted everyone with whom we came in contact to have a courteous experience. So we would say, "I'm afraid we do not permit our young ladies to visit that hotel" or "I'm sorry, our young ladies are not permitted in that neighborhood." We always stayed in character, still referred to the girls as young ladies, and extended the same polished and polite telephone experience to everyone. Believe it or not, it wasn't unusual for a hotel client to pack up and move to an acceptable hotel!

Stay in Character

One of the elements we downplayed in the Fantasy Experience (which, as I've mentioned, was the business we were *really* in) was that this was a commercial transaction. Part of the fantasy was to give the client the feeling that he was calling his friend Sheila or his friend Ashley and they were introducing him to one of their beautiful girlfriends. Therefore, we needed to be very diplomatic when discussing the business aspects. We never ever used the words price, money, pay, dollars, or charge. Instead, we asked, "How would you like to take care of things this evening?" The young ladies themselves were instructed to avoid discussing payment as much as possible. When she would phone to let us know she was leaving, we would tell her how much he should give her. She would then hand the phone to him and *we* would tell him the amount. "She should have five hundred," or "She will make out the credit card slip for five hundred." The word dollar was to be avoided if at all possible. On the extremely rare occasions a client gave the young lady less than he should have in a cash transaction, she was instructed to say, "I'm so sorry, I thought Sheila told me it was five hundred and I seem to have only four hundred. Would you mind counting it again for me just to be sure?" She was always to take the position that there must be some misunderstanding or an honest mistake had been made. If the extra $100 was not forthcoming, she was to call us and say, "Sheila, I'm a bit confused. I thought you said it should be five hundred, but Mr. Client has given me four hundred. Would you like to speak with him?" At all times, what we said and the way we said it was totally congruent with our plot or story. (For those of you who are wondering what happened on the extremely rare occasion when he didn't pony up the full amount–the young lady always received her full share and the business took the hit.)

Sydney says

These two businesses stayed in character when they posted these signs:

At an optometrist's office:

"If you don't see what you're looking for,
you've come to the right place."

In a restaurant window:

"Don't stand there and be hungry,
come in and get fed up."

Do as I Say, Not as I Did

I'm not proud to admit it, but there were times when I personally took liberties with maintaining The Fantasy. We had quite a few Middle Eastern clients who often took the girls to a very elegant nightclub called Regine's for an evening of dining, dancing, and lots of champagne drinking. These calls usually didn't end until the wee hours of the morning, and I often found myself answering the phone at two or three A.M. when the young lady phoned in to tell me she was leaving. Occasionally the client would balk at paying the rather sizable fee, based on the argument that she had spent most of the evening sipping Cristal. I would have to patiently explain that the young lady was paid for her time, not what she did or did not do during that time.

Every once in a while, the client refused to accept the logic of this explanation and, depending on how disagreeable he was about it, I occasionally became equally disagreeable. "This is not a camel bazaar in the middle of the desert. The price is the price, it is not negotiable, and if you are not an honorable man and are unable to live up to your word, then you will have to call someone else the next time you are in town." Admittedly, the camel reference was unnecessarily snarky, but the language impugning his honor and his word were very deliberately chosen because I knew how very significant those qualities are to Middle Easterners. And yes, I did usually manage to get them to pay in full.

It's All about What You Say and How You Say It

The words you use must always:

- be consistent with the plot or story of your business
- be congruent with the business you are *really* in
- be appropriate for the script from which you direct the "mental movie" you want in your customer's mind
- be chosen for their ability to affect the person to whom you are speaking
- consist of words and terms commonly used by those in that specific market
- resonate with your target market and make them feel, "This is for me."

Whether speaking directly with a prospect or customer, or when writing copy for your website or direct mail piece, always keep in mind that in addition to imparting information, the goal is also to:

- influence the reader or listener's perception of your business
- create an effect

The signs at these two establishments are definitely consistent and congruent with the plot or story of each business:

In a taxidermist's window:

"We really know our stuff."

Sign at a tire shop in Milwaukee:

"Invite us to your next blowout."

- be memorable so that prospects remember you
- inspire the desire to make an appointment, a purchase, or at the very least, request more information
- make the caller or reader feel you know who they are and what they want
- establish trust
- instill the belief that above all others, you are uniquely qualified to solve their problem.

Words, and the way those words are used, are a critical element in everything you and your employees say while interacting with a customer, whether on the phone, face-to-face, or via e-mail, web copy, advertising, and direct mail pieces.

Be memorable. Wouldn't you call this guy if you needed a plumber?

On a plumber's truck:

"We repair what your husband fixed."

Outside a muffler shop:

"No appointment necessary.
We hear you coming."

Have a Sense of Humor!

Everyone likes to laugh. All other things being equal, people are happy to give their business to an entrepreneur with a sense of humor. Most customers like to patronize places that make them smile or don't take themselves too seriously, unless, of course, you are a financial planner or a criminal attorney. But even then, a small funny saying in a picture frame on a table in the waiting room would probably not dissuade anyone from giving you their business and might very possibly be the deciding factor between going with you or going with a competitor.

It's free advertising! They will tell all their friends about your business because you made them laugh.

At an auto repair service station:

"Free pick-up and delivery.
Try us once, you'll never go anywhere again."

In the front yard of a funeral home:

"Drive carefully.
We'll wait."

Targeting Niche and Sub-Niche Markets

There are riches in niches. The more specialized the niche, the easier it is to reach that market and to make a sale—and to charge premium fees. The cosmetics companies are masters at this kind of legerdemain. They take the exact same product with the exact same ingredients, package it differently, and target it to women with dry skin, sensitive skin, Asian skin, or aging skin, for example. Sometimes there might be a minor ingredient added or subtracted, but the product is essentially the same. They could offer a single jar of eye cream to everyone who identifies with any of these skin types, but they wouldn't sell nearly as much. Women prefer to buy a face cream they believe

SYDNEY'S XXX-RATED SALES SECRET #18

They've got to perceive it to believe it.

is specifically intended for their particular kind of skin. And they'll pay more for it because they believe it has been formulated just for them and their skin type.

Shampoos and conditioners in the same product line have identical or all-but-identical ingredients too. Which manufacturer do you think sells more shampoo, the one that has only one option labeled "Moisturizing" or the manufacturer that has a choice of shampoos labeled "dry," "damaged," "frizzy," or "color-treated"? How many variations could there be of car wax? If the can said the wax inside was for a BMW or a Mercedes, Porsche, Viper, Ferrari, Lamborghini, or even a Cadillac, would someone who owns one of those cars pay an extra $5 for it as opposed to going for a generic can of wax? You better believe they would. Same wax inside, all you have to do is put the name of a particular car on the label and watch it fly off the shelves.

All of these are legitimate companies that didn't spend quite enough time to consider how their online name would appear!

"Experts Exchange" is a knowledge base where programmers can exchange advice and views at:

www.expertsexchange.com

Need a therapist? Try "Therapist Finder" at:

www.therapistfinder.com

"IP computer" software:

www.ipanywhere.com

NICHE YOUR PRODUCT

Feng shui is described as "the Chinese art of placement." The concept revolves around everything relating to energy flow. In interior design, where a chair is placed could block the flow of energy to and from a room, where your bed is placed can have an impact on your marriage and your sex life, and where you place your home office in relation to the compass points impacts how creative you will be and how successful your business will be.

One of the members of the Platinum Mastermind group I am in is a feng shui expert and has contributed a couple of stories to this book. She has a product she packages and markets to people who live in apartments. Do you see how she could use the exact same materials but put them in a different package and market that expressly to students living in dorm rooms? Information on how to properly feng shui an office space could be broken down into a product for women, for men, or for a home office. She will need to do a little tweaking for each one, but 90 percent of the product could easily remain the same.

Identical or nearly identical services can be marketed to different niches too. Again, perception is reality. When a customer perceives that a service is something that has been customized for their individual needs or circumstances, they will always choose it over a generic service that does the same thing, because they believe it to be more uniquely qualified to be appropriate for them. The point I am trying to make is, the more niched, specialized, customized—choose whichever word you like—a product or service appears to be, the more likely the customer is to think, "This is for me!" Not only will the customer buy it, she will gladly pay more for it. It matters not that very often the only "customization" is the packaging and the words used on the label, as well as the copy used to advertise it.

One of the most practical ways to create a sub-niche market is to go over your current customer list and break that down into distinct subgroups. You already know you appeal to them and they already know, like, and trust you.

Study how these different groups think about and talk about the issues they desire to address or the problems they need to solve. Use those same words and terms every time you interact with them on the phone, face to face, on the internet, via direct mail, and in all your advertising and marketing.

Words: Deal Makers or Deal Breakers

Here are some classic examples of words you should use instead of ones which might sour the deal:

- meeting or visit, *not* appointment
- investment or amount (preceded by the word "total" where appropriate), *not* cost or price
- monthly investment or monthly amount, *not* monthly payment
- agreement, paperwork, or form, *not* contract
- own, acquire, choose, or take, *not* buy
- OK the paperwork, approve the form, or authorize the agreement, *not* sign here
- clients or people we serve, *not* customers
- challenge or concern, *not* problem
- more economical, *not* cheaper

As you can imagine, a lot of guys are a little nervous when they call an escort service. They are especially nervous to give their real names, and I can't say I blame them. It made some of them so uncomfortable that they would hang up without booking. You could actually *feel* them shrinking back, stomach contracting, and throat closing. Well of course we had to know their true identity, but if we came right out asked, "What's your name?" we could lose that call. But if we asked, "What name are you registered under?" or "What name is your phone listed under?" they felt much more comfortable giving it to us. It was the same question, but when we asked it more indirectly, it felt a lot less threatening. Isn't that interesting?

I have done some trade show consulting and have noticed that a number of visitors to a booth prefer to have their business card stapled to a sales or contact form rather than fill out all the information by hand. However they do still have to write in their credit card information if making a purchase, especially when the product in question is one for which they will be billed on a monthly basis. I immediately watched history repeat itself: You could feel and actually see them shrinking back when told they needed to write in their credit card number. Some became so uncomfortable they walked away and the sale was lost. But I found that when I suggested the salesperson point their finger and say, "I just need you to fill it in from here down" those words didn't kick in that sense of discomfort. And they did fill it in and my clients did get the sale.

If You Want It Done Right, You Have to Know What "Right" Is

This is why it is so critical for you, the business owner, to personally spend time interacting with customers and selling. You need to see and feel for yourself what works and what doesn't. As the owner, you know what you do or offer better than anyone, and can talk about it better than anyone else possibly could. Once you have figured out which words are the most effective, write up a script, or at the very least, provide your employees with a list of bullet points. Remember–you also want to make it clear to them what words *not* to say!

SYDNEY'S XXX-RATED SALES SECRET #19

If you want it done right,
you first have to do it yourself.

You Are the Director

Dan Kennedy and I like to think of selling as performance art, and every performance needs a script just as every script needs the right words and the best language. He says, "If great direct response copywriting is salesmanship in

Sydney says

For those of you who sell over the internet or by direct mail, you will have to do A/B tests to see which version of two different ones pulls better. Continue to tweak until you reach a conversion rate that satisfies you.

print, why shouldn't selling be copywriting delivered as a performance?" And as with every performance, all the actors need to know their individual lines and their stage directions, and then must perform them as an ensemble.

You, the business owner, are the director and it is up to you to see to it that everyone is on the same page and adhering to the script. You cannot simply call a meeting, hand out sales scripts, and announce that everyone must now say and do things this new way. You have to explain to them why the new script is more effective, do some coaching and role playing, and most of all, make it crystal clear that compliance is mandatory. No one likes change and while they may go along with it for a short time to humor you, they will quickly slide back into their old routine unless they know they are being monitored and that there are consequences for those who don't get with the program.

A FRESH EYES VIEW

John Avolio

johnavolio.com

As a business consultant, my primary focus is on strategic business development for high technology companies specializing in counterterrorism technology, and domestic and foreign businesses and governments who seek to acquire such technologies. This is an account of the impact a Fresh Eyes view had on one of my high technology clients.

A high technology company specializing in explosives detection hired me to work with them on a newly patented technology and prototype product utilizing that technology. While this was originally funded by a federal grant for Defense and Homeland Security purposes, the client was also seeking to develop strategic alliances with compatible partners, outlets in other markets, and applications for this technology in other products and areas. They also needed an evaluation of the prototype product by someone with expertise not only in science and security, but also with knowledge of other technologies and products in the same field, as well as contacts at the governmental agencies and private businesses who are potential buyers of such a product. As one of the principals remarked, "John has the know how and the know who!"

The entire management team was so close to the project and so intent on the original market and application of the technology that they could not see beyond the scope of their original focus. They were directing their energies on what was metaphorically a pile of crumbs, when in reality there was a feast sitting right there in front of them. Initially, the client was focusing on a potential market in need of only a few hundred systems. The additional revenue from both increased sales and the opportunities from ancillary applications would make a huge difference to potential investors or to those who might wish to acquire my client's company.

With a pair of Fresh Eyes, I immediately realized that this product had the potential in the U.S. market alone to sell over sixty thousand systems, and that there were other applications this technology could be used for that had been completely overlooked by both management and the R&D team.

Together, we developed a new action plan that included targeting new markets and identifying additional ways in which their technology could be applied to other products as well as combined with separate but compatible forms of other products and technologies. This client is implementing their new action plan and is on the road to financial success they never imagined possible.

An outside consultant—a pair of Fresh Eyes—can make a significant difference to the future of a business and bring an enormous contribution to the proverbial table.

XXX POWER IDEAS

- **X** Using the right words can create a specific effect or influence a customer's perception of your business.
- **X** Be kind and courteous even to those who do not appear to be qualified prospects; you never know who they might refer or whether some day they might be in a position to become a good customer.
- **X** Always speak (and act) in a manner consistent with your plot or story, and be mindful about "staying in character" at all times.
- **X** When you use language that resonates with a particular niche, they will feel your product or service "speaks" to them and will be influenced to think to themselves, "This is for me!"
- **X** You can sell the exact same thing, or nearly the exact same thing, to several well-defined sub-niches if you use words and language that conveys the impression it has been designed expressly for their issues, interests, or concerns.
- **X** As the business owner, you must take the time to personally engage in the actual act of selling in order to gauge firsthand a customer's response to different words and phrases.
- **X** Every employee must have a clear understanding of not only what to say and what specific words to use, but also how to say it. This must be continuously monitored and enforced.

Chapter 11

SALES CHOREOGRAPHY™

Dance of the Seven Veils

Good Sales Choreography™ can make the difference between having a run-of-the-mill business and one that has fiercely loyal customers who love doing business with you and are willing to pay premium prices to do so. Well-thought-out, well-designed, and well-executed Sales Choreography™ sets you and your business apart from all the others. In many cases, it all but eliminates your competition in the hearts and minds of your ideal prospects and customers, particularly when you cater to a specialized niche market. But Sales Choreography™ doesn't just happen; it takes imagination, energy, commitment, and work, both on your part and on the part of everyone on your staff.

Sales Choreography™ is a relatively new concept; there are some people who have incorporated it into their sales process without even realizing it, but most are still in the dark. The good news is, this gives those of you in the know a tremendous advantage over your competition.

Sales Choreography™ can be physical or psychological. Its purpose is to influence the perception a customer has of you and your business, to influence a customer to make a purchase, *or* to control or influence the way a customer responds to you and your staff. It's too bad the word manipulate has such negative connotations, because when employed in a positive context, that is exactly what well-designed and effective Sales Choreography™ can do.

Physical and Psychological Sales Choreography™ at Work

Let me give you examples of both physical and psychological choreography I designed for my business.

Influencing Perception

It was always extremely important to me that our clients treat our girls politely and respectfully. In fact, one of the reasons we always referred to them as "young ladies" was because we wanted to plant the subliminal message that *we* considered them young ladies and we expected the client to think of them and treat them that way too.

I also made sure the young lady reinforced it herself when she arrived with specific physical choreography. If she was wearing a coat, she was never to take it off herself. Instead, she turned her back and started to slip it off her shoulders, causing him to instinctively reach out and help her with it, just as any gentleman would do. Most of the time the girls wore suits, so if it was too warm for a coat, they did the same thing with their suit jacket.

Influencing First Impressions

One of our biggest challenges was influencing the first impression the client would have of the young lady we sent him. I very meticulously choreographed this too. Beauty is very subjective and no matter how accurately we described her, it was unrealistic to think we could duplicate that movie he probably had playing in his mind. I realized that the only way to control that first impression was to make sure that his first sight of her was the whole picture, not just one of its components, particularly just her face. So after knocking on the door, I instructed the young lady to step back a few feet so his first view was of all of her, the whole package—her silhouette, the way she was put together, the totality of her presence.

GIVE THE GIFT OF LAUNDRY

There are only three or four laundries in New York City that specialize in laundering and hand ironing expensive bed linens from stores like Frette and Pratesi. The prices are pretty steep, $20 and up per sheet, and between $5 and $10 for a pillowcase. Of course if you can afford several hundred dollars for one sheet in the first place, these prices are not likely to deter you.

So how does a company that washes and irons linens use Sales Choreography™ to differentiate themselves from the competition? Instead of returning the linens tightly wrapped in clear plastic, which is how the other laundries do it, one savvy company wraps them in colorful tissue paper and ties a wide grosgrain ribbon around them, just like a present. Not only is it visually more pleasing, it inspires that happy feeling everyone experiences when they receive a present. The psychologically subliminal message is this is a gift, not only from the laundry, but also one that the customer has given herself—the expensive bed linens. There is also the added value of emotional gratification and validation derived from knowing she is able to afford "the best." This service is a bit more expensive than the others, but the pleasure received more than makes up for it. Even something as mundane as laundry can make the recipient feel "special."

If his very first vision of her was just her face through the keyhole, there was the very real possibility his first reaction might be disappointment. But if his first visual impression was the harmony of all her component parts, that first reaction was much more likely to be positive. It set the tone for the whole evening and was a very important part of our Sales Process.

Physical Choreography

Physical choreography is the use of physical surroundings or other visual cues such as dress, for example, to influence the way a person thinks, feels, and/or acts. Physical choreography can also be a physical act, the manner in which you or a staff member interact with or treat a customer. For example, having two waiters place a plate in front of each diner simultaneously is an act of physical choreography. A salesperson in a fur salon who helps a client try on a coat by holding it for her as well as helping her take it off and hanging it up, is engaging in an act of physical choreography. Displaying an iPod along with different earpieces, holders, speakers, and the like right next to it, is physical choreography. In fact, the entire physical design of an Apple store is intended to influence the way the customer thinks and feels about both the company and its products.

Environment

One of the most common ways to use Sales Choreography™ to influence a client's perception of your business is through the physical appearance of your office or store. For example, let's say you have an appointment to see two different dermatologists, both of whom have offices in the same building. You are interested in what they suggest you could do about all the little brown spots that have suddenly appeared all over your face, neck, and chest.

The waiting room of dermatologist number one has gray indoor-outdoor carpeting, metal and "leather" chairs, unmemorable tables with assorted magazines that have seen better days, and ho-hum posters on the walls. The waiting room of dermatologist number two has wall-to-wall carpeting, chairs covered in dark blue fabric, wrought iron and glass tables with the latest fashion magazines neatly arranged on one, and framed landscape paintings on the walls. Which doctor is likely to be more expensive? Which do you perceive as being more knowledgeable about the latest treatment options? If there is no discernable difference between the ages and personalities of the two doctors, which do you feel is more competent? If you were treated well by the staff in both offices and the prices were comparable, which one would you choose to be your dermatologist? I'm willing to bet you'd choose dermatologist number two.

Here's another example. You have just inherited a surprising amount of money from your great Uncle Horace and want to invest it relatively conservatively because you have too many friends who have lost millions in the stock market. You and your wife are interviewing financial planners and you have three appointments set up. The first firm has a tasteful but unremarkable waiting room, and the receptionist and the other employees you see are all dressed in dark suits. Everyone is very polite and professional and all told, there appear to be about ten people in the office. The meeting itself takes place in a conference room and the planners, two men and one woman, all partners in the firm, are also dressed in conservative business suits. They spend time asking you about what your investment goals are and then tell you what they can do for you that will fall within acceptable risk parameters, while still giving you the highest possible yields.

Financial planning business number two is a much larger operation, taking up two floors. The waiting room and conference room are much fancier, the staff is very professional and also nicely dressed. There appear to be at least 50 people working there and everyone seems very busy—phones constantly ringing, numerous people who appear to be clients coming and going. The meeting with two of the planners on staff, one a senior person and the other a junior person, is similar to the first, but the senior person has to go after half an hour, leaving you with the junior person, who is very nice and certainly seems knowledgeable You get the feeling that most of your communications are probably going to be with him. You have basically the same conversation about your investment goals you had with the previous people.

Business number three is located in a large, open loft space in the trendy part of town, the furnishings are very modern and there appear to be approximately six people working there. The meeting itself takes place at a big table in the middle of the room and you meet with the two partners, both in their

Sydney says

It is very difficult for *you* to see and grasp the impact that your physical environment has on your prospect or customer. Conditions in your business that you take for granted, that you don't even notice, can intimidate people, worry people, confuse people, disappoint people . . . and that's why they don't buy. On the other hand, when choreographed effectively, the physical environment of your office or store can reassure people, calm people, inspire trust in people, or arouse excitement in people . . . and these positive feelings motivate them to give you their business. One of the first things I assess during an on-site consulting engagement is the appearance of your place of business, your employees, and all the other minutiae that send out subliminal positive or negative messages to your clients, patients, and prospects.

30s, who are dressed casually, as is the rest of the staff. Their demeanor is fairly casual too. They listen to your concern about investing conservatively and assure you they can do that but don't offer too many specifics. You know from your research that they are extremely successful and have, in fact, made a couple of your friends a considerable amount of money.

Think about the impression you got when reading about these three businesses. All three are successful and all three come with excellent references from people you know and trust. The only differences are the perceptions you acquired from the environment, from the appearance and demeanor of the planners themselves, and from the other people working there.

SYDNEY'S XXX-RATED SALES SECRET #20

You really do only get one chance to make a good first impression.

What is the perception someone coming to your place of business would walk out with? Is this the image you want to project? The physical environment as well as the manner in which you and your staff interact with clients, customers, or patients while they are in your place of business will influence a prospect's perception of your competence, trustworthiness, the level of personal attention they can reasonably expect, your price points or fees, *and how they feel about you.*

Personal Appearance

As the proprietor of your business, you are the lead character. You may, in fact, be the only character. In either case, your appearance, actions, attitude, and demeanor set the tone for the business, both in the eyes of your prospects and customers, and your staff. At heart, you may be a blue jeans and sneakers kinda guy, but if you are in the financial field, you will be much more successful if you dress conservatively when interacting with clients. You may favor leopard mini skirts and skin-tight crop tops—and have the body to carry it off—but if you are a physician, you aren't going to win the hearts and minds of patients or colleagues if you dress like that while on duty at the hospital. When your personal style is out of keeping with the style of dress generally considered appropriate for your profession, think of the clothes you wear for work as a uniform, a uniform that inspires trust, confidence, and respect in a prospect, customer, client, or patient.

Your employees are your supporting cast, and their appearance is important too. One of my most upscale spa clients had a receptionist with purple streaks in her hair who wore scruffy black high-top Keds. It was a horrible contrast to the beautiful and luxurious design and ambience of the spa. If you are uncomfortable asking your employees to dress in a certain way, consider a uniform of sorts, perhaps some sort of smock or knee-length jacket under which they would wear black pants or a skirt. And real shoes, always real shoes, unless you own a sporting goods store.

The personal appearance of you and your employees—clothing and grooming—is a very significant element of physical choreography and has a huge influence on how your clients, patients and prospects perceive your business.

Because appearance is such a personal issue, many business owners are reluctant to set and enforce standards of dress and grooming, and may even be disinclined to set and maintain standards for themselves. This is a huge mistake, considering how strongly personal appearance influences customers. I find this is one of the most difficult reforms my clients have to deal with, and they very often leave it to me to introduce the new dress and grooming code to their employees. This way, the "blame" is shifted away from them and on to me, which makes it easier for both the client and the staff to accept and deal with it going forward.

I was very particular with respect to the kind of clothing I permitted my young ladies to wear. Remember, we were in the fantasy business, and that fantasy was having the prettiest, the most elegant, the most stylishly dressed New York City call girl show up at the client's door. If she arrived in a basic navy blue suit and serviceable pumps, she was not going to meet the client's expectations, and his perception of our entire business was going to go right down the tubes. However, if the young lady arrived in a stylish suit and high heels, that would have a very positive influence on way he felt about her, and about the business as well. It reinforced the Mental Movie our advertising and our Sales Process had already initiated.

SYDNEY'S XXX-RATED SALES SECRET #21

What you wear is not who you are, but what you wear
is who your customers perceive you to be.

Show and *Tell*

In the Time Warner Center in New York City there are a couple of floors where the (very high-end) restaurants are. When you get off the elevator it is not immediately apparent which way you should go and there is a concierge desk staffed with people to ask. While escorting you to your restaurant (simply pointing out the direction is not an option) your chaperone asks you your name, tells you what a wonderful restaurant it is you are going to (validating your choice), walks inside the restaurant with you, greets the *maitre d'* by name, and says, "Miss Barrows will be joining you tonight for dinner." Whenever you get up to go to the powder room, an alert staffer immediately appears and personally ushers you there. The wait staff is attentive but doesn't hover about excessively, and they are exceedingly gracious without being obsequious. You are not exactly surprised at the end of the evening when you get a very steep bill and notice that in addition to the $40 and up entrees, the drinks were $20 apiece. But you have been made to feel so welcome and have been treated so extraordinarily well from the minute you stepped off the elevator you really don't mind and, in fact, are looking forward to coming back again. This is a terrific example of meticulous physical choreography at work.

More and more retail stores are now instructing their employees to escort customers to wherever the merchandise they inquired about is located, instead of just waving their hand in the general direction and leaving it up to the customer to wander around until they find it themselves. More and more frequently in the better professional practices, the receptionist or nurse comes up to the patient directly to tell them the doctor is ready to see them, and escorts them to his office or an examining room. Contrast this with having that same nurse or receptionist calling out your name from across the room, announcing that the doctor is ready to see you now, then instructing you to go to the third door on the left.

Actions Speak Louder Than Words

I saw a little article in a newspaper recently about how Nordstrom now has their salespeople come around the counter to personally give you your purchase, instead of just handing it to you over the counter. A salesperson who brings in a couple of tops that match the pants you are trying on is hoping to influence you to buy a top as well. The offer of a beverage is likely to keep you in the store longer, increasing the chance that you will make a purchase. Having samples of products out for customers to play with and try greatly enhances the likelihood they will buy something. Computer imaging that shows what a patient will look like after a procedure makes the transformation feel all that much more believable and real, propelling many patients to make the decision to say yes. In designer boutiques such as Chanel and Armani, the customer is encouraged to think of a particular salesperson as "her" salesperson, and that salesperson cultivates a relationship with her by attending to her needs when she is in the store, sends little thank-you notes and invites her to special events. Taking the puppy out of the cage and encouraging the customer to play with it is a classic example of physical choreography, and all but guarantees a sale.

SYDNEY'S XXX-RATED SALES SECRET #22

It's not just what you do,
it's how you do it.

Little Things Add Up

Small impulse items are positioned by the cash register for a reason. A clean waiting area in an auto repair shop will encourage the patronage of more women than a shabby or dirty one. A website that shows you other items that people who have ordered the same thing you just did often influences you to purchase the same additional item(s) too. Research has shown that direct mail sales letters that get the reader actively involved by directing them to attach a sticker to the order form have a higher conversion rate. Once they have spent $100, Sephora, the make-up store, gives a little gift to Sephora cardholders every time they make a subsequent purchase. All of these little actions influence a prospect or customer's perception of your business and induce them to make a purchase or return to buy something again.

It's Easier Than You Think

These are the differences Sales Choreography™ can make. It doesn't have to be complicated, and as you can see from some of these examples, it doesn't even have to cost anything. You can achieve a significant competitive advantage by writing effective physical choreography into your script. If you need help getting started, find an expert who knows how to do it to give you some ideas and demontrate how to implement them.

SELLING AS PERFORMANCE ART

Harmony Tenney
harmony@businessempowerment.com

I once "shadowed" a rep from our radio group who wanted to sell a sports sponsor package. After we arrived, he and the female owner spoke for about 45 minutes about their families, their friends, etc. When she left the room to help a customer, I had my colleague move his chair close to her desk. I asked him to take out his proposal. I told him that when she came back, he needed to go thru each page (mostly sports event photos) and then fold the proposal to the signature page, and hand her the pen. He almost got distracted again, but once he handed her the pen, she signed immediately. My "choreography" focused the final minutes of the meeting and got the sale.

Business owners can talk and talk and talk without getting to the point . . . it's a defense mechanism. Salespersons have to keep the attention of the business owner long enough to fully engage their awareness of what's being offered, and to keep directing it to the desired outcome–a sale.

Even sales managers can have this problem. I once had a manager shadow me, and to my complete detriment, he spoke with the business owner about golf for 55 of our 60-minute allotted time. I wasn't allowed to interrupt or speak. And of course, the sale did NOT happen. I didn't take him on another appointment unless he demanded to come.

Psychological Choreography

Psychological Choreography can be defined as subliminally influencing the way a person thinks, feels, and/or acts. Psychological choreography is directly associated with feelings and the influence these feelings have on the target in question, in this case a client, customer, or patient. Some offices, particularly doctor's offices, bake cookies on site—not just to give them to the patients, but also for the effect the fresh-baked aroma has on them. Scents that evoke positive feelings and memories have a calming effect and reduce tension and fear—which can be very important for many doctors' offices and certainly for dental practices. Using language during a sales presentation, either verbal or written, that promotes the feeling that the customer already owns the item or has received the benefits of the service is psychological choreography. Addressing someone by their last name with an honorific, e.g., Mrs. Smith, Mr. Jones, evokes a different feeling than calling them by their first name. Having an audio feature that automatically starts playing when a web page is opened can incite such a negative feeling that the viewer clicks away as quickly as possible, and yet other viewers find this appealing. Being greeted by a receptionist sporting a lip and/or eyebrow piercing might not cause alarm if the business is a music store, but it would likely be very unsettling if the business is the office of an estate planning attorney. A dispenser of Purell on the bathroom wall of a physician's office sends the subliminal message that this practice is very fastidious about cleanliness and is, therefore, "safe."

Psychological choreography subliminally stimulates *feelings*, and these feelings influence the way in which someone perceives how trustworthy you are, how competent you are, how comfortable they feel with you, and whether or not you are someone with whom they want to do business. Psychological choreography can prompt a prospect to make a purchase, take the next step (whatever that might be), or provide them with the confidence to sign up for a five- or six-figure treatment plan. This is an element of the Sales Process that is completely unknown by the majority of businesses out there. You will be able to capture a greater share of the market if you incorporate it into your script and make sure all your employees work as a team to execute it.

Advertising and Marketing

There are so many factors that go into creating the mental movie that a prospect or customer has about your business. The first input is usually the impression they form from your advertising and marketing. The colors, the images, the words, the type, the layout—they all create a perception of not just what you do, but even more importantly, "who you are." You've observed how some ads create the impression that the advertiser is very upscale and very expensive while others make it clear that theirs is the place to shop for bargains.

The words and phrases used in a direct mail piece or on a website can very effectively transmit "who you are" and also who you want or expect your customer to be. Someone looking for bargain prices instinctively knows that using the words "lavish" or "sumptuous" is not a place where you are very likely to get a deal. Copy that trumpets "Come on in today and take advantage of our easy payment plans!" is not selling luxury goods. "Call 555-1212 to make an appointment with your own Private Wealth Advisor" is going to attract a very different customer than, "One of our customer service representatives is ready to help you now."

The Telephone

Doesn't a business that has a receptionist who answers the phone with a very proper British accent communicate a totally different image than a business whose receptionist speaks with a very strong Brooklyn accent? Both people may say exactly the same thing word for word, but their accent is going to influence your perception of that company. The warmth and interest an employee transmits, her attentiveness, the words she uses to ask a question or impart information—all these things and more can be employed to create feelings that influence the perception a prospect or customer has of you and your company. This is why scripts are particularly important. Because certain words are so much more effective than others and arouse feelings that lead the caller to perceive your business in a specific way, the wise entrepreneur will

SYDNEY'S XXX-RATED SALES SECRET #23

Hearing is believing.

Are your callers hearing what you want them to believe?

take the time to craft telephone scripts that send exactly the image he wishes the caller to receive.

When your advertising and marketing is designed to purposely influence a prospect or customer in a certain way, that is psychological choreography. When a company consciously designs scripts to create a certain impact and trains employees to interact with callers in a particular manner in order to influence their response or action, that is psychological choreography.

The Sales Process

There are an almost infinite number of ways to subliminally influence a customer to make a purchase. A sales presentation, whether on a website, in a direct mail piece, or face-to-face, that conveys the feeling the product or service in question uniquely addresses that customer's specific situation or needs, will incline that customer to buy from you. The more respectfully you speak to and treat someone who is looking at a high-ticket item, the more likely you are to get the sale. Verbally "weaving a spell" that helps a client fantasize what it will feel like once she has experienced the service usually influences them to make it more than just a fantasy. Having seats in your store for those unfortunate husbands or boyfriends who have been dragged along for the ride reduces the psychological pressure on the woman to "hurry up so we can get out of here" and gives her time to select more items and spend more money. Donating a certain percentage of the proceeds from a sale to the local ambulance corps creates an incentive to patronize that sponsor because it makes the buyer feel good about spending her money.

Think about what you could do to cause a prospect to feel your product or service is intended especially for them. Is there a niche market in your business that might be more responsive if spoken to or written to using words that resonate with them and make them feel, "These people understand who I am, what I want, and have the ability to give it to me"? Do you and your employees understand the concept of "weaving a spell" and do you have scripts or guidelines so you all can master it? Would customers spend more time in your store if they did not have to look after their children or worry about irritating their significant others? How might you play on the desire of many people, especially women, to "do good" because they have spent their money with you?

When It Feels Right, They Will Do It

The most effective Sales Process leads the customer to say "yes" because giving you their business *feels* right. They *feel* confident they are making the right choice, they *feel* they can trust you, they *feel* you are the most competent, they *feel* you understand them, they *feel* you are uniquely qualified to satisfy their needs, they *feel* comfortable while in your place of business, they *feel* good when they interact with you or your employees. Psychological choreography promotes positive feelings and those positive feelings influence your clients, customers, and patients to want to do business with you and only you. These positive feelings add meaning and value to what you are selling and because of that, your clients, customers, and patients will be willing to pay more for it.

Alexandria Brown, who penned the foreword to this book, wrote a story in one of her monthly newsletters about a shopping trip she and her mother went on in Los Angeles. Nearly every store asked her if she would like to be on their mailing list, which she declined. Then one asked her if she would like to be a VIP member, the benefits of which were being notified when certain merchandise came in or there was a sale. She relates how her "ears perked up" at the prospect of being a VIP member, although in fact, the "benefits" were exactly the same as being on the mailing list at all the other stores. This is excellent use of psychological choreography; the boutique is very likely to get future business from her and possibly her friends, too. And it didn't cost them a penny.

IT'S ALL ABOUT ME!

If you believe Frederic Fekkai is in the hair salon business, you would be only partially correct. I had a psychological Sales Choreography™ experience there I still marvel at. Nearly every upscale hair salon in New York City carries a line of eponymous hair products.

continued

IT'S ALL ABOUT ME!, CONTINUED

I have frequented many of these salons over the years. While the various lotions and potions are always on display (but never have price tags on them), no one has ever once tried to sell me any. Nor do the stylists or the assistants who do the shampoos ever tell you much about, or even if they are actually using, any of the salon's products on you.

I had no expectation that my experience at Frederic Fekkai would be any different. After a brief consultation with the stylist, I was seated in front of a wash basin to wait for someone to come up behind me and tell me it was time to put my head back, as is standard operating procedure in every other salon I have ever visited. So it was a surprise when someone approached me from the front to talk with me first. Before she gets down to business, she wants to ask me about my hair: What kind of hair do I have, do I have any problems/issues with it, what products am I currently using, what am I looking for in a shampoo and conditioner? It was all about me, me, me.

Then she suggests a particular Fekkai shampoo and conditioner that she thinks would be great for my kind of hair and would give me the results I had told her I was looking for. It turned out there was a downside to her first choice she hadn't anticipated, so she then told me about two more, all in terms of what they would do for my hair and how beautiful they would make it look. I made my choice, and as she is doing the shampoo, she casually mentions a bit more about what these products are going to do for me, building up in my imagination how great my hair is going to look and behave. Still all about me, me, me.

Of course by the time she's finished, I'm fantasizing that I'm going to walk out of there looking like a model from a l'Oreal commercial—and, if I want to maintain that effect, will have to continue to use these products. Never once did she ever try to directly "sell" me, and because of that MO, I never felt even the slightest bit of resistance about wanting to buy. Of course I made a beeline to the product area just before heading to the front desk to pay my bill, and there was a dedicated person there whose only job was to help clients make a purchase; you did not have to go looking for anyone to pay attention to you. She, too, only talked about the products and what they would do for *my* hair and

continued

IT'S ALL ABOUT ME!, CONTINUED

how fabulous they were going to make *me* look. At all times these two gals were very clear about what the features were, but they described them only in terms of the benefits to me.

I was startled by the size of the tab when I found out a bottle of shampoo was $35 and the conditioner $40, not to mention the two other products I was also convinced I needed that added up to another $60. But they had done such a terrific job of making me want them that I absolutely had to take them home with me because I *felt* they were going to make my hair so lustrous and beautiful. I may have cringed a bit at the final bill, but I still didn't hesitate to fork over the money. And it is very clear why they choreographed their Sales Process so carefully: You aren't going to sell too many bottles of $35 shampoo unless you have made the customer *feel* that she absolutely has to have it.

HAIL, BRITANNICA!

Darnay Hoffman
darnay@darnayhoffman.com

Years ago, between college and law school, I answered a help-wanted ad in the *New York Times* for salesmen to work for the *Encyclopedia of Britannica*. Remarkably, this experience turned out to be one of the most valuable in my life, not only as a lawyer, but as a businessman with an MBA, as well. *Britannica* had managed to create a highly structured and beautifully choreographed sales process that would allow even a chimpanzee to successfully sell encyclopedias to families in their homes. I've never seen *Britannica's* home sales technique described in print anywhere, so this is probably a first. Here is how it worked.

Lead Generation. *Britannica's* lead generation was done with print and television advertising featuring a premium gift of a boxed, three-volume paperback set of reference books (e.g., a dictionary, thesaurus, and book of quotations) just for inquiring about the *Britannica* and allowing a sales representative to "preview" the *Britannica* in the prospect's home.

Appointments. As salespeople, we made our appointments by phoning people's homes to arrange meetings from the leads we were given from those who had written in asking for the free three-volume reference set. These meetings were usually in the evenings when both parents were home ("one-legged" sales, in which only one parent was present, almost always resulted in a cancellation the next day by the absent parent). Sometimes we would just stop in on them cold at the address listed on the lead cards to "drop off their free paperback books gift" while in the area. There was a simple rule of thumb for scheduling appointments: Whenever you went out in an evening to sell, you had two pre-set appointments made on the phone plus one lead card with an address in the same area of the two pre-sets. If one or both pre-sets cancelled when you got to the door, you could go to the drop-in.

There was also another rule of thumb: The salesman was in more control of the sales process when giving the presentation in the prospect's home rather than in the workplace, where there was a greater chance of interruption and where the prospect would feel in more control. No one teaching the sales force could explain why this was so, but it seemed to be borne out in the field from practical experience.

The Warm-Up. Upon arrival at the prospects' home, we were encouraged to "warm-up" the prospects by making small talk or even rolling around on the floor with the pet dog or cat if that would help us make a sale. The first order of business was to notify the prospects that there was a monthly contest in which a thousand dollars would be awarded for someone's college fund. We would then produce a pen and a contest entry form and would instruct one of the parents to fill it out with their name and address. The importance of this psychologically was the simple fact that the prospect was being conditioned in a non-threatening way to take a ball-point pen from a salesperson and sign their name, at the direction of the salesman, in what would be a preview of the final order-taking process at the end of the sales presentation. The joke among salespeople was always that if the first time a pen appeared was at the end of the sales presentation, the prospect would think "and then he drew a knife." Sales people were also encouraged to use the pen as a pointer all during the presentation in order to continue increasing the prospect's comfort level with the pen.

The Read-Off. Next, a prepared, over-sized, color-illustrated narrative in story book form explaining the *Britannica*, which was known as a "read-off," was read out loud to the customer, who would follow along while the salesman would run his pen along each sentence as a pointer. Periodically, a rhetorical question, such as "wouldn't you agree?" was asked of the prospect during the reading. We were trained to never leave out the read-off since it was a programmed presentation that did not require the salesman to memorize or think about what he needed to say in order to sell. More importantly, because the prospect was usually reluctant to interrupt the reading of the presentation, it meant that the salesman had complete control of the selling process. Psychologically, the prospect was helpless and incapable of preventing the inevitable forced march to a closing and to the eventual sale of the encyclopedia, especially if the salesman directed most of his attention and instruction on the use of the *Britannica* to any school-aged children in the house. If either parent objected, the salesperson would pause, nod in agreement stating that the *Britannica* was not right for everyone, and then slowly begin removing any materials he may have given the children, such as a sample volume of the Britannica. The child would usually look mournfully at the parents until they relented and agreed to buy.

The Broadside. During the "read-off" presentation, we would quickly unfold a plastic sheet the size of a small tablecloth with a life-size photo of the complete set of *Britannica* that dramatically demonstrated what the set would look like in the home. This device was known as a "broadside" and was designed to be dramatic sales showmanship at its best. The broadside would have a spectacular effect, sometimes literally taking the breath of the prospect away, who audibly gasped when seeing it.

The Prospectus. The prospectus was a single, demonstration volume of the encyclopedia with many more color pictures than the average volume (rumor had it that almost every color plate in the entire set could be found in this volume). Gilt-edged pages bound in a luxurious dark leather-like cover gave it an extraordinary feel. We would spend time encouraging any of the school-aged children present to open the volume and to look up some of the topics contained inside. By the time the presentation was finished, it would seem to the parents as if the kid(s) actually felt comfortable using an encyclopedia, demonstrating an immediate educational benefit in owning a set to the parents. (Note: It was difficult *not* to sell to a family with school-aged children. The parents were usually already feeling incredibly guilty that their kids, either in public school or elsewhere, were not getting the education they needed to compete for college scholarships. So they gladly bought the set in order to assuage any guilt feelings they might have.)

Selling Down and the Per-Volume Close. By the end of this 20- to 30-minute presentation, we would then begin discussing price. The customer had the choice of three bindings—plain brown, dark burgundy, and a gold—with prices to match. The ultra deluxe set cost $10,000 and was a limited edition (almost nobody bought this, which was the main idea). Already, the salesperson could see the crestfallen faces of the family. The next model was $5,000 (again, more heartache), and finally, the "budget" set, which was priced around $1,200. Although the faces were more hopeful, it was still no sale—until the salesperson showed how the set could be bought for $29.95 per volume. If there were objections by one of the parents, the other usually would step in and close the sale for you.

Closing on "Greed." As an extra inducement for agreeing to purchase the *Britannica* that evening, we would offer the prospect a free, or nearly free (i.e., $1 per volume), set of *The Great Books of the Western World*. The only catch was the customer had to order right then and there. The temptation of receiving all of those additional books for free was invariably too tempting to resist.

KISS (Keep It Simple Stupid). At the end, it was simply a matter of filling out an order form, while assuring the customer that they had made a wise purchasing decision. The customer had a three-day cooling off period during which they could cancel, but most sales would "stick" if you followed the programmed sales methodology *Britannica* created. Nothing could be simpler.

Honestly, when I look back at it today, it was one of the easiest and most enjoyable jobs I ever had.

XXX POWER IDEAS

- **X** Most business people are totally unfamiliar with the concept of Sales Choreography™, which gives you a tremendous advantage over the competition.
- **X** Sales Choreography™ can be psychological or physical.
- **X** Well-executed Sales Choreography™ influences the perception a prospect or customer has of you and your business.
- **X** Well-executed Sales Choreography™ can control or influence the way a prospect or customer responds to or behaves towards you and your staff.
- **X** Well-executed Sales Choreography™ can influence a prospect or customer to not only make a purchase, but to gladly pay more for it.
- **X** Physical choreography is the use of visual cues to influence the way a person thinks, feels, and/or acts.
- **X** The physical environment prospects or customers find themselves in strongly influences their perception of your business.
- **X** Your appearance and that of your staff plays a big role in how people perceive your business.
- **X** The manner in which your staff treats and interacts with your customers is a strong influence on what and how your customers think and feel about your business.
- **X** The physical placement of the products you sell influences whether a customer makes the purchase and whether they make a multiple purchase.
- **X** Psychological choreography begins with the first impression a prospect or customer receives from your advertising and marketing.
- **X** Psychological choreography subliminally influences the way a person feels about you and doing business with you.
- **X** Never underestimate the influence created by those who answer your phones.

XXX POWER IDEAS, CONTINUED

- **X** Effective psychological choreography influences prospects and customers to make a purchase.
- **X** Good psychological choreography promotes positive feelings and influences clients, customers and patients to want to do business with you and only you.
- **X** When customers feel good about doing business with you, they are more willing to pay premium prices.
- **X** There are myriad opportunities to incorporate psychological choreography into your Sales Process.
- **X** Sales Choreography™ doesn't necessarily add to your cost of doing business.

Chapter 12

ARE YOU AN AMATEUR OR A PRO?

Dan S. Kennedy

The world in general, and the sales world in particular is chock full of amateurs. Overrun with them, like New York alleys were overrun with rats during the last big garbage strike.

I was there. I saw it. I *heard* it. I see it and hear it everyday with salespeople and business owners, and I have the very same reaction I did to seeing the big, wet, filthy rats scurrying about, hearing them chewing through garbage bags: a chill runs up my spine and bile born of disgust boils in my gut.

Just as I was writing this, the branch manager at a bank where I recently opened several accounts and bought CD's called me to follow up on a brief conversation I'd had with him about getting documents needed from my CPA to open a new LLC's checking account. He had invited me to fax them over so all the paperwork could be done for me ahead of time, so I all I'd need to do would be sign at the x's whenever I came in. Now, three days had passed and he still hadn't gotten the fax. He was calling to follow up. WHAT?!? Yes, a banker calling a customer. Oh, this *should* be routine customer service, especially for customers of my value. But I assure you, it is not. In fact, in the past ten years, conducting a substantial amount of business with 11 different banks in 4 states, I have never once had a banker send me a thank-you note or birthday card, call me to solicit more of my business or see if there was anything he might do to be of service, call or write to try selling me investments or in any other way proactively provide service or acknowledge my existence. And that had happened here, with this banker too. If you are not yet a millionaire and you think millionaires get a different kind of service than you do, 'tain't necessarily so. So, finally, after all this time, I have encountered a young banker who is acting as a sales professional. I am stunned. I will reward the initiative.

In my book, the *No B.S. Guide to Marketing to the Affluent*, I have a whole chapter about how business owners and salespeople can attract, keep, and multiply we particularly affluent clients. The sales pro banker has done two of them: show initiative and follow up. Such behavior is rare, unique to the few pros, foreign to all the amateurs.

In this chapter, I'd like to take you through a short checklist of other differentiators between the rare pros and the mass of amateurs, and I will. But first, a few words about why you should strive to be a pro.

Why You Should Strive to Be a Sales Professional

First, the pros make a lot more money than the non-pros. Much is made in media and political dialogue these days about the ever widening income and wealth gaps between a small percentage of the population at the top and a big, fat percentage of the population far below. This exists for many reasons, most of which are choices made by the people, not mysterious forces beyond their control nor some evil conspiracy among the rich.

For example, ask any poor person you encounter for a list of the last ten books they read about subjects that could help them not be poor, the dates they were read, and the ideas extracted from them and acted on. When their answer is few or none, you will have a clue to the true causes of their financial poverty. You might just ask when the last time they went to the *free* public library and studied there to improve their lot in life versus the last time they sat for hours and played a video game.

In sales, the income gap is even wider, as are the behavioral differences between the mediocre majority at the bottom and the small group of pros breathing the rarified air at the mountain's top. In most sales organizations or in most sales fields in any industry—insurance, financial services, cars, real estate, industrial supplies, spa treatments, you name it—80% of all the income is concentrated in the hands of 20% of the salespeople. Everywhere you look, where there are 5 salespeople, there will be 1 making a great deal more money than any of the other 4, often more than the other 4 added together. Further, within the 20%, the majority of that income is earned by 20% of the 20%. These top earners do not necessarily work harder or longer hours or have genetic, educational, or other advantage. Often they work less. Often they overcome handicaps their less successful peers do not have. They earn so much more because they make themselves into consummate professionals, go about their business with a commitment to professionalism, and present themselves to their clientele as a pro. By doing so, they garner infinitely more access, acceptance, trust, respect, appreciation, loyalty, and referrals. They get a lot more leverage out of each relationship by being recognized as a pro. Their secret is this leverage, not harder work, longer hours, better leads, or luck.

Second, pros have better lives. They get a lot more respect and are treated much better by their clients. They have much higher self-esteem and self-confidence, so they feel better about themselves, the work they do, and the rewards they earn. They are neither guilt-ridden about success or anxious or fearful about failure. They enjoy greater prestige in the organizations in which they work, the industries and their associations to which they belong, and in the communities in which they live. Finally, full circle, because they earn so much more money, they can provide a better home near better schools and better support and lifestyle for their family, buy better health care when needed, assist friends when those needs arise, better support charities or causes, and invest in order to develop financial security.

One of my friends, a client, and a partner in one business is a dentist. The average dentist earns about $75,000.00 a year. The average cosmetic dentist as much as twice that. My partner earns over $1-million a year, and only practices part-time. Is he a better dentist than most? Possibly, but not by a 10 to 20 to 1 spread. But he is a much better sales pro than most other dentists. That has not only created his much greater income, it has propelled him to prominence within his profession as an author, lecturer, and business coach, led to his being sought out for and involved in other interesting and lucrative businesses by leaders in other fields (like me), and helped him create a life of great rewards, security, respect and prestige. Being a sales pro pays many rewards.

What Being a Sales Pro Is Really All About

First and foremost, it is about treating selling as a profession, so that you approach it with the same necessity for and dedication to knowledge, skill, and performance as you hope any surgeon operating on you or a loved one approaches his profession. This is about your attitude about your work. This attitude matters a lot. Only you can devise and enforce demanding standards for your study, skill development, preparation, practice, performance, follow up, and results. If you allow yourself to be casual or sloppy or to just show up and wing it, no one will stop you. If you were a surgeon behaving so badly, eventually the hospital administrator or a regulatory body would step in and stop you.

But salespeople never get prosecuted for malpractice. They commit it constantly, but are only indirectly punished for it by the erosion of their income, opportunities, and self-worth.

Second, it is about attention to detail, something that Sydney has been impressing on you throughout this entire book. It is what first and most impressed me about Sydney and her descriptions of the lessons learned and sales and business practices created for her first business. I was in awe of her attention to minute detail, and I'm very rarely in awe. Pros pay thoughtful and thorough attention to even the smallest of details that in any way affect or might affect their prospects' and clients' perceptions of them or the actual performance of selling. The deliberate choice and use of one word or phrase in place of another, a practiced gesture, the crease of the trouser leg . . . the research and information gathered in advance about a place, an industry, a person . . . the facts known exactly, to be cited authoritatively . . . the systematic organization of customer testimonials so one can be retrieved at a moment's notice in precise response to any specific question or objection. If people come to your office, every detail of its environment–sight, sound, smell, touch, taste; the titles of the books visible spine out on the shelf behind you, the apparel of the person at the front desk–should be well thought out. And on and on.

I've been privileged as a speaker to work with some of the very best–and famous–sales pros of my time: Zig Ziglar, a legend to four generations of salespeople; Tom Hopkins, probably the most famous sales trainer in the real estate industry, and well-known throughout the sales world. I toured with both, speaking–and selling–at 25 to 27 major events a year for 9 years, addressing audiences as large as 35,000. We've also had both speak at Glazer-Kennedy Insider's Circle™ events. As I said at the very start of this book, Zig, Tom, and other traditional sales experts tend to approach selling as a very mechanical process, quite differently than the focus of this book. But that's neither here nor there when we are talking about the behavioral differences between pros and amateurs. So, let me give you a behind-the-curtain peek and tell you something instructive about each one of these great pros.

Even though Zig delivers basically the same speech every time and has done so thousands, probably tens of thousands of times, the morning he spoke at our event just a few years ago, he was downstairs early, at a table, reviewing his notes, rehearsing his speech, practicing his gestures.

Tom Hopkins pretty much delivers the same speech, too, and has thousands of times. But in every city where we caught the same cab or limo from airport to hotel, I observed Tom pleasantly quiz the driver about the local weather, business, sports, economy, landmarks, and most current and topical news and events. He then worked several of those references into his speech. Such a little detail. Certainly not necessary. But it might engage the audience a tiny bit more. Somebody might notice and appreciate that extra effort, that professionalism. If, on an average day, it caused only ½ of 1% of the audience to pay closer attention and like him more, so that they bought when they would otherwise have not, that would mean between $25,000.00 and $50,000.00 extra to Tom. Multiplied by 25 of those engagements in a year, $625,000.00 to $1,250,000.00. Multiplied by 9 years, $5.6-million to $11.2-million. *Not* such a little thing after all.

In Chapters 10 and 11, Sydney directed you in two applications of this extreme attention to detail: Sales Language and Sales Choreography®. These chapters are worth a thousand times their weight in gold. They define how a sales pro prepares, practices, and performs. Being sold to by such a pro is a genuinely pleasing and reassuring experience. Some of us, actually many appreciate it quite consciously and very deliberately reward it. Others may not recognize it for what it is, but are profoundly, positively influenced by it subconsciously nonetheless.

These chapters can be a treasure hunter's map for any business owner, in uncovering a long list of little and not-so-little opportunities for improvement within his business. A client of mine made a list of 115 things he called "profit-boosting turnings-of-the-screws" for his business as a result of the information in these chapters and then, acting as a dedicated pro, prioritized them and developed a step-by-step, day-by-day plan to implement them all, one every two days, over 230 days. If you are willing, you too can use this information to, as Sydney described it in Chapter 2, be your own "Fresh Eyes Consultant" and unearth hidden opportunities.

These chapters can be a roadmap to elevated selling professionalism, to consummate pro status, for any sales professional. And that means anyone who should be a sales pro as one of the roles in their businesses—the chiropractor, dentist, or cosmetic surgeon, the accountant, banker, or lawyer, the hair stylist or barber, the waiter or waitress working a restaurant, the plumber. It means YOU.

This book promised a radical new approach to selling, and I think it delivered. Most approaches to selling are mechanical parts bolted together like a toy made with an Erector set: Opening lines for cold prospecting. Get past the gatekeeper phrases for B2B prospecting. A key story. Five trial closes. This or that technique. A toolbox for a ham-handed worker. Not a palette for an artist.

This book is about artistry. About a sensitivity for selling. About an infinitely more professional performance. It is not about adding a few new gadgets to the toolbox, but about changing the way you perform as a sales pro.

The reason hardly any other author, expert, sales trainer, coach, or consultant talks about selling as Sydney has in this book and does in her Sales Design® tele-coaching programs and in personal training is that most salespeople are and will lazily remain amateurs and therefore prefer a simplistic, shiny new gadget to a complex and sophisticated new way of selling that requires thought, time, commitment, and dedication to master. You have obviously persevered at least to the point of reading most of this entire book.

HOW TO BE A SALES PRO

- Treat selling as a PROFESSION
- Enforce STANDARDS of professionalism
- Pay extreme ATTENTION TO DETAIL
- Use SALES LANGUAGE carefully
- Use SALES CHOREOGRAPHY® creatively
- Consider selling as a PERFORMANCE

You've arrived here because you haven't bailed out yet. The question now is whether when you have finished, this will merely be the end of an interesting read, or the beginning of a process of elevating your skills, style, status, and success in selling.

The End.

The Beginning?

That's up to you.

X X X X X

DAN S. KENNEDY is the author of 11 books, including the popular "No. B.S." series with Entrepreneur Press as well as the editor of four monthly newsletters including *The No B.S. Marketing Letter*. He can be contacted ONLY by FAX at 602-269-3113 or by mail at Kennedy Inner Circle, Inc, 5818 N. 7th Street, #103, Phoenix, AZ 85014. Information about Dan's books at NoBSBooks.com.

Chapter 13

HOW MUCH?

Eliminating PRICE as an Object

Unless you sell items pre-priced by the manufacturer, you will have to make the decision as to what to charge for your product or service. How do you arrive at that price? Do you look around to see what others are charging and then charge a little less or a little more? Do you calculate how much the product cost to make or how much the service costs to deliver and then multiply by X? Perhaps you "know" that "nobody" will pay more than X dollars for a product or service like yours. Or you feel guilty charging more than you probably could because that would be greedy and unfair.

None of the above qualify as a sound reason to assign a price to what you do or sell. Unless you are in the commodity business, which might hobble but does not entirely eliminate your ability to charge more than the competition, you are welcome to set your prices at whatever rate your customer will pay. Note that I said *your* customer—not anyone out there who might ostensibly be in the market for your product or service. You must determine who your ideal client, customer, or patient is, and customize not just what you sell, but the way in which you sell it. Then you can charge what you believe it is really worth—or more!

Make Price Irrelevant

There are numerous reasons a customer, client, or patient might choose to pay more for a product or service. If you can engineer the content or the perceived content of your product or service in such a way that it strikes an emotional chord, you can usually command a higher price for it. When you design the sales process so that your customers can easily and enjoyably navigate their way across your bridge, they will gratefully pay you more for that pleasure. Give your customer a memorable or meaningful Experience while using your product or service and they will pay a premium price for the privilege. How many of the following ways to make price irrelevant can you apply to your business?

Little Luxuries

Who ever thought you could sell a cup of coffee for $4, particularly when the local diner or deli charges $1? A cup of coffee is a cup of coffee, right? Well, yes and no. The person who pays $4 and up for a cup of coffee is not just buying a cup of coffee—they are buying the *experience* of purchasing, and if they wish, imbibing, that coffee in a special place, a place with a particular ambience and atmosphere. Howard Schultze, the CEO of Starbucks, took something as basic as a cup of coffee and built what is now a worldwide empire of gourmet coffeehouses.

According to Taylor Clark who wrote the book, *Starbucked,* Americans work an average of 160 hours per year more than they did 35 years ago. One of the ways they cope with working more hours than workers in any other Western country is to treat themselves to "affordable luxuries . . . to . . . make them[selves] feel more accomplished and satisfied with their lives." Schultze's original target market was high-income urban professionals aged 18 to 45, who were stressed from working long hours, had disposable income to spend on affordable luxuries, and who needed "to feel their all-consuming work has yielded something meaningful." Starbucks' target customers' desire to indulge themselves and be a part of a group of others just like them made the price of that cup of coffee irrelevant.

There are many little luxuries people will pay for because they have the need or desire to indulge themselves. You can get wire clothes hangers for free from the dry cleaner but many people choose to pay up to $12 apiece for decorative fabric or painted wood hangers. A bar of soap can be had for less than a dollar, yet a seemingly infinite number of stores successfully charge anywhere from $6 to $20 for a bar of their soap. Candles can be found for $10 a dozen, but there is still a brisk business being done in candles that start at $10 apiece and can go much higher. I could go on a lot longer and still not cover all the little luxuries for which we pay whatever the price tag reads because we want them, feel we deserve them, and we can afford to buy them. The price is irrelevant compared to our desire to give ourselves a little treat and walk out of the store with that item in a shopping bag.

When Only You Will Do

There are some people whose area of expertise is so specialized that they are literally the only one who does, or can do, what they do. Dan Kennedy tells a story about a fellow who repairs the cracks in the hooves of racehorses. Apparently he has some sort of proprietary glop as well as a secret technique for applying the glop. And because he is the only person who can fix the hooves so that these racehorses can continue to compete, he is able to charge whatever he pleases—and apparently it pleases him to charge a lot. Racehorse owners pay it since he is the only one they believe can effectively apply this highly specialized glop. People who are the only ones able to repair something are in a perfect position to ask for whatever amount of money they choose; when the customer really *really* needs or wants something fixed, the cost is irrelevant.

The model Naomi Campbell is notoriously difficult to work with, so much so that she is the only world-famous supermodel who has never (to the best of my knowledge) done a campaign for a major fashion designer or luxury brand. She only occasionally still does fashion shows and is booked primarily for her ability to attract the press and get publicity for the designer in question. If you are a new or struggling designer who needs press coverage, having Naomi walk in your show is an all but guaranteed way to get it. Since there is no amount of money that could buy that kind of media exposure, the size of her fee is irrelevant.

Dr. Charles Martin, one of the guest authors in this book, is a dentist who specializes in fixing patients whose dental problems are extraordinarily severe. Patients fly in from every state in the union because he is one of the few dentists in the country who has the expertise to handle cases this serious. His fees run in the mid- to high-five figures and occasionally more, but if you are in a truly dire situation, you'll pay whatever he asks.

Sally Hershberger is a "hairstylist to the stars" and is most well known for the shaggy hairstyle she created for actress Meg Ryan. If you want your hair personally cut by Sally Hershberger, you can expect to fork over the better part of $1,000 for that privilege. To those for whom no other hairstylist will do, the price is irrelevant.

Status

There are so many status fashion accessories around these days it is a niche industry unto itself. Designer handbags, sunglasses, watches, jewelry, shoes—the list is endless. Every single one of these status items has a much lower-priced option that serves the same function, and often just as well. But status items make the owner feel special and confirm to them, and to others, they are in-the-know, operate at a certain taste level, have the money to afford it, and/or are part of the special group of other people who own the same thing. Any or all of those feelings are so treasured that the cost is irrelevant.

Certain items identify the owner as being part of a certain group. Lilly Pulitzer dresses are worn by women in a very specific social set and are a very clear signal to others in that set that they, too, belong. Being admitted to certain clubs bestows affiliation or status on its members, both to themselves and to outsiders. Those who summer in Bar Harbor or Fishers Island are a very different crowd than those who summer in East Hampton or Martha's Vineyard. Both confer a certain status and even though the nature of that status is quite different, it is very significant to those who seek it.

Hiring a caterer who is known for catering events for Old Hollywood celebrities like Elizabeth Taylor or Sean Connery confers a different status than using a caterer who is known for doing events for Lindsay Lohan or Toby Maguire. Being on the board of the American Ballet Theatre is prestigious, but so is being on the board of City Meals on Wheels. A dress by Azzedine Alaia holds a distinctly different cachet than a dress by Valentino. All of these examples confer status on those who use, own, or are associated with them, but all have totally different constituencies. All carry very high price tags and are worth whatever that number is to someone who desires the association with the particular status they bestow.

Personal Satisfaction and Validation

The list of things people buy because it makes them feel good about themselves is long and varied, and very idiosyncratic. $500 face creams, $12 clothes hangers, $200 sneakers, $8 cookies, a $150 automatic watch winder—all are purchased because they make the purchaser feel good about him/herself.

For the woman to whom such a thing matters, to be able to look in her closet and see a dozen dresses all hung on matching satin and lace hangers causes a delightful *frisson* of pleasure and satisfaction. For the man who has a collection of expensive watches, to have a beautiful rosewood or leather watch winder box in which he can store and display them is a satisfying reminder of his accomplishments and success, as well as the feeling of pride of owning the watches themselves.

Walking onto the tennis court in state-of-the-art tennis shoes can feel immensely gratifying to the man for whom owning the latest and most technologically advanced tennis shoe is important. And who knows whether it is really the design of the shoes or the confidence they give the wearer that causes him to play a better game? La Mer is the most expensive face cream on the market in spite of the fact that no scientific study has ever shown it to be superior to a face cream one-tenth of the price. But jars can be found in the medicine cabinets of women all across the country, not only because it makes them feel they have "the best," but because it validates them as being in-the-know as well as someone who has the discretionary income to afford "the best."

Knowing you were able to arrange to have a troupe of performers from Cirque de Soleil perform at your daughter's birthday party can feel immensely satisfying to a parent whose child is an aspiring gymnast. Having a celebrity chef like Wolfgang Puck or Emeril do the food for your husband's 40th birthday validates your superior effort to make the occasion extra-special and feels very gratifying because you are able to give your spouse (not to mention your guests) such a special and memorable birthday experience. Engaging decorator Bunny Williams to redo your living room is extremely gratifying to a couple who has admired her style for years in numerous home magazines, and serves as validation to themselves that they have "arrived." In all of these examples, the personal satisfaction derived from owning the item or experiencing the service renders the price irrelevant.

How might you position what you do or sell in such a way that having or using it makes purchasers feel proud of themselves for making the purchase because it validates that they have reached a personal milestone or goal?

Peace of Mind

Insurance brokers of every kind are very much in the peace-of-mind business. Retirement planners, funeral homes that sell pre-planned funeral arrangements, pest control companies you contract to do a twice-yearly assessment of your home, those who sell smoke and carbon monoxide detectors, the physician who performs yearly physicals—every one of them deliver peace of mind in addition to their primary service.

Is there a way you could incorporate an element of peace of mind in the product or service you sell? There are innumerable people for whom feeling safe and protected is worth whatever it takes to obtain it.

BUSINESS STARTED BOOMING ONCE WE STOPPED SELLING INSURANCE AND STARTED SELLING PEACE OF MIND

Jan Drake
jcdrake@optonline.net

For the last 20 years my husband, Chris, and I have owned an independent insurance agency in Bethpage, New York, selling property and casualty insurance. Business was good but we had lots of competition from direct writers.

Enrolling in Sydney's Sales Design class brought a huge boost to our bottom line. She helped us realize that we were not in the business of selling insurance, we were really in the asset protection business. Affluent homeowners became our target market. We developed an 11-step direct mail campaign that resulted in a 153 percent ROI.

The campaign addressed prospects' fears, anxieties, and peace of mind. I pointed out that Chris was a Vietnam veteran and had 10 years of insurance experience as a claims adjustor with Hanover Insurance. We explained that during his days as an adjustor he found that more than 25 percent of the homes on Long Island were grossly underinsured and many claims were not paid. For most people, their home is their biggest asset; they don't want to find out that they do not have the insurance coverage to rebuild. Because two-thirds of all policy holders do not know what they are covered for they need to rely on their agent for guidance.

We noted that when disaster strikes, many agents can't help the homeowner because they don't know how the claim process works. Clients want to hear "you're covered" in any loss. They want the peace of mind of knowing that in the event of a lawsuit, accident, burglary, or house fire, Chris and I have made sure they have the proper insurance so that their assets are fully protected. We can assure our clients that their policies are comprehensive because we are able to write them from a claim adjustor's point of view. Very few other agencies have this expertise.

Getting a review of your insurance policies is about as popular as having a root canal. In order to help prospective clients be more comfortable with the process, we tell them in advance exactly what to expect when they schedule an Asset Protection Review with us. In the mailing we send out before the meeting, we talk about privacy issues and confidentiality, the questions we will be asking during the review, and we assure them they will not be subjected to a pushy salesperson or a hard sell. We promise they will walk out with a comprehensive written proposal, a free scheduled appraisal of their home, and a full understanding of what their coverage does and does not include. Also in each mailing there is a full page of testimonials, including ones from a well-known local politician and the editor of our local newspaper.

One of the things we always tell a prospect during the meeting is how Chris negotiated an additional $213,455 for a client from an insurance company after the client's home was destroyed by a pipe burst. We show before-and-after pictures and explain just how he was able to get that additional money. And we offer a 100 percent triple guarantee to any client who is unhappy with our services.

One way we motivate prospective clients to act immediately is by offering free reports, scheduling only a limited number of Asset Protection Reviews each month, and a free gift if they respond by a certain date.

Sydney's Sales Design Program was so successful for me that I was a finalist at the Glazer Kennedy Inner Circle Super Conference in April 2008. I presented my marketing plan in front of 1,200 members. As of September 2008 we have had a 28 percent increase in business.

Time and Convenience

My housekeeper saves me several hours a week by cleaning my apartment and doing the laundry. She has a set of keys, she often comes when I am out of town, and I know she is completely and totally honest and trustworthy. My assistant not only saves me untold amounts of time by doing the majority of the administrative work necessary to run my business, she pays my bills, has all my credit card numbers and passwords, and knows much more about my personal affairs than I do. If she got hit by a bus, I'd be in a whole heap of trouble. Having a housekeeper and an assistant makes it possible for me to focus on growing my business and spend my time working on the things that generate income. The time I do not have to spend doing housekeeping and

THE CONVENIENCE PREMIUM

People will definitely pay for convenience. If I had to buy whole kiwis and mangoes, wait for them to ripen, and then peel them and cut them up myself, I'd never eat them. But I can buy a container of cut-up kiwis and mangoes at my local specialty food market, and while they are easily twice the price, I'd pay four times more to not have to do it myself.

administrative tasks is time I also have to allocate to personal pursuits. Both of these women are worth every penny I pay them.

If you are a person with limited mechanical skills, having someone assemble your new baby's crib is a service you would likely pay just about anything for. When someone has to unexpectedly go out of the country and their passport is just about to expire, does it matter what the only passport expediter in town charges when the only alternative is standing for hours in line themselves? There are people whose primary source of income is the money they make from walking other people's dogs. When a product or service is something a customer very much wants or absolutely has to have, the price being charged for it is irrelevant.

Pleasure and Enjoyment

Pleasure and enjoyment are areas where many people will spend unlimited amounts of money; the opportunities are endless. Men buy luxury sports cars such as Vipers, Ferraris, and Lamborghinis, with no hope of ever being able to drive them at 100 miles an hour on public roads. There are entrepreneurs who organize a day or even a weekend at a racetrack where those who own such cars can learn how to drive them safely at high speeds and then are let loose to spend hours doing so. Unusual travel opportunities and destinations are very popular and can command astronomically high fees. You can even arrange to be blasted off into space in a rocket ship if you have the $200,000-plus to pay for it (and can pass the physical).

Putting together performances of all sorts, particularly those that hold special or nostalgic meaning, can be very lucrative. Baby boomers spend millions to attend concerts by bands like the Rolling Stones, theatergoers paid hundreds of dollars for seats to *The Producers* when Nathan Lane and Matthew Broderick played the lead roles, and any performance in which someone's child appears is a guaranteed multiple sale. People have been known to spend top dollar on entertainers for children's parties and ridiculous amounts of money for milestone birthday parties. There are all sorts of opportunities to sell complementary products, and services, too. Memorabilia commemorating all of the above is a hugely lucrative business.

Spas—day spas, hotel spas, and destination spas—have become so popular that there are several magazines devoted solely to the subject. And when was the last time you saw a woman wearing sandals who did not have a pedicure? Some towns have more nail salons than banks. Fresh flowers are as much of a necessity as bread in some households. Computer games, stereo systems and televisions, iPods, CDs, DVDs—the list is endless. Companies that supply these kinds of businesses or provide technical support, installation services, and/or repair these products have an opportunity to do very well.

Golf, sailing, boats of any kind, horses, dogs, and all the ancillary products and services that go along with them are things on which people spend untold amounts of money. Swimming pools (and pool maintenance services), lessons of any kind (tennis, cooking, ceramics), places where parents can take their children to have fun for a few hours—you are limited only by your imagination as to services and products you could provide.

Sydney says

Remember, the money is not just in the product you sell or the service you provide. The real money is in the experience you provide the customer while he or she is buying it or using it. And where applicable, there is a great deal of money to be made on memorabilia the customer inevitably buys to memorialize and remember the experience.

Most people work so hard they feel they deserve to have some fun and relaxation, and they are willing to pay for it. And anything that involves children or pets is a goldmine; parents and pet owners will pay incredible sums for "stuff" and services of every description.

Self Improvement

Self-improvement products and services is a vast and extremely lucrative area for entrepreneurs of all kinds. When your prospect believes that the product you sell or the service you offer is going to help make him or her a better version of who they now, you have a sale. The business you are *really* in here is the aspirational business and the hope business. Anything having to do with physical fitness (the list of products and services is endless), appearance (ditto), psychological/emotional health and awareness, and improving one's ability to make money are all guaranteed winners. If your gizmo, magic potion, or personal enhancement program will enable the purchaser to move closer to being or actually becoming the kind of person he always wanted to be, or possess the physical attributes she always dreamed of, the price to achieve that idealized state becomes totally irrelevant.

Sex

You didn't think I was going to leave this one out, did you? It's an irrefutable fact: Sex sells. It's interesting that the vast majority of the customer base is male, but that is a matter beyond the scope of this book. *Playboy* and *Penthouse* magazines made their founders millions and in the case of the former, spawned an entire empire. X-rated movies have been raking it in for decades (and is one of the only industries in which women substantially out-earn men) and pornographic websites have made money since the inception of the internet. Countless trees have been felled for books on sex; ads for 900 numbers abound.

Gentlemen's Clubs, as they are euphemistically called, can be found in every major city and in just as many minor ones, and employ tens of thousands of workers of all kinds. "Working girls" can be found on the street, in so-called massage parlours, staffing "houses of ill-repute," in the phone book, on the internet, in various print publications, and by word of mouth.

Victoria's Secret stores didn't become ubiquitous because women needed another place to buy panties. And their models are worldwide celebrities. There are dozens of lingerie manufacturers who do very well, thank you, making pretty unmentionables, some at prices equally unmentionable (how many $80 g-strings do you have in *your* underwear drawer?). They may have cleaned up New York's famed Times Square, but there are still discreet sex shops in every neighborhood in the city, even the toney Upper East Side—and in neighborhoods all across the country. Google "sex toys" and you will have 24,700,000 results to choose from (as of this writing). You can take pole-dancing classes at the gym (it's great physical exercise—honest!) and it could be argued that a great many women go to the gym in the first place in pursuit of a sexy body.

Hooters has 435 locations in 42 states and 24 countries as of June 2008. Wet T-shirt contests are a staple at bars in spring break hot spots. There are scantily clad women in car and beer commercials for a reason. And the tabloid press would go out of business if sex scandals were to dry up. Hmmm. I suppose a lot of high-falutin' lawyers would see a drop in their income too . . . The moral of the story (you should excuse the pun) is that men in particular and women to a lesser extent spend millions of dollars a year on sex-related products and services.

Of course the *hope* of having sex or the *aspiration* of being perceived as sexy is what more people actually spend money on than they do on the real thing. Many perfumes ads intimate that men find women who wear this particular brand of perfume more alluring. (In the interest of full disclosure, my summer fragrance is Chanel's *Allure.*) Underwear ads for Calvin Klein are clearly intimating that men who wear their briefs are extremely virile, so if you aspire to create the same impression on your target market, you will buy their product. Ads for many vacation destinations feature a couple in bathing suits cozying up to each other, stimulating the imagination that they are just minutes away from taking them off and getting it on. There are an infinite number of ads for myriad grooming products in which the model is scantily clad and in a come-hither pose, sending the not-so-subtle message that if you want to inspire another to view you as just as appealing, that product will do the trick. Those of you on the wrong side of 50 will recall TV commercials featuring

Swedish-born model, Gunilla Knutsen, suggestively cooing, "Take it off, take it all off" for Noxema shaving cream. And a recent magazine ad for BoConcept beds reads, "If nothing happens in this bed, don't blame us."

This kind of advertising is not appropriate for everyone or for every niche in your market, but you may wish to consider whether or not your bottom line might benefit from generating a little hope that some action just *might* occur due to using your product or service. For many, the aspiration to be perceived as desirable and sexy, or the hope of finding themselves doing the horizontal mambo in the very near future, is so compelling that the price they have to pay to achieve it is irrelevant.

FEAR OF LACK OF SEX SELLS, TOO

Kathryn Weber
kweber@redlotusconsulting.com

Some years back I worked in marketing. The communications company I worked for specialized in marketing communications for patient compliance programs with major pharmaceutical companies. Our client asked us to develop a marketing campaign for an erectile dysfunction (ED) drug. The challenge with an ED drug was not how to get more men to use the brand—but how to move ED away from the perception that ED only affected elderly men and position ED as a more common occurrence. In short, we wanted to make ED "everyman's disease." The marketing was all aimed at exploiting men's fears and self doubts about their performance and their ability to fully satisfy their partner.

We showed capable, active, and yes, virile, men as possibly having a hidden problem, a very effective ploy if you are one of these guys and do have a problem. The ads intimated that an occasional misfire or sexual radio silence could very well be a "sign" of a "larger problem." Even the healthiest and most responsive man can have an off day, so the tactic was to create the doubt that this might be just a temporary thing and that if they wanted to be sure it did not occur again, then Brand X would save the day, or rather, the night. Playing into those singular moments cast the net to an ever-wider pool of fish.

Another ED treatment misconception is that ED drugs create erections, which is not, in fact, true. ED treatments enable an erection to occur, they don't create them. However, this was a fallacy the company was happy not to debunk. If men believed they would experience raging erections because they swallowed this little pill, that was fine with the drug company! The ED marketing lesson? Play on fear, play on doubt, and exploit weak moments for gain. That fear drives an emotional buying decision rather than an intellectual one; this particular purchase, or prescription, plays on men's greatest fear—the fear of the inability to perform. A fear they will pay just about anything for to keep it from happening to them.

SYDNEY'S XXX-RATED SALES SECRET #24

Sex sells. 'Nuff said.
Just keep it legal.

FENG SHUI SUPPORTS SEX—AND LOTS OF IT!

Kathryn Weber
kweber@redlotusconsulting.com

Most people don't think of sex when they think of feng shui. Most people think feng shui is all about colors and symbols and how to arrange the furniture. However, authentic feng shui is very much focused on the bedroom.

As a result, I often use sex to sell feng shui. Why? Well, besides the old saw that "sex sells," it's because to get clients to buy into using me for feng shui, I have to overcome the resistance of one of the partners, which is usually the man.

When I meet with the couple, I can almost hear the man's eyes rolling because he expects my consultation to be a touchy-feely kind of interaction with nothing but talk of incense and woo-woo and good chi. But, traditional Chinese feng shui is most decidedly in favor of the man. It's the man's job that must be protected (if he's the breadwinner), his environment must be supportive for him, and the frilly bedroom most women favor is completely opposite of feng shui principles.

One of the primary concerns in feng shui is making sure there is enough rest and sufficient opportunity for sex. Suddenly, when I relate this information, I have the man's attention. That's when I know I'll have the woman as a solid customer—when her husband suddenly sees the value feng shui brings to him in the form of sexual satisfaction.

Selling women can be tough, especially when you're a woman yourself. The sell gets harder when the product or service is typically seen as a woman's interest, such as feng shui, when a man comes into the picture. But when you can appeal to a man's sensibilities through the use of position, money, or sex, the sell becomes much easier and the dollar amounts inconsequential. And everybody's happy.

Strategies for Reducing Sticker Shock

The most basic strategy for reducing sticker shock is to introduce the highest-priced option first and work your way down, making the price of what you were really looking to sell in the first place seem reasonable in comparison. This works in print as well as in telephone and face-to-face sales. But if you are in a competitive market and/or selling high-ticket items, you are going to have to get a lot more sophisticated.

The first strategy is to ensure that you are attracting your ideal customer, and part of that customer profile is someone who has the money to spend in the first place. In addition, it must be someone who is in the market for what you are marketing; the more you have refined the niche you are marketing to, the better your success rate is likely to be.

Scripting that mental movie you want your prospect to have playing in their mind starts the process of creating expectations about price and includes:

- the look of your advertising and marketing pieces and the manner in which you convey that you have the solution for the problem they need to solve and can deliver the benefits they are looking to obtain
- the words you use in print and in every interaction anyone in your organization has with a customer
- the careful selection of products and services the prospect has to choose from

- the appearance of your place of business, yourself, and your employees
- the sales choreography, both physical and psychological, that you have written into your script
- the experience you have designed and religiously implement before, during, and after the sales process

If you have written a script that incorporates all of these elements, the script is viable (as in realistically doable), and everyone adheres to it, by the time the subject of price comes up either the prospect will be expecting it or it will be irrelevant. But remember, the majority of people do not buy during their first encounter. Have a marketing program in place in order to remain in contact with the prospect and a variety of ways in which to "touch" them. Different people respond to different words, methods, and stimuli, so be creative, don't send out the same boring sales letter over and over again.

SYDNEY'S XXX-RATED SALES SECRET #25

When you have put all of the interlocking pieces of the puzzle together correctly, the issue of price evaporates.

THE GREAT AMERICAN SEDUCTION

Patrice Dickey
patricedickey.com

I always love it when my longtime PR client, gynecologic surgeon Dr. Tom Lyons, wins another "outstanding citizen" award for his post-professional-football-career contributions to the sexual well being of women.

It's no secret—sex sells. And so does football. What great marketing partners!

Dr. Lyons has racked up numerous sports awards, including two-time All-American with the University of Georgia Bulldogs. And sports made his many goals possible. He financed his medical education playing several seasons for the Denver Bronc each football award came another big round of publicity. And another flurry o patients.

"Nearly every patient–I'd say 99 percent–comes in with a problem related to sexua function," said Dr. Lyons–hardly a surprising statistic for a gynecological surgeon. These problems often interfere with intimacy, and may lead to significant self-esteem issues and depression.

His goal with surgery is similar to the goals of marketing:

- Fix the problem
- Generate reproducible results
- Make sure it's safe
- Improve recovery times

The marketing corollary:

- Improve brand image
- Implement systems
- Make sure the systems work well
- Increase profits

Whenever Lyons lectures on the procedure he developed that allows women to more quickly regain (and enhance!) their sex life after gynecological surgery (which previously might need to be postponed for as much as 12 months), he says, "I ask the surgeons in the audience, 'What's the big deal, postponing sex for up to a year?'" Lyons knows firsthand that any sports figure at the top of his game would think, right, like losing the championship game. There's always next year.

Big deal? You bet it is.

XXX POWER IDEAS

- **X** When you consciously attract the ideal prospect, customize your product or service for that particular niche market, and sell it in such a way that the customer has a wonderful experience while buying it or using it, you can pretty much charge whatever you like.
- **X** Selling a lot of little luxuries can mean banking a lot of big dollars.
- **X** If you are unable to position yourself as being the only person who does or sells what you do, then find a way to do it differently than everyone else.
- **X** Brainstorm with your mastermind group in order to come up with a way to have your product or service perceived as a status item.
- **X** Position your product or service, or add some element to it, so that having, using, or owning it makes customers feel validated and good about themselves.
- **X** If you are not already in the peace of mind business, add on something that will give your customer peace of mind.
- **X** Identify ways where what you sell could save a customer time, or offer the convenience of not having to do the work themselves.
- **X** There are unlimited opportunities for products and services that provide a fun and pleasurable experience.
- **X** Many people are on an ongoing quest to improve their lives, inner selves, and physical appearance, and are always on the lookout for new and different avenues to achieve that.
- **X** Sex sells. There may or may not be an opportunity for you to capitalize on that, but it is worth thinking about.
- **X** A really tight script will create really terrific results.

Part Three

OUTSIDE INFLUENCES: GUEST CHAPTERS

This special section allows readers to benefit from the breadth of experience of many business men and women that I admire. Each chapter addresses the topics we have talked about so far in this book. Enjoy!

Chapter 14

IT SHOULD BE GREAT (THE CUSTOMER'S EXPERIENCE) EVEN IF IT STARTS OUT BAD!

Directing the Movie in the Customer's Mind

Daniel D. Cricks, Results Marketing LLC

Many readers may need to understand some background regarding the business I will be talking about. Some of you may be able to relate to it already. In the auto repair business not long ago (in many cases still today), repair shop owners thought that they were doing the consumer a favor by just being *available* to repair their cars for them. There was no consideration given to the customer having a good experience.

But we had a different philosophy in our shop; this difference contributed to my auto repair shop being wildly successful. We knew that our business was *not* just about fixing cars, it was about providing them with a *great experience* every time they visited our shop.

Even though my business was in a highly competitive market place, in a not so great location, during a time when many repair shops were going out of business at an alarming rate (right after September 11, 2001), we still managed to grow. Given all of these challenges, we experienced *growth rates of over 20 percent for three consecutive years.*

During this time, I was attempting to empower my top employee (Bob) to make decisions on his own. He had already demonstrated an unusually high level of understanding of the importance of great customer service. He embraced it and enjoyed the fact that we had the type of business that allowed him to treat people in such a fashion. I began to allow him to provide his input for solutions. If it was in line with my philosophy, I allowed him to go with "his" way of doing it. If not, I knew that the only way he would learn was to continually be exposed to the "right" way.

Here was the situation: I was in my office working on (i.e., not in) my business, when Bob came in frazzled and upset. He informed me that one of our employees was driving a fleet truck that we had just finished servicing to the front of our shop, misjudged the truck's size, and hit another customer's car. Turns out, it was one of the most expensive cars we had on the lot at the time—not just a Cadillac, but a Cadillac with a *pearl white paint finish*, which is much higher quality paint and costs more than most normal paint finishes.

I asked Bob how bad the damage was and his response was, "pretty bad." After surveying the damage (and looking for some Tums), I went back into teaching mode with Bob. When I asked Bob what he thought we should do about our dilemma, his answer was to be honest, call the customer, and tell him what happened. I asked him what he would say to the customer. This was his answer: "Mr. Jones, one of our guys was pulling another customer's truck around and hit your car damaging the rear of it. You might want to call your insurance company." I coached Bob on a better way of handling this situation.

Here is how things actually played out. We called the top body shop in the area and explained what had happened. We asked if they could get the vehicle in and move it to the front of the line. We also got a commitment from them on a time frame as to when the vehicle would be repaired and returned back to us. Then we called a rental car agency in the area that we had a relationship with, found out the availability of a vehicle, and asked that it be delivered to our client at his office, and made sure they knew that we would be taking care of the bill. Another detail that we made sure to include when it came to the rental car was that we didn't want their cheapest, smallest car. This client normally drove a larger car and we didn't want to subject him to a small inexpensive vehicle for the few days that he was already going to be inconvenienced. This was no time or place to try and save a few dollars!

I felt that it was important for Bob to call the customer for several reasons; mainly so he could continue to learn, but also because this client was very comfortable dealing with Bob. I knew it was especially important that we get the language right. This was the script Bob used when he called the client at his office:

> Hi Mr. Jones, this is Bob from Brookgate Tire & Auto Center. We had a little mishap here at the shop. Our lube technician was moving another client's vehicle and accidentally bumped into the rear of your car. We have made arrangements with the best body shop in the area to get your car in tomorrow and take care of the damage. They should have it finished in three days. We have also scheduled a [vehicle type] rental car to be delivered to you at your office this afternoon before it is time for you to leave. Of course we will be taking care of all of the expenses involved and I really apologize for any inconvenience that this may cause you. Is this OK with you?

You may notice some of the changes in language Bob used that made a huge difference. Instead of referring to our employee as "one of our guys" we referred to him as our lube technician; we come across as more professional. He said another client's "vehicle," instead of another customer's truck. A "client" infers more value than just a customer, and "vehicle" doesn't sound as bad as having his car "hit by a truck." Saying he "bumped your car," sounds pretty benign compared to "hit your car."

Part of the *choreography* was how important it was that we let the customer know immediately that everything had been arranged as far as repairing his car and providing him with transportation. It was vitally important that we informed him at once that there would be no expense incurred by him. Finally, it was of the utmost importance that there be a genuine apology. I scripted the call in this manner, anticipating the "Movie in his Mind" and tried to address all of the concerns that would be part of that movie as Bob told him what had happened. After Bob asked him if this was OK, his response was, "I guess so. You guys have taken care of everything, and there isn't anything I can really be angry about, since you have already handled it all."

The real measure was the results. We had a *nice* rental car delivered within in an hour and called after we knew it was delivered to make sure it was acceptable to him. Then we delivered his car to the body shop and followed up every day to make sure it was done on time. When we called Mr. Jones to let him know that his car would be done the next day as promised, he responded by telling us to take as much time as we needed, he was enjoying driving the rental car!

The day his car was ready, all he had to do was drive to our shop and pick up his car. When he got there, we immediately met him to go over his car and make sure he was happy with it. To his delight, he couldn't even tell where the damage had occurred and said it looked better now than it did before. Part of that was because we also had the interior detailed while it was at the body shop!

When the client came inside the shop he asked how much he owed us for the repair he had brought the car in for originally and pulled out his checkbook. After we took care of that business, he thanked us for being so professional about the way we handled what could have been a real pain for him.

Mr. Jones stopped by a few days later just to tell us that we could damage his car anytime! His wife couldn't believe how much better the Cadillac looked after having been "damaged." He once again thanked us and immediately referred two of his co-workers to our shop. We knew at that point that we had provided this customer with the best possible experience given the circumstances!

There were several elements that made this customer experience a positive one as opposed to, in a best-case scenario, *only* losing a good client. We spent time designing and choreographing the whole process before we called the client. This made a tremendous difference. We also paid careful attention to the language we used. We told the same honest story to the client, with a slight change in the language but with a much better feel to the scripted story. Another key element was that we trained the employee at the same time.

This isn't something we can assume our employees will know; most simply have not been properly trained and coached. Bob immediately realized how different the two versions were; he just needed the awareness!

X X X X X

DAN CRICKS is an Independent Business Advisor with Glazer-Kennedy Insider's Circle in Cleveland and Akron, Ohio, and Mastermind Coach. Dan is also a Marketing Guru and Business Coach to the Auto Repair Shop industry and various other types of businesses all over the world. Contact him at greatresultsmarketing.com, freegiftfrom.com/dancricks, DanCricks.toolstoachieve.com or by fax at (877) 376-2321.

Chapter 15

WEDDING PLANNER LEVERAGES THE STAR POWER OF THE PLAYBOY MANSION

Making Your Business Irresistible

Ciara Daykin, Firefly Occasions, Inc.

Everyone knows the name, but how many people can actually say they've been to one of Hugh Hefner's parties at the Playboy Mansion? I can! My husband Simon and I got to attend the EXCLUSIVE Kandyland party at the end of June 2007.

I own Firefly Occasions, Inc. a wedding and event planning company based in Calgary, Alberta, Canada. In my three short years in business, I've risen to the top of my industry in my area. I attract affluent brides who are willing to spend a lot of money to ensure that their weddings days are out of this world, unlike all their friends, completely unusual and fun.

Getting to the point where I could charge $10,000 to plan someone's wedding, as compared to my competition that charges $2,000 to $4,000, didn't just happen by writing new packages. I had to find ways to leverage to position me as the *crème de la crème* of wedding planners. I was well on my way by summer 2007. I had written my new packages, raised my prices, I had pictures of me and famous wedding planner Preston Bailey on my website, my e-zine list was growing all the time and subscribers were loving the content I was providing. But I really had to come up with more to impress the bridal eyes that were viewing my company day after day.

A colleague runs a concierge company in Calgary. Late one night that summer, I was on Facebook and I got a message from him. "Do you and Simon want to go to the Playboy Mansion next weekend?" Normally, I would have said no, no, NO. After all, I'm Catholic, married, and in public, kind of a prude. But my husband was looking over my shoulder and, being a man, he went ballistic so we started talking about this invitation.

I was concerned with how a trip to the Playboy Mansion would be perceived by my market if they ever found out? I market to women who've just gotten engaged, have their married lives ahead of them, and love the man they're with probably more now then they ever will in the future (sad but true). What would their reaction be to seeing the wedding planner that they'd come to trust at the Playboy Mansion? Aren't they in the stage where they're hiding the *Playboy* magazines and cancelling their subscriptions? I was honestly, really, really worried about this. But my husband said to me, "The Girls Next Door is one of the biggest shows on TV right now. And according to last month's *Playboy* the highest percentage of viewers is women. And, Ciara, you read my *Playboy* magazines just as much as I do."

He was totally right. I really like *Playboy* magazine and we've had a subscription for years. But isn't something like that supposed to be kept secret between husband and wife? So I picked up our latest copy and flipped to the party section where they show all the people that have been at their parties. And of course, picture after picture is featuring big time CELEBRITIES. If I had to tell you the one, sole thing that influences my target market the most, it's celebrities. They are absolutely obsessed with them (and so am I! I can't keep off of PerezHilton.com or TMZ.com). So I finally got it—by associating myself with a place that is a haven of celebrities, by being pictured alongside of them, my celebrity stock would go waaaayyy up. BINGO! I was convinced and really excited. We were going to the Playboy Mansion and I was adamant that we were going to leverage this trip as much as we possibly could.

We started off our fabulous Beverly Hills weekend with a shopping trip on Rodeo Drive. And of course, for a wedding planner, no trip to Los Angeles is complete without a stop at the Monique Lhuillier bridal salon where past brides such as Kevin Costner's wife and Britney Spears had their wedding gowns designed. Simon and I also checked out Hollywood Boulevard and lunched on the patio of The Ivy. What a lot of people don't realize is that these places that are associated with celebrities are not off limits to the public. You just have to act like you belong there. The Ivy is where tons of hot stars are seen, in fact Kimora Lee Simmons and her boyfriend, Oscar nominated Djimon Hounsou lunched a couple of tables over from us. All I did was make a reservation for us to sit on the patio and there we were, lunching among celebrities.

When Saturday night finally came I was a nervous wreck. I had purchased two smoking hot dresses for the Mansion. I had decided on this gold sheer number that left little to the imagination. I was almost ready to go when my whole dress started to run and the damn thing was so sheer that it completely fell apart. Of course tears followed and it meant I was on to dress number two. I'm telling you this because dress number two ended up being a big part of this incredible night. This dress was BCBG Maxazria. In Calgary, it's probably one of the most expensive places you can shop. And I was still worried that it wasn't good enough for the Playboy Mansion. Was I ever wrong!

This dress was smoldering sexy. It was a short black halter style dress with a plunging neckline that almost went to my belly button (so I needed lots of double-sided tape). The neckline was covered in silver metallic material that really made it sparkle. I wore black high heels that shimmered when I walked.

When we got off the shuttle and stepped onto the grounds of the Playboy Mansion we really felt like we'd arrived in the big time. The entire mansion was done up in with amazing Kandyland decor including giant lollipops, candy canes, and mushrooms. They even had Oompa Loompas waiting for us when we arrived. And I was getting compliments on my appearance left, right, and center from the predominantly male guests.

We edged our way toward the tent where Hugh Hefner was sitting and of course it was mobbed. But one of his girlfriends, Kendra, was standing near the outside of the tent and she looked over at me and said, "That's a hot dress." So I struck up a conversation with her and asked if she'd mind if my husband and I took a picture with her. As soon as she heard that we were a married couple at the Playboy Mansion she went into mega conversation mode. She was so excited that we'd come here together. We got our picture taken with her and then she called over some Playboy bunnies and told them to pose with me as she shouted out, "She actually brought her husband here. Isn't she cool?" The dress (and my husband) worked.

We spent the rest of the night schmoozing with a ton of other celebrities, including the Red Hot Chili Peppers guitarist and host of Rockstar Dave Navarro, Michael Clark Duncan, Kevin Federline, Steve Valentine (Dr. Nigel Townsend on Crossing Jordan), Kato Kalene, Ron Jeremy, and of course the beautiful Playboy bunnies.

We took tons and tons of pictures of our time there. The trip in itself was totally unbelievable but it's what we did with the pictures from the trip that really made it worth every penny.

As soon as we got home I did a huge blog posting on the trip. Then in my bi-weekly e-zine I shared pictures and stories with my list. Plus we have a Facebook group for the company and the pictures went up there as well. The response was amazing. People were so enthralled with the fact that we'd gone to the Playboy mansion that there were tons of comments back to us about the trip. And the dress! People could not stop talking about the dress. It was the topic of conversation for weeks. I realized just how valuable that dress had been for me.

After promoting our trip to the Playboy Mansion I got a flood of new customer inquiries. These weren't just your typical brides, these were the caliber of brides that I'd set my sights on. I signed a client from California that had seen the pictures and I ended up planning their huge anniversary party back in Calgary. This was an event that helped me to establish a really strong relationship with a high-end hotel in Calgary and has led to more clients and speaking engagements. The trip to Playboy immediately resulted in five new affluent customers and a new business venture. After being at the Mansion my husband came up with the idea of targeting grooms with an e-zine, much like I do with the brides. He quickly launched GutsyGroom.com and began promoting stags to the Playboy Mansion. We sent one guy and we still get a thank-you note from him almost every single week! That venture has now turned into a business that is successfully sending grooms on once-in-a-lifetime stag adventures.

In our office we have pictures up of the trip as well, the most notable, a print of a Playboy bunny in front of the Playboy insignia. While in Beverly Hills we went to an art gallery on Rodeo Drive and purchased a limited edition print done by Victoria Fuller. You might remember her and her husband from the Amazing Race (they were the ones that brutally fought all the time and got a lot of flack for it). She is a former Playmate and the only artist Hef has ever licensed to use the Playboy insignia of the bunny. We also received a signed dedication from her on the certificate of authenticity by making friends with the saleswoman at the gallery. She had Victoria come in and do this especially for us and then shipped it to Canada. It was the ideal souvenir and sparks a lot of questions when we have clients in our office.

I think that every business owner needs to increase their celebrity stock. Whether it's pictures with celebrities, being at the same parties as them, or frequenting celebrity hot spots, they all increase your status in the minds of your customer base. My target market is the echo boomers, the children of the boomers who are now coming of age in the digital decade. They live their lives online and they are obsessed with celebrities. They are constantly logged into blogs discussing what celebrities are doing. When I posted our Playboy adventure online through my own channels my target market also read about the party on their favorite celebrity blog. In their mind, I might as well have been up on that celebrity blog pictured beside their favorite celebrity. It all meshes together for them and becomes dinner conversation. Months later at a Bridal

Fair I had women coming up to me telling me how much they loved my dress at the Playboy Mansion and asking us how we got to go there. And I'm sure they went home and told someone, "I just met that wedding planner that went to the Playboy Mansion." I had another client telling their friends at their actual wedding, "This is my wedding planner, she's been to the Playboy Mansion." It's six degrees of separation and it works. People want to be as close to celebrities and model their consumer purchases after celebrities. I'm cashing in on that fact. You can be sure that the next time we're invited to the Mansion, I won't be thinking twice about RSVPing YES.

X X X X X

CIARA DAYKIN is the Event Choreographer for Firefly Occasions www.fireflyoccasions.com. Ciara runs a successful wedding and event planning company based in Calgary, Alberta, Canada, and plans events such as The Canadian Juno Awards (Canada's version of the Grammy's). Ciara's career has taken her to international locations such as Australia, Mexico, Ireland, and the Playboy Mansion. Ciara provides brides with engaging tips for tying the knot without coming undone in her bi-weekly e-zine and her free report, "The Top 10 Things a Bride Can Do to Take Her Wedding from Ordinary to Extraordinary!" She also gives tips and tricks for hosting an event in her free report "5 Things I Hate About Your Party." Ciara's newest venture is rockstarwedding planner.com where she coaches other wedding planners to attract high-end clientele and lead a rockstar wedding planner lifestyle.

Chapter 16

CREATING AUTHENTIC TRUST

Dialogue Not Sales Push

Ari Galper, Creator of Unlock The Game® and ChatWise®

Here's a radical thought: What if you could completely let go of trying to close a sale with a "prospect" and instead, connect with them at the human level as someone who authentically wants to help them solve their problems?

No, I don't mean ask them more "qualifying" questions, I mean *really* create a connection with them so they feel that you really care about their well-being.

Don't focus on making the sale, you say! How can you be in sales if you are not focusing on the "sale"?

To be truly successful for the long term, making this shift in mindset from "the sale" to authentically connecting with your potential clients, is one of the most important pillars to creating and sustaining profitable long-term relationships.

Why? Because when you let go of your own agenda (trying to close, close, close), you'll find yourself creating real trust and drawing sales into you by the mere fact that you have a deep understanding of the problems that you help your prospects solve.

If you can make this shift in mindset, then you'll find yourself talking with them without your mind racing ahead in an effort to move them in a direction they may not want to go. When you're present with them, they trust and believe you more.

As the economy shifts, you're going to discover that your leverage will no longer just be about your ability to "make the sale," but rather your ability to create authentic trust; and ironically, *authentic trust between a seller and buyer creates more sales!*

The "Wake-Up Call" that Created New Sales Mindset

My guess is you'll be able to relate quite well to my story that triggered this shift in my own mindset. It happened about seven years ago when I was doing direct selling (after having spent several years studying all the great sales gurus), designing sales training for UPS, Qualcomm, and other major companies, and finishing my masters degree in Instructional Design, which focuses on studying how people learn. On that fateful afternoon, I was on the phone doing an online demonstration with the top executives of a software company. Have you ever had a sales call that felt like a "love fest"? This one was like that. Everything was going by the book. They were interested, they were asking me tons of questions, I had all the answers at my fingertips. At the end of the call, they thanked me profusely for my time. And the vice president's final words were, "We'll definitely be getting back to you." I was so proud of how well things had gone that I could almost feel my head swell as I started to hang up the phone. But then . . . instead of pushing the "off" button on the phone, I accidentally hit the "mute" button. I didn't realize it until I heard them continuing to talk. They hadn't hung up, but they thought I had. And what do you think they were saying about our oh-so-promising phone conversation?

"OK." It was the vice-president's voice. "So we're definitely not going to go with him. But keep stringing him along. Get more information so we can get a better deal with another company."

Ouch. I was devastated.

My first feeling was outrage that they had lied to me. I felt hurt and used, but the feelings of rejection that swept over me were even worse. "I'm a good guy," I told myself. "I did everything right. I've studied all the best sales programs in the world. I didn't cut any corners. Why are they treating me this way?"

Then I remembered a lot of other times when I had gotten a gut feeling that something was "off" about how a prospect was reacting to me. I could never put my finger on it, but at some level I knew that everything I had learned was incomplete. But I ignored that nagging discomfort and kept on doing what I had been doing–until that "wake-up call."

You know, a lot of sales programs today would look at that call and say: "If a prospect lies to you, it's okay to lie back. If they're aggressive to you, it's okay to be aggressive back, because that's how you can control the situation. If they try to box you in, it's okay to force them into a commitment."

But this buyer and seller conflict, battle, whatever you want to call it, just felt so wrong.

It took me a long time to figure out one basic truth that none of those "fight-back" sales programs ever talked about:

The problem wasn't with the prospect. It was with me. There was something fundamentally wrong with how I was approaching selling. And I needed to change.

It was at this point that I was finally able to let go of the outrage and rejection and take responsibility for having tried to sell the "wrong" way. Once I shifted my thinking from focusing on them to focusing on what I was doing, the answers started to come. I realized that the old ways of selling had everything backward. And that freed me to begin thinking about what ultimately became the Unlock The Game® Mindset.

They knew I had an agenda for that call, which was to make them buy what I had to sell. I tried to do it by going with my script, developing it, dealing with their "objections," pushing subtly to move things forward . . . you know the drill. They seemed to be playing along, and I wouldn't have known any differently if I hadn't accidentally hit the "mute" button that fateful day.

The problem was the whole dynamic of trying to "make the sale." *I was on that call to make a sale, and the implicit sales pressure I was exerting with every word I spoke made them feel it was okay to lead me on and even lie to me.*

Would they have lied to me if they trusted I wouldn't exert sales pressure on them regardless of their decision? Probably not. So that's really the day that this new sales mindset that I call Unlock The Game® Mindset was born.

A Direct Challenge to Traditional Selling

If you flick through the pages of business magazines and sales training material, you'll find a constant flow of messages like, "Focus on closing the sale"; "Overcome objections"; "Be relentless"; "Accept rejection as a normal part of selling"; "Use persuasion to get useful information about your prospects"; and "Chase the sale." *In short, get the sale at the expense of the human relationship.*

There is a much better way to succeed in selling—stop selling and start building authentic relationships based on trust, authenticity, and integrity. When you treat people as people, not prospects, and reveal your trustworthiness, they will start to trust you. They will see you as a problem solver focused solely on their needs. From there you have the basis of a long-term relationship—the true competitive advantage. This is not a technique, it's a way of communicating with people. You can't fake being trustworthy.

"Salesy" Language Breaks Trust

There are many common sales lines that have become so "salesy" that they can lose a sale at the very beginning of the process. They sound innocent enough, but because prospective clients are so tired of feeling manipulated by salespeople, they hear these tired old phrases and run the other way. Phrases like, "Would you be interested" or "Explore possibilities" or "Follow up" have now become pressure triggers for prospects. Regardless of your intentions, these words portray you as the negative "salesperson" stereotype, even if you truly want to help the prospect. This is why it's time for a whole new sales mindset with natural language, so that trust can be built rather than triggering rejection.

Here are some "trust-based" phrases you can use to replace old traditional sales languaging:

- "Would you be open . . ." (instead of "Would you be interested . . .")
- "Where do you think we should go from here?" (instead of "Why don't I come over and show you what I have?")
- "Hi, my name is Ari, and I'm hoping you can help me out for a moment?" (Instead of "Hi, my name is Ari, I'm with XYZ Company, and I'm calling to see if you'd be interested in . . .")

Aikido: The Foundation of Unlock The Game®

You're in a crowded bar when all of a sudden, a fight breaks out between two men who've had too much to drink. One of the men turns as if he's going to take a swing at you. What's your first instinct? Most of us will do one of two things: try to step away or raise our arms to deflect him and fight back (which can result in harm to you or your attacker). However, if you were trained in Aikido, the Japanese martial art that focuses on diverting an attacker's energy, you could quickly defuse the situation by immobilizing him without harming him in any way. In essence, you're neutralizing the energy that he's using to attack you in a way that takes the conflict out of the situation.

Traditional selling focuses on closing by presenting or, in many cases, pushing solutions onto prospects. When you focus only on making the sale before discussing the prospect's problems first, something happens—they feel as if you are attacking them, you trigger their suspicion, and they start "pushing" back. This pushback is the resistance or the energy that Unlock The Game® teaches you to defuse. When you get rid of this pressure you can then open a natural dialogue that will determine whether it makes sense for you to work together.

If you're open-minded and willing to "detox" from your old-school sales thinking, then you're only a few small steps away from experiencing sales success in ways you never thought possible.

X X X X X

ARI GALPER is an international speaker, author, and creator of Unlock The Game®—a truth-based sales approach that takes the pressure out of the selling experience for both the seller and buyer. Ari is also the creator of ChatWise®—an online sales conversion system using his truth-based sales approach via live chat. Visit UnlockTheGame.com and ChatWise.com for a FREE TEST DRIVE.

Chapter 17

LITTLE HINGES OPEN BIG DOORS

Using Fresh Eyes

Bill Glazer, Marketing Advisor, bgsmarketing.com

As you've undoubtedly discovered, this book is a lot about how to properly systemize your selling process in order to achieve *extraordinary* results. This is what Sydney Barrows has trademarked as Sales Design™.

During my over 34 years of being an entrepreneur, first as a retailer and then during the past 10 years running marketing, publishing, coaching, and consulting companies, I have discovered that often making a small change to the sales process can make a huge difference in results.

I first heard this clearly stated by Dan Kennedy in 1997 when he sent out his famous "No B.S. Marketing Letter" with a small metal hinge glued to the top of the first page. That was a visual that I will never forget and it really hit home with me. He wrote an entire issue about how "little hinges can open up big doors" which illustrates the BIG LESSON of this chapter: identifying and making small changes in your sales processes can make a big change in your results.

Let me give you five little hinges, tell you how I have applied them to my businesses, and at the end of each I'll provide you with a smart question for you to ask yourself about each of them.

Little Hinge #1: Greetings

One of the biggest struggles that retailers have is engaging prospects in conversation when they walk into their doors. Think about what normally happens when you walk into a retail store. The salesperson typically approaches you and opens up the conversation with the five words *"How Can I Help You?"*

Most people are conditioned to respond with the five words that salespeople hate to hear: *"No Thanks, I'm Just Looking."* This disengages the prospect in conversation; a salesperson can only do her job and maximize the opportunity to sell the prospect if there is a dialogue.

So, after years of doing it the way I just described, I made a little hinge change which was to change the script of the salesperson's greeting. Instead I say: *"Hello. What Brings You Into the Store Today?"*

This might not sound like a big change, but it was. Now the prospect would give a much more lengthy response which would allow the salesperson to follow up the conversation, often with a follow-up question.

SMART QUESTION: What changes can you make to your live or by phone greetings that will engage the prospect?

Little Hinge #2: The Perfect Sales Presentation

I first saw this little hinge perfectly implemented by Joe Polish who provides marketing and sales advice to the Carpet Cleaning Industry. Let's use a Carpet Cleaner as an example.

The salesperson enters a home, looks at what needs to be cleaned, and then attempts to sell the homeowner his services. Many salespeople struggle with the sales presentation, especially in delivering a presentation that will maximize the opportunity with the prospect. Joe changed his tactic: Before the carpet cleaner walks around the house determining the extent of the work, he pops a DVD in a portable DVD player and allows the owner to watch the "perfect" presentation about why his company offered the most thorough cleaning and see all of the microscopic bugs and organisms that are living in their carpets. So, now when the Carpet Cleaner finishes his walk through (which is typically at the same time the short video is completed) he returns and only has to write up the order. This approach can also be applied to the retail environment.

SMART QUESTON: How can you automate all or part of your sales process to deliver the perfect pre-recorded presentation?

Little Hinge #3: Follow-Up Phone Appointment

When Dan Kennedy and I are looking for new Independent Business Advisors (IBAs) for our Glazer-Kennedy Insider's Circle™, we send out a mailing to all of the Members who live in a specific area and ask those who are interested to fill out a brief application. Then we follow up with them by phone, go over their application to make sure we think that they are a fit, and send those that do a two-hour DVD to watch which explains the entire program. But we found that many people who asked for the DVD never got back to us; in most cases when we called them, they had not watched the DVD.

So we added one more step to the process: When we told them their application looked good and we were going to send them out the DVD to watch, we required a $500 refundable deposit and scheduled a follow-up phone appointment with them after they watched the DVD to answer any questions they may have.

This completely changed everything. With an appointed follow-up time, they made the time to watch the DVD. And, of course, the deposit helped because if they weren't interested in the program, they still had to keep their appointment in order to get their deposit back.

SMART QUESTION: What step can you place in your sales funnel that will get your prospects to take action?

Little Hinge #4: Live Chat Online

This is one of those little hinges that can really open up a BIG DOOR. If you have a website that is getting traffic, there are a lot of people who are leaving without buying or taking whatever action you want them to take, and there is not much you can do about it—until now.

The way most people try to improve online conversion is to constantly tinker with their sites by changing headlines, color, font, add video or audio, add testimonials, etc. While these can all be helpful, they are typically not the key to the vault that we are all looking for.

Ari Galper, who is one of our Glazer-Kennedy Members living in Australia, decided that he wanted to add the "human touch" to his website, meaning that if his visitors could chat with him through his site he could help them feel comfortable about ordering, answer their specific questions/objections, and more importantly find out why they're not buying. So Ari installed a "live chat" box on all of his website pages and started to engage his visitors in conversation.

He discovered several important things.

First of all, when it was done correctly it created a genuine trust with his visitors. People couldn't believe that someone online cared about them and wanted to help them.

Secondly it informed him of specific areas of his website where people were stumbling and he needed to go back and fix.

Thirdly and most importantly, it boosted his overall conversion rate 10 times of what he was experiencing in the past.

However, if you are going to install a chat function, you need to take it seriously if you want to make it profitable. You can't just outsource it and forget about it . . . it's too important not to take under your wing or assign it to someone who will take it seriously.

Ari makes his "live chat" product available to others and is a terrific resource. You can find out about it at Chat-Wise.com.

SMART QUESTION: How can I install "live chat" on my websites in order to increase sales and where else in my marketing can I add ways for people to communicate with me so I can overcome objections and close more sales?

Little Hinge #5: Survey

Often when I'm consulting with a client, I'm presented with a product or service and I'm asked how they can better sell it. Unfortunately it's really the wrong question. A much better way to sell something to your prospects is to figure out what your prospects want and then give it to them.

For example, a Member in my coaching group wanted to increase the fee he was charging to provide information. I told him to follow a three-step formula that has always worked well for me and my other clients.

> *Step one*, send a multiple-choice survey to his Members, telling them that he wants to add more value to his service to them and asking what else they would like.
>
> *Step two*, present the results of the survey to his Members. It's important that they see not only what they are asking for, but what others are asking for as well.
>
> *Step three*, present the "new" program to the Members. You can now raise prices because these additional services are what they have asked for, not what you have chosen to provide them. It also shows them that you care about their needs, which positions you as someone who really cares.

My client hit a homerun with this little hinge and was able to move a large percentage of his Members from a $197 yearly program to a monthly $397 program.

There is one other significant advantage to surveying your customers and prospects from time to time. You can actually learn some very useful information.

SMART QUESTION: *How can you survey your customers and prospects to discover what else you can provide them with and also find out how they currently enjoy doing business with you?*

The two big ideas that you should take from this chapter are

1. "How I can implement these concepts in my business?"
2. "Where are the holes in my own sales funnel that if (and when) I plug them can lead to opening up big doors for me?"

X X X X X

BILL GLAZER is the Number-One Most Celebrated Marketing Advisor specializing in the Retail Industry. Retailers should visit his website at bgsmarketing.com. All others should visit dankennedy.com to sign up for The Most Incredible FREE Gift Ever (over $600 of pure Marketing and Money-Making resources) for any business.

Chapter 18

OUR TEN-STEP PROCESS TO SUCCESS

Sales Choreography in Action

Christopher G. Hurn, President, Mercantile Commercial Capital

Dan Kennedy introduced me to Sydney some time ago, and while she is the one who asked me to contribute to this book, it is Dan that has told thousands how I have a "performance advantage." Now, despite the suggestive phrase, Dan has never meant anything sexual when he tells others about his favorite commercial lender. What he's meant by "performance advantage" has a lot to do with our focus, speed, discipline, follow-up, attention to details, and fanatical service . . . but none of those things by themselves would give us the "performance advantage" of which Dan speaks. Collectively, those attributes, plus my very purposeful choreography of our sales process, has led to countless national and local awards (including a place on the 2007 *Inc.* magazine's list of America's 500 Fastest-Growing Companies), tremendous growth and profits, and raving Clients and Referral Partners. Like most things in successful businesses, the more attention you pay to the little things affecting your Clients, the more success you'll experience.

Crawl Inside Their Minds Like a Psychologist

The first tactic I'd suggest you adopt in your business is psychological. By this, I mean really trying to get into the heads of your prospects and understand what they're thinking, how they're dealing with it, and what their next concern(s) might be when using your product or service. Anticipate where their thinking will take them and neutralize their typical response to "defend" themselves against your selling. While this may appear basic and even clichéd, my experience is that far too few business owners and/or salespeople actually do this. Most don't stop long enough to truly consider what it's like on the other side of the table.

For us, we know that when borrowing money, everyone feels some anxiety about "getting approved." There also exists a growing suspicion of ordinary bankers among entrepreneurs and a reluctance to accept their slower, methodical ways even though we've entered the 21st century. Knowing this, we implemented what we call our "Pre-Approval Process" which guarantees, in 24-hours or less, the issuance of a pre-approval letter (assuming qualification and the submission of seven basic documents) that can be relied upon by our prospective borrowers. We do this in order to neutralize their anxiety, but we also do it because hardly anyone else *can* do it in the commercial lending arena. (You can see our Pre-Approval Application and Checklist by visiting TheSmartChoiceLoan.com/preapproval.) We've actually trademarked this business process of ours as our "Guaranteed, 24 hours or less, 39-step Pre-Approval Letter Process™."

Get Physical and Seduce Them with Your Language

Design and create the most perfect physical representation of what you're selling, while you choose the precise words to stack the odds of your sale in your favor. As you've read in this book already, the chances that you can be successful just selling the "thing" (the product) is slim to none; you need to sell the experience, the dream, your one-of-a-kind expertise and so forth. We aren't selling money in our business; we're selling the smart fulfillment of an aspirational dream.

Here is an example of our carefully crafted office tour when someone local comes to visit. Much like a Broadway play, the performance occurs in *exactly* the same way each time:

- *Step 1.* Receptionist greets the person with, "Welcome to Mercantile! My name is Ken. Who are you here to see?" He knows they wouldn't be here if they weren't here to see someone in particular. "Please have a seat while I personally tell them you're here."
- *Step 2.* The receptionist directs them to be seated in the plush office chair against the east wall to face our large *Inc.* 500 wall plaque and flatscreen television that is continuously playing a long, full-color slide show of properties we've financed with a bullet point slide listing the benefits of working with us that appears after every three slides shown. This conveys our credibility while demonstrating social proof. They "cook" there for up to five minutes with nothing else to look at or read, other than the things we want them to see.
- *Step 3.* Before leaving to go find the person being met with, the receptionist points to our revolving, vertical newsmagazine stand that's stocked with some of our past issues and encourages the prospective Client to browse through them and feel free to take them home to keep and/or share.
- *Step 4.* After the receptionist returns, he says, "Mr./Ms.____ has asked that I escort you to our boardroom, as they're finishing up with

another Client's phone appointment. They'll be happy to meet with you shortly. Please allow me to show you the way."

- *Step 5.* The receptionist then leads the prospective Client a few feet along the lobby's hardwood floor and stops near our Controller's office, facing the inner core of our offices which has three rows of large, full-color photographs of projects we've financed with the Client company name, city, and state listed. More social proof is clearly given here, perhaps even overwhelming proof.
- *Step 6.* Walking slowly enough that the prospective Client can easily observe the pictures on the walls, the receptionist then says as he gestures to the walls, "You probably recognize some of these photos of local businesses and buildings that we financed. You've certainly come to the right place for smart commercial property financing." Reassurance and more social proof have now been given again.
- *Step 7.* Continuing down the hall, the receptionist gestures toward the large "Currently Under Construction" board that lists over 30 construction projects currently in process all around the country, lifts one of the magnetic strips and says, "Rather than having a dummy photo of a bulldozer for every one of our many construction projects, we just use these handy magnetic strips with the project name on it. Once a project is complete, we take a photo and add it to our wall collection." Still more overwhelming proof has been given, plus a demonstration of practical sense.
- *Step 8.* "Now, this is our Wall of Fame, which contains most of our awards and a small fraction of the articles written about us in publications like the *Wall Street Journal*, the *Orlando Sentinel*, the *Orlando Business Journal*, and many others over the years." More reassurance, independent credibility and social proof are the point of all of this carefully crafted language.
- *Step 9.* Stopping at the Boardroom door, the receptionist shows the visitor the chair he wants her to sit in (the one closest to the credenza where she can directly watch another large flat screen television). A DVD called *Leading Experts* will already be playing; in this DVD I'm discussing smart wealth creation strategies for business owners and am

being interviewed by an independent third party on these matters. The receptionist says, “Please enjoy watching this nationally televised interview with Chris Hurn, our company’s President and CEO. We like to show this particular DVD because it answers a lot of the questions you might have about us and the process of buying commercial property in a smart way. We’ll be happy to give you a copy if you like. Mr./Ms.___ will be right with you.” This, again, is meant to demonstrate expertise, credibility and reassurance.

- *Step 10.* The receptionist then says, “By the way, may I offer you a drink? We have coffee, water, and various soft drinks.” He gets the drink if she accepts, and now we’ve begun some level of reciprocity. He then checks his watch, closes the door halfway, and then lets the MCC staff person know they have five minutes before they should go to greet the prospective client. This gives the prospective client some time to watch the DVD and “cook” even further.

The key to this choreography is that it happens *every* time in *exactly* the same way. It is nothing short of a true performance, but is there any doubt we’re now the equal of any national bank with branches on every street corner in the minds of our prospective clients? In fact, I’d argue we’ve blown well past the perceived creditibility level another ordinary banker might have when compared to us . . . just by choreographing the “tour” of our office when a prospective client comes to visit.

If you haven’t put this much thought into the experience someone has when they visit your offices, you have a template on which to model! In fact, we’ve put this much fore-thought into the choreography of virtually ALL of our business processes. Doing this level of choreography will surely increase your sales and help put you on the path to phenomenal business success.

X X X X X

CHRIS HURN is the President/CEO/Cofounder of Mercantile Commercial Capital (MCC), the nation’s leading 90 percent loan-to-cost commercial loan provider. His firm has been named to *Inc.* magazine’s list of 500 fastest-growing companies in the United States, and he has been named the “Banker of the Year” by his industry’s only trade association, was named the “Marketing Guru of the Year” by Coleman Publishing, and was the Small Business Administration's "Financial Services Champion of the Year" for Florida and for the 12-state Southeast region. He is a serial entrepreneur and regularly speaks around the country on smart wealth creation strategies for business owners and entrepreneurs. Visit TheSmartChoiceLoan.com, call (866) 622-4504, or e-mail info@mercantilecc.com for more information.

Chapter 19

SATISFACTION GUARANTEED

Making Them Eager to Come Back for More

Barry Lycka, Spa Consultant, Cosmetic Surgeon

Imagine this scene. You get out of your business meeting later than you wanted to. The meeting didn't go well and you didn't get the contract. The best you could do was get them to meet with you again. Maybe a waste of time, but at least it's a chance.

That moron you had to deal with was the brother-in-law of the owner. To say he was stupid would give him too much credit.

Now you're stuck in rush-hour traffic trying to make a flight. Horns are honking, tempers are flaring. Your cabbie gets cut off and shouts a string of obscenities. You're not going anywhere. Forget that flight, it's not going to happen.

You call and get a later plane. Which means no sleep. And tomorrow's meeting will likely go like hell too.

Now, let me share another reality, the polar opposite of what we just witnessed. Just steps away from rush-hour madness is an oasis of calm, a place where your cares melt away. Imagine this scene.

You step off of the crowded main street into a doorway that says Corona Rejuvenation Centre and Spa. Immediately, your nose is greeted with a fresh, pleasing odor, like a fresh bouquet of freshly cut flowers.

You climb down the short stairway. At the end, you are instructed to please remove your footwear. You do and you replace them with a comfortable set of slippers.

You open a second door.

Immediately, your stress vanishes. Gentle, calming music caresses your ears. The room you are now in is one of the most beautiful you have ever seen. The walls are a light green but have a faux fern pattern; the floors are Brazilian cherry wood.

You have a "Wow Experience." You feel as if you belong and your cares were left on the street.

You approach the main desk. The receptionist is on the phone but she immediately puts the call on hold. She greets you by name. "Mrs. Smith, how are you?"

You lie. You don't want to ruin this moment. "I'm OK."

"And how's your dog Pinky?"

"Fantastic. He'll be waiting for me when I get home"

The receptionist is sweet, bubbly, and kind. She reaches out and cuts through your sour mood. You're amazed she remembered your dog.

"We are so glad you could make it. Welcome to Corona Rejuvenation Centre and Spa, where your cares and worries evaporate. Here's your key to your locker. Your personal assistant will meet you as soon as you're changed."

You walk a short distance to your locker room. You pass a beautiful fountain in a central, circular courtyard. It's made out of Italian marble, imported from the same quarry where Michelangelo obtained his marble. Beautiful. It sets the scene for your spa experience, especially considering that the word "spa." is short for Salus per Aqua—Good Health through Water. How fitting.

You open your locker. Inside is a thick Turkish bath robe. It's warm, just out of the dryer. It smells heavenly. You disrobe and let the robe caress you. It smells fresh, like it just came out of the dryer. Again your stresses feel as if they were never there.

You enter the relaxation room.

The lights are muted. The sound of gentle music and running water fill your ears. Calm, gentle tones. You feel loved, cherished. You deserve it, you think.

The room again has beautiful hardwood floors. The air is of fresh floors. Your attendant arrives.

"How are you Mrs. Smith?" she asks.

"OK."

"Can I get you a glass of glacial water?"

The water is cold, it revitalizes you.

"Now follow me. Your room is waiting"

You are taken to your treatment room. On the treatment table is a towel and a candle. The attendant takes the candle and puts it on the shelf. She takes the towel and spreads it on the treatment table. She puts another on top.

"You're here for your massage, right?" The same routine would have been in place whether you had a facial, a Thermage, or a Fraxel treatment.

"Then please slip out of your robe when I leave the room and get under the towel. I'll be back in when your ready."

You follow her instructions. She's back in just a minute.

"Any areas really sore today?"

"Yes, my neck. It feels like a giant monkey fist."

She proceeds with the best massage you ever had. Firm, but gentle. She relaxes the opposite side of your neck before working on the sore side. The massage lasts for 45 minutes but you feel like it lasts forever.

At the end, your therapist gives you more water. Then you are given a moment to get into your robe and your therapist returns.

She tells you about all the wonderful things Corona has that helps to draw the poisons out of your body. Soothing bath salts, invigorating creams, home massage units.

You acquiesce and buy it all.

You come back into the relaxing room. Another glass of cold glacial water. Then you go to change. Your clothes are impeccably folded in your locker. A chocolate is on top. A little card is there saying, "We want you to have a nice day." It's signed by your attendant.

The world outside the door is no longer such a savage place.

X X X X X

DR. BARRY LYCKA is one of North America's foremost cosmetic surgeons and consultant to the medi-spa industry. He helped to pioneer this area and has developed an area-specific program for spas with Sydney B. Barrows. Find out more at BestSpasSite.COM.

Chapter 20

INSIDER COPYWRITING SECRET TO DEEP, LASTING CONNECTIONS

Finding Your Ideal Customer

Lorrie Morgan-Ferrero, RedHotCopy.com

Imagine getting a ticket to visit a colony of creatures living on Mars. Would you simply go there without doing any research on their culture, their habits, or their sensibilities? Of course not!

Yet many marketers erroneously waste their time spewing out generic messages to their prospects. They are not aware of how often these prospects leave the fold, never to return again. That means money pouring out faster than it comes in.

Let's bring things back to Earth. Ever notice how different language appeals to different people? How you speak to one group makes a big difference in whether or not you'll connect. Using the word "sick" to a nurse means someone is ill. Using the word "sick" with a teen means something is a *good thing*. You never want to mix up the lingo. Using the right language with the wrong prospect isn't going to get you anywhere.

As a marketer, where do you begin to dig for this connecting information? You start by connecting to the person on the other side of the page . . . the person reading.

Before we go one step further, you need to understand this concept:

Copywriting is a team sport.

There is YOU, the writer. And there is HIM or HER, the reader. Here's the deal: The reader gets to decide when the game is over. As soon as the reader is gone, nobody is reading your copy anymore. So you must anticipate what's going to keep them interested and intrigued with the copy ahead of time.

First of all, when you want to connect with somebody, you have to know where they're coming from. Say you're interested in someone of the opposite sex; to get the best results, you're going to need to do a little research, right? Hopefully you wouldn't just approach the object of your desire without knowing a bit more about him/her. (That's why the movie "Fatal Attraction" was made.)

This goes the same with your target market for your business. You need to dig a little bit and do some research in order to get the best results. Here are some things you need to know.

For starters, you must know the education level of your target market to reach them effectively. In general, even educated people don't mind reading simple words. *Simple means clear.* But there's a fine line between talking down to your target market and using simple language. For example,

- Instead of "at this point in time," write "now."
- Instead of "subsequent to," write "after."
- Instead of "on the grounds that," write "because."

- Instead of "in spite of the fact that," write "although."
- Instead of "whether or not," write "whether."
- Instead of "make inquiry regarding," write "inquire."

You get the idea. (Lawyers may not appreciate copywriting but your prospects will.) So anytime you can simplify the language in your copy, by all means do it. You're not insulting your reader at all.

For the most part, Americans read between the 11th and 12th grade levels. Did you know that best-selling books are written for the 8th to 10th grade level? *Reader's Digest* aims for the 10th grade level, while *Time* and *The Wall Street Journal* reach for the 11th grade. So remember to KISS it . . . *Keep It Simple, Sweetheart*!

Once you establish the education level you need to know more about how your target market lives day to day. How do you do that? I'm glad you asked.

One of my favorite ways to dig deep into the lives of my target market is to prepare a fact sheet just for them. Here's what I do. I look into who my past clients are as well as my ideal future clients. Then I meld those demographics together to find out who my ideal customer really is. This deep research makes all the difference in whether or not you will connect with your "tarket."

The word tarket comes from combining the words "target" plus "market." I coined the term because it's CRITICAL you think in the singular, not plural. *Target market sounds like a mob. Tarket is one person.*

"Target" + "Market" = "TARKET"
Target Market is Plural
TARKET is Singular

Before you do anything . . . I mean ANYTHING, you MUST know how to collect the critical info targeting your market.

Once you have a grip on your average target market, you're ready to eliminate all but one. Don't worry. No one gets hurt. It's just for your copy.

You're going to narrow your target market down to a specific *tarket*!

Do you know who Volvo's tarket is? A 35-year-old mother of two. Not a female college student. Not even a 35-year-old *father* of two. That's not to say one of those other people might not buy a Volvo . . . but Volvo knows the power of focusing on ONE specific tarket.

How about *USA Today*? They tarket a 40-year-old male businessman who travels. Do other people buy *USA Today*? Of course!! But you can only market effectively to ONE person at a time.

Got yours in mind? Now you need to imagine the hair color, gender, age, health, marital status—everything you can think of—regarding your particular tarket. At the end of this exercise, you should have an imaginary friend to sell to.

You should go as far as to name your tarket. It really makes your copy sound personal when you envision somebody real. Now, literally find a picture of your newly born "tarket" either from your own pictures or from royalty-free clipart. (Don't worry . . . it's just for you.)

The point is to make him or her as real as possible. Here's my tarket; her name is Nikki and here's her story:

> Nikki Stanton is a 37-year-old divorced entrepreneur with a web conferencing business. She's internet and business savvy, invests most of her profit back into the business, and lives in San Diego in a gated community with her 10-year-old daughter, Madison. Nikki is involved in her daughter's school and drives her to dance classes. She has a home office and makes approximately $117,000 per year. She jogs three times a week in the neighborhood. She loves to find bargains on designer clothes, *and she dreams of visiting Italy with her daughter someday.*

When I'm writing my copy, I have Nikki pull up a chair and I tell her what's on my mind in a way she can hear me. Then I write it out. Works like gangbusters. There is so much feedback sent to Red Hot Copy from people feeling as though I'm talking directly to THEM. Of course I'm not, but they are feeling the CONNECTION.

That doesn't mean I don't have male clients or women who are either older or younger than Nikki. It's just a powerful trick to get me to focus on marketing to ONE person—MY tarket.

The following checklist will get you started, but don't limit yourself. Throw yourself into the experience of everything your target market lives everyday. Be VERY specific. That's the only way you're really going to connect.

- *Age* (pick one)
- *Gender* (pick one)
- *Education level* (do they have a high school diploma, a college degree, an MBA, etc.)
- *Family status* (married, single, divorced, etc.)
- *Child status* (do they have children)
- *Religion* (what are their beliefs)
- *Fitness level* (how important is their health)
- *Pets* (do they have them)
- *Socioeconomic status* (how much money do they make per year)
- *Profession/occupation* (how do they make money)
- *Hobbies* (do they fly planes, do scrapbooking, grow exotic plants, etc.)
- *Geographic location* (what country, state, city, suburb, etc., do they live in)
- *Media they consume* (what websites, blogs, magazines, television shows, etc. do they take in)
  - favorite TV shows
  - favorite movies
  - magazines they read
  - newspapers they read
  - favorite celebrities
- *Where they shop* (do they go to the mall, order online, visit WalMart, shop sales, visit department stores)
- *What credit cards do they own* (think about what is in their wallet . . . credit cards for what establishments)

Remember, you won't make everybody happy unless you write boring, milquetoast copy that's easy to ignore. The first recipient of the Pulitzer Prize, Herbert Bayard Swope, wrote, "I can't give you a surefire formula for success, but I can give you a formula for failure: try to please everybody all the time." Enough said.

X X X X X

LORRIE MORGAN-FERRERO of RedHotCopy.com is among a handful of the most highly sought after copywriters in the information marketing industry, appealing particularly to female entrepreneurs. To date, Lorrie has helped her clients generate millions of dollars in sales using her rapport-building style of copywriting. A direct descendent of Ralph Waldo Emerson, clients hire Lorrie to write for them or to learn her easy proprietary, step-by-step system for themselves. Download her free special report, "7 Deadly Mistakes to Avoid with Promotional Web Copy" at redhotcopy.com.

Chapter 21

AGREEMENT THINKING TOOLS

Making It Easy to Say "Yes"

Dr. Charles W. Martin, DDS

Easy. That's what we all want. Life's hard enough already. As an influencer, your job can be unnecessarily harder than it has to be. In this chapter, I'll give you vital persuasion thinking tools that, when properly and consistently applied, will give you the key to the hearts and minds of your prospects. When the key is turned gently, those hearts and minds gladly yield to what you offer. Which makes things much easier.

If you're like me, you sometimes think to yourself, "Everyone is entitled to my opinion." While it's a humorous sentiment, its also full of truth. You, like me, want people to *agree* with you. You want others to think as you do, to see as you see, to value what you value, to feel as you feel. And your prospect is just like that, too. Keep this in mind, and you have a persuasion "easy" button you can utilize to smooth the sales process—for you and your prospect.

Yet many selling encounters, particularly those that employ tricks produce disagreement, angst, and frustration. It is enough to give selling a bad name—a label that will stick as long as the inept, poorly trained, and unprofessional resort to any means possible to wrench dollars out of the forlorn wallet of embittered prospect. Yeech. No wonder mommas don't won't their children to grow up to be salesmen. It need not be this way.

Which Side of the Table Are You On?

Imagine you are sitting opposite your prospective buyer at a table. In one respect, the scene looks like a face-off. A standoff. This is the typical adversarial buyer/seller scenario.

Now move yourself around the table and sit beside your prospect, much like a friend would. You are now occupying the Point of We, rather than the adversarial point of You versus Them. The Point of We is an advantageous position that turns your sales battle into a joint effort—a partnership to find agreement to let the buyer buy.

The Point of We helps you help your prospect buy what will help him. It is a position of duty and honor. It requires finding and using your prospect's viewpoints to persuade him to do what he ought to anyway, willingly.

One of the major components at the Point of We is Agreement Thinking, which includes finding agreement, consciously and actively with your prospect and rendering disagreements obsolete.

When properly applied, the principle of Agreement Thinking reverses the angst, disappointment, and dislike of the selling encounter every time.

Sounds cool, huh? *So what is it exactly?!*

Agreement Thinking is finding the obvious and less obvious agreements, values, ideas, and realities that a prospect holds dear. The next goal is showing your prospective buyer how your offering "agrees" with what he most values; how that offer solves a problem, supplies what is missing, fixes what is broken, or creates a new opportunity for all manners of profit: financial, feelings, ego, positive publicity, love, legacy, future, security, memories, experiences, knowledge, bragging rights, revenge, admiration, and dozens of other possibilities.

Warning: these are powerful techniques. Use them wisely and with honor. Think of them like a surgical knife: wielded with competence and integrity it can save lives and create a greater good and likewise to great damage in the hands of the incompetent or the unscrupulous.

Here are three of the many essential Agreement Thinking Tools used at the Point of We to find the agreements that empower your buyer to feel he bought for *his* reasons.

One: Please Understand Me

If you have a chance to interview your client, customer, or patient, you'll be miles ahead of your competition. But be advised: It's how the interview is performed and how in depth it goes that matters. You are looking to find out what really matters to your prospective customer, client, or patient.

Once the first answer is given to a question, ask a series of add-on questions: "Tell me more about that," or "Why do you think that's so?" or "What else can you tell me about that?" The first answer is the logical one the prospect likely practiced in mental rehearsal before meeting with you or is the standard answer to questions like yours. *Prospects are un-rehearsed for the probing, add-on questions.* Each subsequent question carries the answer force provided by the prior answer. A sort of probing momentum develops and carries you and your prospect along as he reveals more.

As the interview continues, your prospect will reveal more. Most everyone likes to talk about himself. Most people are at ease in such a situation. Finally, someone is listening to what he has to say!

As the prospect talks he starts to trust you. No one else takes the time to listen. But you've granted him the importance he feels he deserves. You will auto-magically be regarded as someone who can be trusted. Your likability quotient skyrockets. People *buy* from those they like and trust.

If you go in imagining that your prospect is thinking: "I am important and deserve to be heard," in essence, you're agreeing with him. Agreement leads to further agreement, as you'll presently see.

Two: Little Agreements Open Big Wallets

How do you get someone who seems diametrically opposed to you and your offer to eventually agree to buy from you? It's all about speed and agreement.

There are two levers here. The first is time—time needed to chisel away slowly at the hardened view. This must be done with a certain lightness that does not arouse the sleeping, unthinking parrot named NO, living in the prospect's limbic system. When these "chiselings" accumulate over time they can add up to significant change. Time is the lever of the patient person who understands the task.

What is the second lever? *Finding what you can agree on* with the person with a divergent view. Then, find more you can agree on. And then more yet. Once the opposing view starts agreeing with you, his intransigence declines. He'll like you more as you agree more. He will trust you more because you agree. And like answer force and its subsequent momentum during an in-depth interview, the agreement force and momentum increase for finding even more things on which to agree. The smart person applies the second lever concurrently with the first.

Together, the two levers synergistically induce acceptable change. For some this can mean getting that special account that seemed locked up by the competition forever. For others, it can mean one's first big break into the field of his dreams. And for some, it means convincing that patient in denial to go ahead and get the treatment she needs.

In sales, the direct application of this is to sell just the next small step. Then the next one and then the next one. Eventually a parade of small steps leads you all the way to the "Yes Zone"—where customers, clients, patients, and you all win because you cared enough to make the sale happen.

Three: Make My Day . . . Please

My younger sister has the talent of gregariousness—in spades, mind you. Her husband quips that Kay has only three degrees of separation with the rest of the human race instead of the customary six! I have yet to go any place with her that she doesn't find *some* connection with the formerly perfect stranger. It may be a bit circuitous, but by God, there is one.

So how does Kay the UberConnector do it? She starts with easily agreed upon small talk. Agreement. Then she compliments and finds something to like about the other person. More Agreement. Her enthusiasm, already contagious, spreads like a fire through the peopled area. Other people outside the conversation chime in, hoping to be included. Kay admits all to the inner circle of "feeling good in the neighborhood."

Kay uses agreement and uplifting enthusiasm to bring her own unique energy to the scene. It's like a rising tide that carries all ships. But this tide is made of positive mental energy that makes others around her feel good about themselves.

Kay is not in sales—which is a shame. She is a living agreement seeker and finder. She leaves people around her feeling better about themselves and their world. She brightens their day. It is a gift that more can and should deliver. Can you?

Unknowingly, Kay utilizes the *cultural agreement* shared by all Americans that outgoing, enthusiastic people who make others feel good about themselves should be heard, welcomed, and supported. You can, like Kay, make it your way to brighten the days of others. And with that, when done genuinely, your sales will explode.

Apply Agreement Thinking to every situation where you need to move someone to your prospective, to your side, to your offering, to buy what you purvey. Yes, this is the *persuasion easy button*. Happy pushing.

Summary

- Move to the Point of We—selling as if you are partners.
- Seek agreement and use it to get further agreement.

- Seek to understand others if you want to be liked and trusted and make a sale.
- If you wish to change someone or get his agreement, do it bit by bit by finding things you can agree on.
- Make someone's day—your sales will increase.

X X X X X

DR. CHARLEY MARTIN, an active practicing clinician since 1979, is a high performance practice management coach and consultant. He founded Affluent Practice Systems to serve dentists committed to technical excellence and compassionate care who want to go to the next level. Affluent Practice Systems helps dentists in the areas of practice growth, strategic planning, practice marketing, exceptional case presentation, personnel selection, performance metrics, profitability, and mastermind groups. He can be reached at cmartin@martinsmiles.com, by phone at (804) 320-6800, or at AffluentPracticeSystems.com. For more on the concepts discussed in this chapter and a special free offer, go to charleymartin.com.

Chapter 22

TELEPHONE MYSTERY SHOPPING

What Movie Are You Currently Playing?

Chris Mullins, Mullins Media Group

"We have met the enemy . . . and he is us!" —POGO CARTOON

Every point of communication with a customer is a sales opportunity. The business owner must embrace this fact.

The telephone is the most critical tool, often the first point of entrance in your business. The purpose of telephone mystery shopping (inbound/outbound) is to identify lost sales opportunities, to fix what's not working with staff training. The telephone is the one tool that opens or closes the door to the business. IT MUST BE DONE WELL.

Have you ever said to yourself, "I should be doing better?" Start investigating by doing mystery shopping of your business. You'll quickly uncover who's really part of the sales team or the sales *prevention* team. Brace yourself because by doing telephone mystery shopping you're putting your whole sales process under a microscope. You will uncover lots information that will be extremely useful to your bottom line.

Here's a real lost sales opportunity example: While placing a telephone order with the customer service call center of a large corporate stationery business, I hear what sounds like a bird chirping. I finally ask, "What's that noise?" "Oh that's my cell phone," she says, proudly. "My daughter calls me every morning at 9 A.M." Next, I hear another strange noise, what's that? "Oh (laughing) that's my daughter leaving a message." Then, shortly after I hear what sounds like a regular telephone ringing, "That's my daughter trying to get me on this line."

Now, the customer is questioning their whole relationship with this company . . . "Have I always been charged the right amount? Why haven't I ever been offered discounts? I wonder if they know what they're doing?"

Here's another lost sales opportunity example: An automotive repair client asked us to do telephone mystery shopping and was devastated by what we uncovered. The front desk person said to a prospect that was calling to schedule an appointment, "I'm going to give you the name of another shop down the road, friends of mine, they have a much nicer reception area for you to wait." By the way, this individual was, according to the owner, "our best salesperson, right hand guy, been with us for ten years." Your staff feels it's their responsibility to SAVE the customer from spending money with you for every reason you could possibly come up with.

Fresh eyes to your business is critical to achieve improvements. As the owner, you're too close to the daily operation of your business. The staff has heard from you over and over again on what to fix, but rarely hear how to fix it because that step requires time. The staff views you as not understanding them, just not getting what they go through with customers on the telephone and in-person. They do expect you to have intermittent outbursts, then you'll stop. They don't feel like you listen to them. Before you know it you start to think like them. They've convinced you that the list you gave can't be fixed, our business is different, it's just the way it is, it's always been like this, it's the cost of doing business.

Many owners have good intentions but this just isn't your area of expertise. When you try, your staff will sabotage your efforts and not trust what you say. You'll be so angry at what you've uncovered, you won't be able to communicate your feelings in a way that will get you the desired results. Sure, even the outside experts will have to deal with some sabotage efforts, but they have experience in this. By the way, it's not your staff's fault, unless of course you've been giving them ongoing coaching and training.

Here's another lost sales opportunity example with a retailer that specializes in bra fittings for all women. The business owner is the salesperson. She starts out great at giving one-on-one attention to a shy customer in a private room. This customer told the owner that she wears sports bras for running but didn't know if they fit right. That's as far as it went; the owner never tried to measure for the right sports bra. Then the phone rings with another prospective customer. The owner is now distracted, attention goes to the phone, the customer leaves buying only one bra not three as intended, and made a quick decision which led to the wrong size which of course leaves hard feelings. No trust, no relationship, no referrals, no upselling, no repeat business.

X X X X X

CHRIS MULLINS, CEO of Mullins Media Group™, LLC, expertly attacks a very significant problem area costing almost every business large sums: the handling of inbound telephone calls. For mystery shopping, analysis, and staff training contact Chris Mullins at (603) 924-1640 or Fax: (603) 924-5770. Visit: MullinsMedia Group.com and GreatBottomLine.com.

Sydney Barrows has arranged for you to have a
"Complimentary 15-Minute Consult"
with Chris Mullins, the Phone Sales Doctor™
to talk about what's happening in your business regarding the telephone.
Call 603-924-1640 to schedule your consult.
Be sure to say that "Sydney" sent you.

Chapter

23

MAKING THE DEAL

Matchmaker, Matchmaker, Make Me a Match

Sheila Spangler, President, Capital Stategies

You find certain people, places, or things attractive. You may not even be consciously aware of WHY you like something or someone. You just do. What causes attraction?

Some say pheromones, others say looks, sense of humor. Can attraction be developed and delivered on cue? Sure. Just ask anyone that sells something on commission. They have to learn to do this or they don't eat.

Selling a product, service, or even selling your business requires attracting the right people. You attract them through advertising and marketing that is targeted to your specific audience. Then you must be able to "seduce" them into consummating the deal.

I am a match-maker . . . a relationship-builder. I facilitate sales and financing of businesses. Many people would call me a "business broker." I meet owners who want to sell their companies, oftentimes for more than the value. However, many owners haven't created an exit plan, have no clue who will buy, or how to sell it if a buyer does show up.

From the buyer's perspective, buying a business is a HUGE commitment. The smart sales person helps them with the logic of buying. How do you help your buyer get interested, stay interested, and finally close the deal?

Show the buyer how his future is going to look using your product or service. Build a relationship in order to create trust. First and foremost, people do business with people *they believe* they know, trust, and like.

How does a buyer believe they know you? You ask questions. Draw out information about them.

You find out what interests them. What are their hopes, dreams, and desires? Once you understand your prospect, you'll understand his emotional hot buttons. You can gently push these buttons to help him justify his decision.

Help the prospective buyer think but don't jump in and try to force him to do something. Asking your buyer questions should take up 80 percent of the meeting time. You are building trust. Trust is everything. Your ability to sell is only as great as your ability to create trust.

In order to get someone to buy anything, you must "see" it with their eyes. What is the buyer really experiencing? If you were the buyer and walked into your store for the first time, what would you notice? How are you treated? What words are said to you? How do you FEEL?

As a business intermediary, I know that many buyers of businesses are seeking a better life for themselves. They believe owning a business will provide them with Nirvana. In many cases, they're right.

So, if you want to sell your business, you'll need to find out what the prospective buyer wants, what is their definition of Nirvana? Then give it to them.

When selling businesses, I encourage the seller to help the buyer feel the DESIRE to own this business so badly he'll do just about anything to buy it!

Is all this a mind game? No. It's about giving people what they want. You get what you want (to sell) and the buyer gets what she wants (to buy). All you are doing is helping the process along.

Plan what you will say, how you will say it, the words, the questions, the timing. This is sales as performance art. Choreograph the business tour and presentation. Give the buyer an experience that she will not likely forget. Pull the heart strings.

Buying anything is NOT just about numbers. It's about FEELINGS first. Even for people who have a lot of money. Billionaire Kirk Kerkorian decided to buy Steve Wynn's Mirage Resorts because of a comment that Mr. Wynn made in *The Wall Street Journal*. The comments that Mr. Wynn made indicated a vulnerability to Mr. Kerkorian.

Vulnerability is a feeling about weakness, exposure, susceptibility. As it turns out, Mr. Kerkorian was right. Steve Wynn did really want to sell his hotel and the two made the deal happen. Kerkorian just knew that the time was right to buy. Steve Wynn's words gave him away.

Is there a way to overcome the hard, cold facts on the financial statement with the emotional, non-logical feelings of what the buyer REALLY wants? Yes. Tell the story about your business by describing the experience rather than stating the facts.

Here's a real life example (with names changed):

> My clients Doug and his wife Darlene were ready to sell their business after starting it from scratch and running it successfully for 18 years. Some business acquaintances of theirs, Fred and Betty, wanted to stabilize the peaks and valleys of cash flow they had experienced over the years. So they began talking about a deal.
>
> Doug and Darlene came to me and asked for my help in putting the two businesses together. They had a "walk-away number" they wanted for the sale of their business. A professional valuation report

was obtained. The report showed that the business was worth $450,000 to a financial buyer. However, the range of value to a strategic buyer was $750,000 to $950,000.

Wow! Why would Doug and Darlene ever settle to sell their business to a financial buyer when it was worth so much more to the right, strategic buyer?

In the beginning, Fred and Betty didn't see why they should pay MORE for this business than a financial buyer would. Even their CPA and tax attorney couldn't understand this. (This is why you should have a professional business intermediary on your team when buying or selling. End of shameless plug.).

I was able to show Fred and Betty how their business would benefit by merging the seller's company into their company. I helped create the "movie in their minds" that I wanted them to see by showing them the combined financial picture of the two companies. I showed them how the ups and downs of past cash flow would be eased by the new company's product and service sales. It would reduce the gaps of the more lengthy sales cycle of their business. Until they saw it and felt it, they couldn't believe it.

I had to build a considerable amount of trust with Fred and Betty, especially since they had received negative comments from their attorney and CPA. I spent several hours over several days going over the details, to their satisfaction, until they finally said, "Okay. Let's do the deal."

They purchased the business only after they saw the "picture" and "felt" how the future would look—easier cash flow, more stability, less worry, greater customer base.

Until you have a picture of what you want, you'll be wandering aimlessly here and there. Build trust, help your buyers see the "movie" you want them to see, plan, write and direct the "movie" about your business—then watch the crowd continue to show up day after day.

X X X X X

SHEILA SPANGLER is President of Capital Strategies, a business intermediary and financing firm. She provides coaching and consulting for business sales/acquisitions, valuation, planning, and exit strategies. You can contact her directly by fax at (866) 425-7160 or e-mail at business@sheilaspangler.com, or visit sheilaspangler.com.

Chapter 24

MAINTAINING POSITIONING WITH CLIENTS AND PROSPECTS FOR MAXIMUM LIFETIME VALUE

Harmony Tenney, MBA

Maximum Lifetime Value should be the focus of every interaction with a client. It brings to an end cold calling, uncertainty, and tons of extra hours. How does it work?

Each customer is an asset that can grow. Each is a living entity, able to contribute to a long-term, sustainable, and mutually beneficial relationship.

Many salespeople think of the "sales" they've made as a logged number of dollars on a contract or spreadsheet. The human element completely escapes them.

Here's the math. A new customer signing a $36,000 contract at 15 percent net margin is going to yield $5,400 to your income the first year. If that same customer stays with you for five years, your income from that client increases to $27,000. AND, if he refers one similar new customer to you each of those five years, that client has now brought $108,000 to your table! Five such referring clients, and six figure annual incomes are easy as pie!

Have an Angle

Most salespeople approach prospects with no idea what will happen, guessing their best and trying to make it to the end of the interaction without being rejected. The problem with this is that it sets the salesperson up for failure–right off the bat. The preferred action is to *choose* the approach to a prospect–newspaper writers call it the "angle" to their story (otherwise, it's just words on a page). For salespersons, the "angle" is a tangible, logical reason that they're approaching one prospect over another.

- "I've been in several times, and really enjoyed my experience here . . ."
- "I was looking at a list of family-owned businesses locally, and came across your name."
- "Most of my clients have three or more children . . ."
- "Three of my best clients do business with you. We definitely should meet!"

This "angle" must then lead right in to what is being offered–it must align with the Unique Selling Proposition (USP). The approach with an angle and use of a USP hints to the prospect that "this salesperson might be different–someone who should be given further consideration." It also opens the door for the salesperson "just enough" to feel around a bit more, and to begin unfolding expertise for the prospect's inspection.

Be Consistent

An expert salesperson has a prepared method for taking every prospect (and re-taking each client) through the "ropes" of working together. Make sure that there is a checklist of what must be communicated in the first meeting. Set expectations for delivering referrals and for working together long term. Prepare specific questions for the prospect that show you've invested your time in getting ready for this meeting, so that the meeting is NOT about bringing YOU up to speed, but rather WHAT you both can do together from this moment forward. The people you meet with *expect* that you've Googled them, that you've concluded an exhaustive tour of their company's website, and that you actually have something to offer that will move them from their present situation to another, improved one. Finally, don't leave without determining what "success" measurement will be utilized.

Once agreement is reached on what is to be done, lay out the best path for "how" it's to be done and why. Most clients and prospects will simply agree, because of demonstrated experience and track record . . . but others will agree if the "why" can be articulated. Put thought into each situation and have sound reasoning behind "how it has to be." Clients don't need "yes" men. They need, and are paying for, a guide with fresh eyes.

Keep in Touch

Long-term memory works best when specifically stimulated and paired with emotion. Strategically place emotional triggers in your dialog, correspondence, and offers. Co-brand with a Wild Card such as a celebrity, an industry leader, a super-hero—even success—anything that builds positive emotional affinity. This strengthens your long-term relationship with clients, helping you to become—and remain—a valued part of their Everyday Economic Reality™.

Just as in contests where "you must be present to win," you MUST keep yourself in the mind of your clients, prospects, and in larger organizations, all decision-makers (it takes all of these to comprise your market). *All* decision-makers may seem like overkill—but it is imperative—here are two examples:

1. A local bank was sold to an even bigger banking group. By maintaining relationships with all decision-makers from the first interaction, the business relationship remained intact. They are still my clients, and I now also include their two advertising agencies in my contact system.

2. An auto dealer went through three General Managers in 18 months. By having contacts in all areas of the dealership (sales, service, parts, finance, executive support), I was able to begin a relationship with each new GM and to back my expertise with the firsthand knowledge of all the persons in the dealership.

Be strategic in your communication.

1. *Fuel the market's interest.* Clients are notorious for becoming "bored" and wanting to "change it up a bit" even when *what* they're doing is working *really well.* They'll jump ship, if only to feel saltwater on their body and look sharks in the eye. You have to create adventure for them by offering new experiences/ways for them to get additional pleasure from what's going well.
2. *Help clients "feel the pleasure all over again"* . . . replicating their best successes in new settings, your client newsletter, or client events.
3. *Remain in the picture.* Keep yourself poised to take advantage of change in your clients' businesses. It's critical. You *must* be on hand to witness changes, to participate in them and, when you can, to direct them. Missing participation means YOUR investment in the long-term relationship is open to *someone else* harvesting available customer/market cash! You want first dibs (legitimately) on the maximum harvest.

Align every interaction to the relationship's purpose–improving their business. You need to:

- create and maintain a client contact system that includes at least monthly contact (more often is better).
- clip and send articles with an explanation of its relevancy and application.
- e-mail at midnight with ideas–it shows how much the client matters to you.
- offer to help with a grand opening, trade show, etc.
- become a resource that shares the "latest and greatest" with them.
- share about your family and personal successes–they must want *more* of you.

Lend Extra Resources and Opportunities

I offer to write press releases, and to distribute them to my press contacts. I also ask to be sent copies of any press releases and to be notified of any community involvement. I offer to help get gift certificates and prizes for my clients' events—from my other clients—and to weave in available resources. This saves each business owner time and establishes additional benefits to being one of my clients.

Strengthen the Business Owner's Relationship with His Customers

Look for and take advantage of every chance to make an impact in the bottom line of each and every client. This inclusion helps advertisers increase brand and customer experience with their company. You might provide point of purchase materials for a retailer, provide an article for a corporate newsletter that shows how the two of you working together will make a difference (publicly commending the client), or even offer your availability to join them in visiting key accounts. Many sales reps "can't be bothered" with such "extras," as they don't seem directly related to money coming to their pockets—I can state (with certainty) that it absolutely has a direct relationship.

Positioning Your Client for Success

As a sales representative for your company, it makes sense to give your client every opportunity for achieving the desired (and agreed upon) improvement in their business through your products/services/interactions. Choosing prospects mindfully and applying your expertise allows you to quickly establish a group of very happy clients—ones that will refer and support you over time—as you consistently provide the "what" in the "what's in it for me?" business query.

X X X X X

HARMONY TENNEY is a Senior Marketing Consultant with the Charlottesville Radio Group. In 2006, *Radio Ink* magazine recognized her as a Top Ten National Finalist for Account Executive of the Year. She has helped small business owners in many industries achieve double-digit growth through profitable marketing initiatives—even in flat markets. Her clients call her "The Profit Panther," and both her undergrad and graduate classmates voted her Most Likely to Appear on the Cover of *Business Week*. Ms. Tenney offers her clients a guarantee and proven results from her "Powerfully Profitable, Done-for-You Radio Advertising." She also offers consulting and several info products for businesses seeking to utilize Radio Advertising most effectively in their marketing arsenal. Contact Harmony at: (540) 255-5686, or by e-mail: harmony@businessempowerment.com.

Chapter 25

PRESENTATIONS MAKE THE SALE

It's a Performance

Ted Thomas, Marketing Master Mind

Most of the salespeople you meet feel they are good at sales presentations. Because they think they are good, most of them end up doing poorly. Here's how to make the sale and take a bundle to the bank.

Most salespeople don't understand that the presentation is the "Show," the entertainment, the performance. Observation reveals, that for most salespeople their idea of an effective presentation is to tell the audience or prospect all the good reasons why they should buy the product or service and when they finish talking they expect the buyers to be impressed with the salesperson's delivery and sales pitch. That doesn't make sense, but that's how salespeople think.

The Sale Is Made During the Presentation

When you present you're "on stage," even if you're one-on-one in someone's office. At this point, you're the star of the show, just like a solo vocalist on the platform or a pianist playing Carnegie Hall. Those entertainers are like you, they're on stage and like you, they create a result; only you can produce successful sales results. When you make a presentation you're at the arena, you're the only performer. What you say and do will make you big money. Everything counts. You are alone, by yourself. What you don't do will count against you. What you do right will count for you. This profession is not for people with thin skin. You won't like the rejection that comes with your failure and you won't like the empty pockets that come from your lack of performance. The audience grades you; if you are persuasive, they vote with their wallets. The steps of selling/closing and follow-up reselling will be enormous. This is not a business or a profession for the weak or faint-hearted or lazy. It's summed up in a Four-Letter Word—Work!

The Lonely Salesperson

You'll be alone. No one can help you with this performance. It's up to you to prepare, practice, and to stand tall and bring home the sales for yourself, your company, and your family. Reading a few brochures and trying to be spontaneous on the platform or in the prospect's office will net you zero. You must plan and rehearse your presentation to show benefits to the prospect.

Presenting is like the trial lawyer in the filled-to-capacity courtroom attempting to free his innocent client, where the media publicity has convicted the client, and the client's friends and family have turned away. The performance requires skill; the process is complex and requires preparation and knowledge. If you're not prepared to rehearse and put in hours into the preparation, rewriting and adapting, this business of sales is not for you. If you thought sales was the easy way to go because you already know how to talk and communicate, you've made a mistake! Sales is a lot more than talking—this is a performance, every minute counts. Survival depends on business acumen, training, and the skill of the salesperson. It doesn't take much to fail. Sales is a serious business and the good presenters leave nothing to chance. Sitting across from a client, you're "on stage" every moment. In sales, you play for keeps, no excuses. You produce results or you fail. There's no second place.

Successful presenters blend the sales process into a well defined and prepared presentation that includes demonstrations that excite, educate, and persuade. Prospects won't admit that they don't understand your premise so keep it simple.

In your presentation you can lose the sale if you move too quickly, so move slowly; the details of your offer and your product are important. If the prospect doesn't understand exactly what you are selling you must explain in detail how it benefits the prospect or you'll lose the sale. In the sales arena, "The confused mind always says no."

Keep in mind, the prospect wants solutions and you want to provide maximum benefits and create peace of mind along with enjoyment for the client. Convincing and persuading takes time and requires you, the salesperson, to break down the presentation into easy-to-understand words and verbiage the customer can understand. That means ask questions and test for comprehension with trial closes, friendly little phrases like, "Is this making sense to you?" "Can you see yourself doing this?" Timid prospects won't tell you they don't understand, they don't want to look ignorant or be made to feel stupid. Assume they don't understand and keep it simple. Numerous salespeople hurry and skip important points; slow down, repeat trial closes for understanding. Ask the questions: "Is this what you had in mind?" Ask: "Would it be okay for me to review this process?" Ask: "Have you ever done this before?" It's okay to repeat this: "Is it okay to do this once more?" If possible, demonstrate more than once, and get the customers and the customer's staff to be interactive. Be friendly, don't intimidate. Be sure they see the benefit. If they don't understand, they won't buy, or if they do, they'll return the purchase.

This is not complicated, with practice, you may demonstrate and trial close simultaneously. Customers buy because they want benefits. Demonstrate, reveal, and show them the benefits and secure their agreement. If the desired benefit is saving them money, point that out. If it's a time saving, point that out. Ask the customers, with a trial close test the waters asking "What if you owned this product five years ago?" Wait for a response. Then, ask them "Where will you be five years from now?"

The presentation is a performance. It's educational, persuasive, entertaining. That's what keeps customers engaged and interested. You must demonstrate in a way that's exciting and easy to understand or you'll scare the customer away. The customer is buying your presentation; make it good but not so good the customer thinks they can't do it. The customer is timid and they won't admit ignorance so make them look smart. The presentation is a performance that demonstrates how your product will solve the customer's problems. The more the customer senses you can eliminate problems, the more business they will do with you. The wise salesperson understands the customer's goals. That's your job. Ask yourself what motivates the customer. Is it less work? More money? Prestige? Recognition? Love? Hate? Ego? Those questions and answers incorporated into the presentation give you the ability to sell the client.

The compensation for salespeople is directly tied to preparation and performance. Salespeople are responsible for their own success. Prepare the presentation with persuasive answers that give compelling reasons, methods, to solve the customer's problems.

The customer wants to know what results you and others are getting; use testimonials to demonstrate and make them visual. The customer is taking the time to listen to you for one reason and that's because they have problems. They will be interested and continue listening only as long as you provide solutions. If your product doesn't solve a problem and you can't demonstrate to the customer the benefits and results, then you need a product that does. Salesmanship is a problem-solving process that narrows down the problems and reveals solutions. The idea is to demonstrate solutions and relieve the customer's pain and you have the sale. The customer will take action (buy) because you can remove discomfort. Your problem-solving product presented with excitement and enthusiasm is . . . persuasion.

Let's Review

The client wants to know "What's in it for me?" The presentation is a show and tell; you explain the benefits delivered in an exciting way, coupled with trial closes. This allows the customer to understand and agree that you're solving their problem. If the prospect can achieve a goal by using the product, then you demonstrate that achievement and trial close, by getting the customer to agree that the product will make their life better, easier, richer. Strong sales presentations demonstrate visually the customer is currently located at A; however, they want to be at C. You demonstrate how your product will get them to C.

The presentation moves the customer from A to C by explaining and if possible, demonstrating that transition process. Simplify the process so there's no question in the customer's mind. Buyers hate risk. Before and after demonstrations go a long way toward eliminating risk for the customer.

Sales presentations have many challenges. For example, the customer/prospect is busy and their heads are filled with things to do, deadlines to meet, and other commitments. That all boils down to the customer/prospect isn't excited, and very well may be distracted or disinterested. That's how most sales calls and presentations begin. You start with a skeptical prospect every time. One step at a time, you need to take the prospect from skeptical to being convinced that your problem-solving product will be the solution the prospect is searching for. This won't be easy . . . . You're on stage. You start with a friendly relationship; ask questions that reveal the customer's needs then transition to the presentation. Assuming you understand the customer's needs, you're basically trying to move them from doubter, skeptic, to a new customer. Salespeople are in the business of customer development. Initially few people will have an interest in your product; if that's the case, they won't buy from you the first time you make a presentation.

Here's one skill that will quickly be effective: THE INFLUENCE OF THE TRIAL CLOSE. This writing isn't meant to tell you when to use the trial close. Although there will be examples from time to time. The trial close process will require some common sense and testing during one-on-one communication and to be effective requires continuous practice and integration into your presentation.

For now, let's look at the form, the actual words and begin to think about the integration process of trial closes. Simple is always best in sales. Inserting the following questions (trial closes) into your presentation will produce positive responses and agreements after making statements of fact or benefits. Try to inject continuously one or more of the following. This takes practice and must be planned. Ask one or more, but not all at the same time.

- Is this making sense to you?
- Can you see yourself doing this?
- This is pretty good, isn't it?
- Should we do more?
- Do you like it?
- Would it be in your best interest to learn this?

These are simple trial closes that are used after a statement of benefit or an astonishing fact, to get heads nodding in agreement.

Here's a few basic short trial closes that could be integrated into your sales presentation. (Modify the word description for your product or service.)

- Can you see how a system like this would be a financial solution?
- In a group meeting ask: "How many of you would like to do that?"
- This is pretty good, isn't it?
- What if you had learned this ten years ago? Where would you be now?

Testimonials are a brilliant selling tool. After a testimonial, use a trial close. Any one of the following could be used regularly.

- Would a few deals like I've just demonstrated make your life better?
- How long would you be required to work at your profession to earn that rate of return on your money?

Can you see how this process would create abundance and cash flow for you?

After you surprise the audience with factual data that's a benefit to them, try these trial closes. They're more like statements; however, they make the point. Use a factual and interesting statement to get attention then say:

As you know, money doesn't fall out of the sky and into your bank account like we all dream it should. Today I'm giving you strategies that will work if you will. I'm giving you the road maps to success.

The number-one reason why salespeople fail to get wealthy is simple. One of the secret formulas for sales success is "be unique." You must offer solutions in products or services that no one else is offering. Most people go into a marketplace and offer what everyone else offers, that's going to get what everyone else gets. I know you want more, which means you must do more by offering and doing what others won't do, only the professionals ever put in the extra time.

If you want premium pricing or market leadership you must strive to make yourself unique by revealing more benefits and solutions and asking for the sale multiple times if necessary. To summarize, the sales presentation when used by professionals is scripted and timed. A presentation that works is improved and refined again and again to bring in higher and higher results. Salespeople who are serious will add and delete segments of the presentation depending on the audience and the economic news. The presentation is the "show." Make it exciting, fast, and filled with solutions, then show examples and beneficial reasons why the customer should take action now.

X X X X X

TED THOMAS is a Florida-based publisher and author of numerous moneymaking Home Study Courses. Ted is the guy people go to when they want to improve their business marketing and sales results. Ted's Marketing Master Mind sessions are attended by the important people that make up the Information Marketing Industry. Ted is a recognized expert and in-demand speaker in the United States and in Canada on the subjects of *Government Secured and Guaranteed Certificates*. His book, titled *The Foreclosure Authority* generates many consulting requests. More than 100,000 students have successfully completed Ted Thomas' Home Study Courses. For those who want to learn more about Ted Thomas' Master Mind membership or private consulting contact: Tedsmastermind@tedthomas.com.

Chapter 26

EMOTIONAL SELLING TECHNIQUES

Scott Tucker, MortgageMarketingGenius.com

It was 1998, and I was driving on the highway in my green Pontiac Grand Am, listening to Tom Hopkins for the first time. I was just about to jump into the mortgage business, as a loan officer, and my friend gave me these Tom Hopkins tapes to listen to.

I was surprised to find how fun selling could be. I was amazed at Tom's "phraseology." The words Tom spoke to me, on those tapes, were like nothing I'd ever heard. I could see how words could appeal to emotions, and at the same time "grease the skids," making the sale automatic.

Back then, I worked at a "real job." I was just finishing up my college education, after having first served in the Navy, and was now working at a professional association in Lansing, Michigan. I remember going to talk to a guy there I liked, who was our association's lobbyist at the state capitol, about the tapes I'd just listened to.

I told him about the phrases I'd just learned from Tom Hopkins. I told him how, using Tom's phrases, I could make the lobbyist agree with anything I told him. It was kinda funny. I did it to him, and just as he was finding himself in agreement with me, he'd turn the tables, and pull the same trick on me, making it to where I was agreeing with him on something or other.

It seems that my friend the lobbyist was very good at "sales" already, as he should be.

In the years since first studying those tapes, I've dedicated myself to truly mastering the use of language that connects *emotionally*, in order to sell anything to anybody–whether consumers, as a mortgage broker, or now to other mortgage brokers, or even to corporate CEOs, as a consultant.

I entered the mortgage business in 1998, in Chicago, just a few months after hearing those tapes. Although I had no idea how to explain the forms, I was familiar with the *benefits* that the borrower would receive. I found myself realizing that I didn't need to be all that well versed in the ins and outs of the mortgage product itself. More than anything, I needed that ability to *listen* to what folks were all worked up about, and then the ability to use what they'd told me about their *emotions*, to help them to do something they already wanted to do.

I found that I could charge, at that time, 7.99 to 10 points (percentage of the loan amount) on a refinance, so long as it solved all their problems. This was 4- to 10-times the fees charged by most of my competitors–but then my competitors were mostly selling based upon price, and competing with each other based upon price like competing street vendors selling identical apples. I was not. I had learned to sell the *same* products and services on a higher level, by concentration on *emotional* connection.

See, their *emotions* about their problems were the most important part of the entire transaction. What was not important were the ins and outs of the commodity, the mortgage that I'd use to solve their problems, and to alleviate their emotional trauma.

People who were knowledgeable about mortgages would stand there in amazement when I'd tell them that I had just been paid 7.99 to 10 points on a refinance, for the fifth time that month. But I'd tell them, "you don't get it. It's about what keeps them awake at night . . . and about how I fix all those problems, and trade them in for all the benefits they so desperately want. It's about their emotions, not about their logic, and that makes price irrelevant."

In fact, the essential elements for being paid top dollar for whatever your products or services or expertise are, are not superiority in the products, or superior product knowledge, but creating trust through an *emotional* connection.

It's somewhat difficult to learn how to get your logic out of the way, and talk to your prospect only about emotions and outcomes. It's very difficult if you're the sort of personality that thinks like an engineer, an accountant, a rocket scientist.

But, when you finally learn how to get *your* logic out of the way, you've learned how to work only with your prospect's emotions, and the sales occur much more naturally and easily.

Today, I coach scores of mortgage brokers all over the United States and Canada. I also provide them with consulting on operations. But one of the most valuable things I do for them is to supply them with marketing that they have exclusive license to use in their geographical area.

And maybe *the* most valuable thing I do is help them change the way they think about *themselves*, the real value they bring to people, and the way they present that to their customers. When you integrate this approach into the advance emotional direct-response marketing, done automatically for them with the tools and systems I've devised, and your own person-to-person selling, when a qualified prospect finally earns the opportunity of meeting with you, fee resistance is gone, and your success at closing sales is multiplied. I've seen this hundreds of times with the mortgage brokers and loan officers I've coached—incomes doubling, tripling, even going up by ten times, while seeing fewer people and actually working *less*.

For example, a Realtor I worked with in Maryland, was able to enter the mortgage business, use my systems to *automate* his emotional direct-response marketing, automate and outsource his handling of inbound prospect calls and online loan applications, delegate the systematized processing of his borrowers' loan paperwork, and get his *weekly* working hours down to five hours! While *increasing* his *monthly* income to $80,000! That's $960,000 per *year*, working five hours per *week*.

Key Points

- *Listen* for what folks are all worked-up about!
- Ask yourself, "What keeps them awake at night?"
- Remember to get *your own* logic out of the way, and talk to your prospects *only* about *emotions* and *outcomes!*

X X X X X

SCOTT TUCKER is an expert in emotional direct-response marketing for the retail mortgage origination industry. Tucker is the creator of a comprehensive mortgage marketing system that is unlike anything else used in the mortgage industry. To learn more, get his free report at MortgageMarketingGenius.com.

Part Four

CONTRIBUTORS AND SYDNEY'S XXX-RATED SALES SECRETS

THE AUTHOR AND CONTRIBUTORS

About the Author

Perhaps better known to millions as the "Mayflower Madam," Sydney Biddle Barrows is a unique American success story. Beginning her business career as a retail executive at Abraham & Straus, at the time the jewel in the crown of Federated Department Stores, she moved on to May Company Corporate and then became the Divisional Merchandise Manager at a nationwide resident buying office.

Six years later she found herself moonlighting as a phone girl at an escort service to supplement her unemployment check after having been fired for refusing to participate in a kickback scheme. It may have been the World's Oldest Profession but it certainly was not being run very professionally, and less than a year later she decided to open up her own agency. Relatively small but very upscale, Cachet prospered for five and a half years until New York's Finest closed it down, only to later publicly concede that it was the most honest and professionally run business of its kind ever operated in New York City.

The recipient of intense worldwide media coverage, her first book, *Mayflower Madam*, went right to the top of *The New York Times* bestseller list. *Fortune* magazine named it one of the Ten Best Business Books of the Year. This book was reprinted 28 times and translated into seven languages; business schools all across the country, including Harvard, included it in their curriculum. *Mayflower Madam* was also made into a TV movie starring Candice Bergen. Sydney has been a guest on every network morning television show multiple times as well as dozens of morning shows in local markets. She was a guest on nearly every talk show on the air through the 1990's, and many of them, including *Oprah, Larry King*, and *Phil Donohue*, more than once. She was the subject of an *A&E Biography*, co-hosted *Saturday Night Live* with Candice Bergen and has appeared on other shows too numerous to mention.

Sydney has also had a very extensive speaking career, guest lecturing at colleges all over the United States, including some in the Ivy League such as Brown and Columbia. Speaking engagements have taken her all over the United States and overseas; she was an extremely popular fixture at Young Presidents Organization and CEO Club events, among others, for years.

She lives on the Upper West Side in New York City and has "no pets, no plants, no children, and no regrets."

Sydney Biddle Barrows is a recognized authority on the Customer Experience, the emerging economic shift to an Experience Economy, and the challenges and opportunities we face in today's ever-changing economic climate. She assists entrepreneurs, businesspeople, and professional practices to re-imagine the way they interact with their customers in order to create unique Experiences that delight and touch them. Because those Experiences add value to the product or service because they are meaningful to the customer, there is minimal resistance to paying premium prices for them. And happy, satisfied customers are loyal customers who gladly spread the word to their friends, family, and colleagues.

In addition to individual on-site consulting, Sydney has also developed the *Customer Experience Blueprint*, a do-it-yourself product consisting of audio CDs, an Implementation Manual, and the actual Blueprint she uses for her private consulting clients. Visit The ExperienceBlueprint.com for information on this and other Experience Design products, consulting services, coaching programs, and presentations about this newly emerging and exciting field.

Sydney Biddle Barrows also does on-site consulting for entrepreneurs, businesses and professional practices who wish to have a Fresh Eyes analysis done in order to identify the "holes in their bridge," which discourage or prevent prospects and customers from doing business with them. If you want insight on how more sophisticated Sales Design™ and Sales Choreography™ can improve your bottom line in the form of increased sales, increased profits and better customer retention, please visit sydneybarrows.com for more information on her consulting services.

Sydney also holds a short-term tele-seminar series on *Sales Design and Choreography*™ featuring renowned guest experts, with additional follow-up programs for those who wish to broaden their knowledge even further. More information is available at sydneybarrows.com.

Successful people are successful because they all do the same thing: they IMPLEMENT. The Implementation Blueprint program is a carefully designed six-month membership program that focuses on *your* business, on *your* challenges, on developing strategies for *your* business and most importantly of all, providing you with the *motivation and drive* to get it all accomplished.

Members get plenty of one-on-one time with Sydney as well as group interaction in the form of monthly virtual hot-seat mastermind meetings. Detailed information on all of the Member Benefits as well as a membership application can be accessed at sydneybarrows.com.

Sydney Biddle Barrows also specializes in consulting services for the spa industry. Learn more about her personal on-site consulting services at sydney barrows.com. Partnering with Dr. Barry Lycka, they offer an area-exclusive coaching and consulting program with focused and ongoing support for day spas, medi-spas, hotel spas, and destination spas who want to provide a superior client experience and distinguish themselves from the competition.

Detailed information is available at BestSpasSite.com or you can find a brief overview of the program and a link to this site at sydneybarrows.com.

Dan Kennedy and Sydney spent a day in a recording studio in New York City where they talked about all the sales and marketing strategies she used in her former business. In addition to those two CDs, a CD of the keynote presentation she gave at the Glazer-Kennedy SuperConference in 2005 as well as a CD of a re-creation of the employee orientation program she held for all new employees of her escort service are included in a product titled *XXX Rated Sales Strategies*. A transcript of their interview as well as that of the orientation CD, which has been personally annotated by Dan, is also included in this package. For information on how to purchase this unusual, one-of-a-kind program, go to sydneybarrows.com.

Join Sydney's VIP program to receive her FREE weekly e-zine so you can keep up to date with what is going on in the fields of Experience Design; Sales Design™ and Sales Choreography™, as well as be the first to hear about free teleseminars and other programs. Sign up today at sydneybarrows.com or The ExperienceBlueprint.com.

About the Co-Author, Dan S. Kennedy

DAN S. KENNEDY is the author of 11 books, including the popular "No. B.S." series with Entrepreneur Press, including *The No B.S. Guide to Marketing to the Affluent* and *The No B.S. Guide to DIRECT Marketing for NON-Direct Marketing Businesses*, as well as *The New Psycho-Cybernetics* and *Zero Resistance Selling* (co-authored with Dr. Maxwell Maltz). Kennedy is also the editor of four monthly newsletters including *The No B.S. Marketing Letter*. Through his newsletters and online publications, network of specialized industry advisors serving over 100 industries and professions, and the network of Glazer-Kennedy Insider's Circle™ local chapters and study groups in over 100 cities, he influences millions of business owners and sales professionals each year. His speaking career has included nine consecutive years on the #1 seminar tour, addressing audiences as large as 35,000, frequently appearing with former U.S. Presidents, Hollywood and sports celebrities, and legendary entrepreneurs like Debbi Fields (Mrs. Fields Cookies) and Jim McCann (1-800-Flowers). He has also appeared with an eclectic variety of other speakers including Donald Trump and Gene Simmons of KISS at Glazer-Kennedy Insider's Circle™ and other client events.

Dan Kennedy can be contacted by fax at (602) 269-3113 or by mail at Kennedy Inner Circle, Inc, 5818 N. 7th Street, #103, Phoenix, AZ 85014. He does not use e-mail. Do NOT e-mail him via any of the websites presenting his information and publications. Information about Dan's books at NoBSBooks.com.

Books by Dan S. Kennedy

No B.S. BUSINESS Success: The Ultimate No Holds Barred Kick Butt Take No Prisoners Tough & Spirited Guide, Entrepreneur Press

No B.S. SALES Success: The Ultimate No Holds Barred Kick Butt Take No Prisoners & Spirited Make Tons of Money Guide, Entrepreneur Press

No B.S. TIME MANAGEMENT for Entrepreneurs: The Ultimate No Holds Barred Kick Butt Take No Prisoners Guide to Time Productivity & Sanity, Entrepreneur Press

No B.S. DIRECT MARKETING for NON-Direct Marketing Businesses: The Ultimate No Holds Barred Kick Butt Take No Prisoners Direct Marketing for Non-Direct Marketing Businesses, Entrepreneur Press

No B.S. WEALTH ATTRACTION for Entrepreneurs: The Ultimate No Holds Barred Kick Butt Take No Prisoners Guide to Really Getting Rich, Entrepreneur Press

No B.S. RUTHLESS MANAGEMENT of People & Profits: The Ultimate No Holds Barred Kick Butt Take No Prisoners Guide to Really Getting Rich, Entrepreneur Press

No B.S. MARKETING TO THE AFFLUENT: The Ultimate No Holds Barred Kick Butt Take No Prisoners Guide to Really Getting Rich, Entrepreneur Press

FREE INFORMATION, SAMPLE CHAPTERS,
and VIDEO DISCUSSIONS
AVAILABLE AT:

NoBSBooks.com

Background and Contact Information for Contributors

John Avolio

JOHN AVOLIO is a technical and business consultant. He serves as a science and security advisor in the area of Chemical, Biological, Radiological, Nuclear, and Explosives (CBRNE) and drug detection to both foreign and domestic industries and Governments. His primary focus is the development of new and novel technologies and methods as applied to counter-terrorism and counter-drug programs. Contact him at john@johnavolio.com and visit his website at johnavolio.com.

Alexandria Brown

ALEXANDRIA BROWN is CEO of Alexandria Brown International Inc., a company devoted to empowering women around the world with the tools to live the freedom-based lives of their dreams via owning a successful business. Her marketing advice has been featured in several Entrepreneur Press books, and she publishes the award-winning *Highlights on Marketing & Success* weekly e-zine with more than 30,000+ subscribers. If you're ready to jump start your marketing, make more money, and have more FUN in your small business, she invites you to sign up for her FREE weekly tips at AlexandriaBrown.com.

Karen Campbell

KAREN CAMPBELL owns Campbell's Scottish Terriers, a rapidly growing niche-market business that focuses on Scottish Terrier and West Highland Terrier collectibles. Started as a catalog/internet-based business, Karen has grown her loyal customer base over the years with her excellent service and a determination to bring new and different types of "Scottie" and "Westie" collectibles to her clients. Marketing strategy has become a top priority as she seeks to keep the customers she has and cultivate new "collectors." Go to campbellscotties.com.

Kim Castle

KIM CASTLE is known around the world as an international columnist for conscious business and as the co-creator of the BrandU® Business Profit System, the world's only process-based results-driven integral approach to business creation. She has helped thousands of entrepreneurs worldwide grow their business from idea to brand to market. While she has worked with Fortune 500 companies including IBM, DirecTV, General Motors, Domino's, Wolfgang Puck, M&M's, Disney, and Paramount, her true passion is helping entrepreneurs grow to big-brand status. Her business has been mentioned in *Inc.* magazine, and she was nominated for the *Los Angeles Business Journal* Women Making a Difference Award. A natural comedienne with six years on the stand-up circuit, she regularly leaves large audiences wanting more of her big-brand strategies for businesses of any size. Find out if you're making one of the "15 Mistakes that Kill Business Success" in her business-saving special report for FREE at BrandU.com. Contact Kim Castle at (800) 457-9713 (U.S.), (310) 827-9720 (INTL) Member Care ext 202, and at BrandU.com.

Dan Cricks

DAN CRICKS is the President/CEO/Founder of Results Marketing, LLC. Dan is an Independent Business Advisor with Glazer-Kennedy Insider's Circle in the Cleveland and Akron, Ohio areas. Dan is also a *Mastermind Coach and a Certified Peak Performers Mastermind Coach* working with entrepreneurs and business owners from many different types of businesses including professionals, business to business and many in different retail establishments all over and outside the United States. Dan is also a public speaker to many different business organizations and chambers of commerce including COSE of Cleveland, Ohio and is a COSE Mind Spring Editor. Dan is also *The Been There Done That Marketing Guru and Business Coach* to the *Auto Repair Shop industry,* working with repair shop owners from all over North America and abroad. Dan's clients have reported business increases of as much as 51 percent after just 30 days of working with Dan's ideas, strategies and coaching. Visit great resultsmarketing.com, call (440) 842-8937, fax (877) 376-2321 or e-mail resultsmarketing@sbcglobal.net for more information about how Dan can help you grow your business. You can get FREE marketing information from Dan at freegift from.com/dancricks, and to find out how you can achieve more in 12 months than you ever thought possible, go to DanCricks.tools toachieve.com.

Ciara Daykin

CIARA DAYKIN is the Event Choreographer for Firefly Occasions (firefly occasions.com). Ciara runs a successful wedding and event planning company based in Calgary, Alberta, Canada. Her expertise stems from years of immersing herself in planning events such as The Canadian Juno Awards (Canada's version of the Grammy's). Ciara's career has taken her to international locations such as Australia, Mexico, Ireland, and even a party at the Playboy Mansion. Ciara provides brides with engaging tips for tying the knot without coming undone in her bi-weekly e-zine and her free report, "The Top 10 Things a Bride Can Do to Take Her Wedding from Ordinary to Extraordinary!" She also gives tips and tricks for hosting an event in her free report "5 Things I Hate About Your Party." Ciara's newest venture is rockstarweddingplan ner.com where she coaches other wedding planners to attract high-end clientele and lead a rockstar wedding planner lifestyle.

Patrice Dickey

PATRICE DICKEY, "Your Guide to Intuitive Wealth," is a Registered Corporate Coach, Registered Yoga Teacher, and multi-award winning author of *Back to the Garden: Getting from Shadow to Joy.* Creator of "Get the Life You Love" for Emory University in 1999, she is an in-demand motivational speaker and sales trainer who has helped thousands bring their passions to life over the past 25 years. A successful PR consultant and creative entrepreneur, she coaches how to "Convert Your Chaos to Cash" and transition to a life of greater personal meaning and legacy.

Visit IntuitiveWealthGuide.com for your Free Special Report—*The Seven Secrets Blocking Creative Entrepreneurs from Getting the Life They Love* at patricedickey.com.

Jan Drake

JAN AND CHRIS DRAKE are experts in marketing property casualty insurance to the affluent. Jan created a nine-step marketing campaign entitled "Sleep like a happy baby with our blanket protection" which resulted in a 28 percent increase in business in six months and a 150 percent ROI based on the lifetime value of a client. Their monthly newsletter "Drake's Decorum" provides education on current insurance issues facing their Long Island marketplace. In the fall of 2008 Jan and Chris will begin to offer coaching to other insurance agents who want to attract and retain affluent clients. Chris is an insurance consultant with ten years of adjusting experience offering clients the maximum money they are due from an insurance claim after an accident or disaster. They can be reached at the Bethpage Insurance Agency, (516) 931-3141, or at jcdrake@optonline.net.

Ari Galper

ARI GALPER is a sought-after international speaker and author and is the creator of Unlock The Game®—a truth-based sales approach that takes the pressure out of the selling experience for both the seller and buyer. His profound discovery of shifting one's mindset to a place of complete integrity, based on new words and phrases grounded in sincerity, has earned him distinction as the world's leading authority on how to build trust in the world of selling. Ari is also the creator of ChatWise®—an online sales conversion system using his truth-based sales approach via live chat. Visit UnlockTheGame.com and ChatWise.com for a FREE TEST DRIVE.

Bill Glazer

BILL GLAZER is the Number-One Most Celebrated Marketing Advisor specializing in the Retail Industry. Retailers should visit his website at bgsmar keting.com.

Darnay Hoffman

DARNAY HOFFMAN is an experienced attorney admitted to practice in New York State and Federal courts. For the past 13 years, Hoffman has been a litigation specialist and appellate lawyer. He is an expert in all aspects of civil practice (e.g., discovery, motion practice, trial), and appellate advocacy.

You can contact Darnay Hoffman at (917) 566-2486 or darnay@darnay hoffman.com.

Chris Hurn

CHRIS HURN is the President/CEO/Cofounder of Mercantile Commercial Capital (MCC), the nation's leading 90 percent loan-to-cost commercial loan provider. His firm has been named to *Inc.* magazine's list of the 500 fastest-growing companies in the United States. Chris has been named the "Banker of the Year" by his industry's only trade association, "Marketing Guru of the Year" by *Coleman Publishing*, and the Small Business Administration's "Financial Services Champion of the Year" for Florida and for the 12-state Southeast region. He is a serial entrepreneur and business coach, and he regularly speaks around the country on smart wealth creation strategies for businessowners and entrepreneurs. Visit TheSmartChoiceLoan.com, call (866) 622-4504, or e-mail info@mercantilecc.com for more information and to receive free DVDs and other special reports. At 504blog.com, you can read more of Chris' thoughts on sales choreography and many other subjects, plus you can also sign up to join nearly 80,000 other members in receiving Chris' free monthly newsmagazine.

Ileana Kane

ILEANA KANE is a Certified Coach and Master Strategist with extensive marketing, sales, and speaking experience. Known best as, "The Million Dollar Muse," she helps people to find their "Million Dollar Idea" and put it into action! Ileana is passionate about helping women move from "working like slaves with mediocre income" to creating their own Pathway to Profit, Freedom, and Breakthroughs. Her systems, passion, and powerful energy has helped women nationwide create a better business while living life on their own terms. For your free report "The 7 Keys to Doubling Your Income in Any Market (. . . without selling your soul!)" go to: milliondollar muse.com.

Larry Lane

LARRY LANE is the principal of Lane Architecture + Design, P.C. Call (212) 594-2007 to receive a copy of his DVD titled, "Secrets of Successful Historical Storefronts" (Free for the first 100 inquiries) where he shares more ways to have a positive experience through architecture. Larry is the author of a book about Commercial Office Interiors, publishes a newsletter called "LAD Sketch Pad," and shares his passion of architecture on Mondays at 5:30 P.M. EST by hosting a weekly radio show at www.blogtalkradio.com/LaneArchitecture. Keep up with current trends by visiting his blog at LaneArchitecture.blogspot.com.

Dr. Barry Lycka

DR. BARRY LYCKA is one of North America's foremost cosmetic surgeons and dermatologists and a consultant to the medi-spa industry. He helped to pioneer this business and is developing an area-specific coaching program for spas with Sydney Biddle Barrows. Find out more at BestSpasSite.com.

Dr. Charles Martin

DR. CHARLES MARTIN is an active practicing clinician since 1979 and a high-performance practice management coach and consultant. He founded Affluent Practice Systems to serve dentists committed to technical excellence and compassionate care who want to go to the next level. Affluent Practice Systems helps dentists in the areas of practice growth, strategic planning, practice marketing, exceptional case presentation, personnel selection, performance metrics, profitability, and mastermind groups. For more on the concepts discussed in his chapter and a special free offer, go to charley martin.com. Dr. Martin can be reached at cmartin@martinsmiles.com, by phone at (804) 320-6800, or at AffluentPracticeSystems.com.

Kurt Minson

KURT MINSON is the Chief Engagement Officer of the Akron, Ohio-based M Group Consultants. The M Group provides unique, Full Engagement directed business development services. Examples include cultural and individual assessments, "Prime Idea" driven strategies, personal and corporate promotions, image and wardrobe consulting, engagement sphere development training and coaching, loyalty and incentive programs, as well as comparative cultural and market intelligence work. The M Group Consultants, 137 S. Main St., Suite 301, Akron, OH 44308, (330) 762-4441—office, (330) 294-1024—fax, kurtminson@MGroupConsultants.com or MGroupConsultants.com.

Lorrie Morgan-Ferrero

LORRIE MORGAN-FERRERO of RedHotCopy.com is among a handful of the most highly sought after copywriters in the information marketing industry, appealing particularly to conscious and female entrepreneurs. To date, Lorrie has helped her clients generate millions of dollars in sales using her rapport-building style of copywriting. A direct descendent of Ralph Waldo Emerson, clients hire Lorrie to write for them or to learn her easy proprietary, step-by-step system for themselves. Download her free special report, *7 Deadly Mistakes to Avoid with Promotional Web Copy* at redhotcopy.com.

Chris Mullins

CHRIS MULLINS, CEO of Mullins Media Group™, LLC, expertly attacks a very significant problem area costing almost every business large sums: the handling of inbound telephone calls. For mystery shopping, analysis, and staff training contact Chris Mullins at (603) 924-1640 or by fax at (603) 924-5770. Visit: MullinsMediaGroup.com and GreatBottomLine.com.

Sydney Barrows has arranged for you to have a "Complimentary 15-Minute Consult" with Chris Mullins, the Phone Sales Doctor™, to talk about what is happening in your business regarding the telephone. Call (603) 924-1640 to schedule your consult, and be sure to say that "Sydney sent me."

James Roche

JAMES ROCHE, The Info Product Guy, is the only info marketer in the world who can "Coach the Product Out of You." He combines his unique background of over 12 years as an artist, coach, and marketing expert to help entrepreneurs get more clients and earn more income using information products like books, e-Books, audio CDs, workbooks, coaching programs, and live events.

James has helped hundreds of experts in over 25 industries including: sales, internet marketing, interior design, business startups, retirement coaching, life coaching, real estate, book publishing, health and diet, holistic health, and many more.

He is also the creator of the Info Marketing Action Plan (iMap), a 90-Day Group Mentoring Program that shows you step-by-step how to create a marketing message, a marketing plan, and info products that get you more clients and sales the fast, fun, and easy way. To get his free Special Report, "3 Secret Steps to Creating an Information Product That Makes You Money" visit: InfoProductGuy.com.

George Sierchio

GEORGE SIERCHIO (The Consultant's Coach) is a business coach for technology-based entrepreneurs looking for the right way to build value into their business by utilizing proven systems and processes in all segments of their company. Go to consultantscoach.com or info@consultantscoach.com.

Sheila Spangler

SHEILA SPANGLER creates financial strategies for business owners by maximizing today's profits so your business can be sold at a premium when you are ready. Plus, Sheila's strategies give you peace of mind about the future, and a better business today so you can enjoy life now! A former bank vice president and commercial lender, Sheila is founder and CEO of Capital Strategies, a business intermediary firm focused on building strategic value. She provides coaching and consulting for business owners seeking advice on sales, acquisitions, financing and exit planning. Like most business owners, your wealth is invested in your business. Find out how to improve the value and access that cash when you're ready. Check out Sheila's website designed especially for business owners like you at sheilaspangler.com. Sign up for a FREE REPORT about increasing the value of your business. You can contact her directly by fax at (866) 425-7160 or e-mail at sheila@capitalstrategies-usa.com.

Harmony Tenney

HARMONY TENNEY is a Senior Marketing Consultant with the Charlottesville Radio Group. In 2006, *Radio Ink* magazine recognized her as a Top Ten National Finalist for Account Executive of the Year. She has helped small business owners in many industries achieve double-digit growth through profitable marketing initiatives—even in flat markets. Her clients call her "The Profit Panther," and both her undergrad and graduate classmates voted her "Most Likely to Appear on the Cover of *Business Week*." Ms. Tenney offers her clients a guarantee and proven results from her "Powerfully Profitable, Done-for-You Radio Advertising." She also offers consulting and several info products for businesses seeking to utilize Radio Advertising most effectively in their marketing arsenal. Contact Harmony at: (540) 255-5686, or by e-mail: harmony@businessempowerment.com.

Ted Thomas

TED THOMAS is a Florida-based publisher and author of numerous money making Home Study Courses. Ted is the guy people go to when they want to improve their business marketing and sales results. Ted's Marketing Master Mind sessions are attended by the important people that make up the Information Marketing Industry. Ted is a recognized expert and in-demand speaker in the United States and in Canada on the subjects of Government Secured and Guaranteed certificates. His book, titled *The Foreclosure Authority* generates many consulting requests. More than 100,000 students have successfully completed Ted Thomas' Home Study Courses.

For those who want to learn more about Ted Thomas' Master Mind membership or private consulting contact: Tedsmastermind@tedthomas.com.

Scott Tucker

SCOTT TUCKER is an expert in emotional direct-response marketing for the retail mortgage origination industry. Tucker is the creator of a comprehensive mortgage marketing system that is unlike anything else used in the mortgage industry. Tucker's mortgage marketing system does not sell "rate and fee." Tucker's mortgage marketing system generates scores of prime and FHA "forward mortgage" refinance borrowers, as well as scores of "reverse mortgage" borrowers, that apply nowhere else. This gives his area-exclusive licensees what he calls "de-commoditization" in the marketplace. Tucker's area-exclusive licensees are viewed by their borrowers as what he calls "non-'mortgage' guys," and financial gurus. What's so remarkable about Tucker's system is that in 95 percent of all transactions, the borrowers never ask "what's the fee?" And in 90 percent of transactions, they never ask "what's the rate?" Tucker tells you more in his free report at MortgageMarketing Genius.com.

Kathryn Weber

KATHRYN WEBER is the publisher of the *Red Lotus Letter* feng shui e-zine and is a certified feng shui consultant in authentic Chinese feng shui. Trained in

Asia, Kathryn helps her readers improve their lives and generate more wealth with the ancient art feng shui. Subscribers receive her FREE Wealth e-book *Feng Shui's 3 Easy Steps to Financial Abundance* (tinyurl.com/5ahylc) and learn the fast and fun way that feng shui can create greater abundance and prosperity. Contact her at (361) 277-2020 or kweber@redlotusconsulting.com. K Weber Communications LLC, P.O. Box 531, Cuero, Texas 77954, (361) 277-2020 business; (361) 676-8800 mobile; (361) 277-8391 fax.

SYDNEY'S XXX-RATED SALES SECRETS

Sydney's sales secrets are scattered in sidebars throughout the chapters in this book but here they are all collected together for convenience.

SYDNEY'S XXX-RATED SALES SECRET #1

Stop! Do not do another thing, do not spend another penny until you have figured out what business you are really in and what your customer really wants.

SYDNEY'S XXX-RATED SALES SECRET #2

So many businessowners let themselves be blindfolded when they fall into the "my business is different" trap. That is not just sensory deprivation, that's opportunity deprivation.

SYDNEY'S XXX-RATED SALES SECRET #3

ALL BUSINESSES ARE ALIKE!!

If the call girl business can pick up viable strategies from the cosmetics business, then your business can implement strategies from an escort service. Just keep it clean and legal!

SYDNEY'S XXX-RATED SALES SECRET #4

The needs and desires of your customer determine what business you are *really* in. What is it they dream about, aspire to, fantasize doing or having? Satisfy these basic, often secret, desires and watch your business take off!

SYDNEY'S XXX-RATED SALES SECRET #5

Mother may have warned you that being easy was a bad thing, but I am telling you that being easy is not only a good thing, it can make you good money too.

SYDNEY'S XXX-RATED SALES SECRET #6

If you do not make sure your employees are fully briefed about your advertising and marketing campaigns, you are just pouring jeroboams (four ordinary bottles of champagne!) of money down the drain.

SYDNEY'S XXX-RATED SALES SECRET #7

You need more than good foreplay to consummate the deal.

SYDNEY'S XXX-RATED SALES SECRET #8

Just because a prospect fits into your ideal parameters, they are still not an ideal client if they are difficult or unpleasant to do business with.

SYDNEY'S XXX-RATED SALES SECRET #9

Time is money, whether you are charging by the hour or not.

SYDNEY'S XXX-RATED SALES SECRET #10

It's not about you. Your customers couldn't care less what you like or what you think they should buy. Customers only care about what *they* want. So if you are interested in getting their money into your pocket, you'd better find out exactly what that is.

SYDNEY'S XXX-RATED SALES SECRET #11

There is no business in which a creative and persuasive guarantee cannot be made. You may just need to dig a little to find it.

SYDNEY'S XXX-RATED SALES SECRET #12

Determine what perception you want prospects or customers to have about your business, and also the *perception your customers want to have about you*. Then work out a plausible story or strategy that will create or enhance those perceptions. If the story includes some "creative" elements (in moderation, of course), don't think of it as being deceitful, think of it as giving your customers the opportunity to experience feeling good about themselves and their choices. They will appreciate you for being the source or catalyst of those positive feelings of pleasure, and validation.

SYDNEY'S XXX-RATED SALES SECRET #13

Regular and frequent contact is key. You don't want to be perceived as the occasional one-night stand.

SYDNEY'S XXX-RATED SALES SECRET #14

It's not just about the money, it's what you have to do to get the money.

SYDNEY'S XXX-RATED SALES SECRET #15

Always have a Plan B.

SYDNEY'S XXX-RATED SALES SECRET #16

You can only fix it if you know it's broke.

SYDNEY'S XXX-RATED SALES SECRET #17

You can satisfy some of the people some of the time and you can satisfy some of the people all of the time, but you can't satisfy all of the people all of the time (with apologies to Abraham Lincoln).

SYDNEY'S XXX-RATED SALES SECRET #18

They've got to perceive it to believe it.

SYDNEY'S XXX-RATED SALES SECRET #19

If you want it done right, you first have to do it yourself.

SYDNEY'S XXX-RATED SALES SECRET #20

You really do only get one chance to make a good first impression.

SYDNEY'S XXX-RATED SALES SECRET #21

What you wear is not who you are, but what you wear *is* who your customers perceive you to be.

SYDNEY'S XXX-RATED SALES SECRET #22

It's not just what you do, it's how you do it.

SYDNEY'S XXX-RATED SALES SECRET #23

Hearing is believing; are your callers hearing what you want them to believe?

SYDNEY'S XXX-RATED SALES SECRET #24

Sex sells. 'Nuff said. Just keep it legal.

SYDNEY'S XXX-RATED SALES SECRET #25

When you have put all of the interlocking pieces of the puzzle together correctly, the issue of price evaporates.

About the Author and Contributors

INDEX

U

V

W

Y